The Electronic Commonwealth

THE

ELECTRONIC

COMMONWEALTH

The Impact of New
Media Technologies on
Democratic Politics

JEFFREY B. ABRAMSON
F. CHRISTOPHER ARTERTON
GARY R. ORREN

Basic Books, Inc., Publishers   *New York*

Library of Congress Cataloging-in-Publication Data

Abramson, Jeffrey B.
  The electronic commonwealth.

  Includes index.
    1. Information technology—Political aspects—United
States.   2. Television in politics—United States.
3. Telecommunication—Political aspects—United States.
4. Politics, Practical—United States.   I. Arterton,
F. Christopher.   II. Orren, Gary R.   III. Title.
HC110.I55A27   1988   324.7'3'0973   87–47783
ISBN   0–465–01878–5

To Our Wives

Jackie, Janet, and Merle

and to Our Children

Sarah, Anna, Cameron, Jamison, Meredith, and Jonathan

C O N T E N T S

FOREWORD

OVER the past several decades, changes in communications technologies have occurred at an ever-increasing pace. The introduction of personal computers, satellites, and electronic mail and telephone networks have substantially altered the ways in which we receive and transmit information. One of the fundamental questions arising from these developments is how the new means of communication have affected our democracy: the conduct of campaigns and elections, governance by officials, and the ways in which citizens participate in their government.

To examine these questions, in 1982 the Institute of Politics at Harvard University received a grant from the John and Mary R. Markle Foundation and undertook a three-year study of new communications technologies, public policy, and democratic values. Three eminent scholars were invited to design and conduct the research and to author the work resulting from it—Professors Jeffrey Abramson, Christopher Arterton, and Gary Orren.

A faculty study group, of which I was the chair, composed of scholars and practitioners from the fields of politics and the media, acted as advisors to the project, helping to shape the work in its initial stages and reviewing the authors' works-in-progress as they went along. The membership of the faculty study group included:

Daniel Bell, Henry Ford II Professor of Social Sciences, Harvard University

Stephen J. Breyer, judge, U.S. Court of Appeals for the First Circuit, and lecturer on law, Harvard Law School

Les Brown, senior vice president, editorial development, *Channels of Communication,* New York

John Deardourff, chairman of the board, Bailey, Deardourff & Associates, Inc., McLean, Va.

Henry Geller, director, Center for Public Policy Research, Washington, D.C.

David Gergen, editor, *U.S. News & World Report*

Winthrop Knowlton, president, Knowlton Associates, Inc., Cambridge, Mass., and former director, Center for Business and Government, John F. Kennedy School of Government, Harvard University

Richard Levine, vice president, Information Services Group, Dow Jones & Company, Inc., Princeton, N.J.

Jonathan Moore, ambassador-at-large and coordinator for refugee affairs, U.S. Department of State, and former director, Institute of Politics, John F. Kennedy School of Government, Harvard University

Roger Mudd, special correspondent and essayist, *MacNeil/ Lehrer NewsHour*

W. Russell Neuman, assistant professor of political science and director, Research Program on Communications Policy, Massachusetts Institute of Technology

Richard M. Neustadt, consultant, Private Satellite Network, Inc., New York

Michael Sandel, professor of government, Harvard University

Professor Ithiel de Sola Pool of the Massachusetts Institute of Technology was a member of the group at its outset. His death was a loss not only to this project but to all who work in the field he helped to pioneer.

The members of the faculty study group contributed a great deal to this work, and the authors and I are grateful to them. The particular contributions of one member, however, need to be mentioned. As director of the Institute of Politics, Jonathan Moore was responsible for nurturing the original idea of this research. His vision and commitment developed the outlines for the inquiry and the funding from the Markle Foundation without which this work would never have been undertaken. He did this within the context of a larger vision, the development of a Center on the Press, Politics and Public Policy at Harvard's John F. Kennedy School of Government. That center, named for journalist Joan Shorenstein Barone, was dedicated in the fall of 1986. Finally, I wish to thank Wendy O'Donnell, the member of the Institute's staff without whose research and administrative skills this project could not have succeeded.

Joseph S. Nye, Jr.
Institute of Politics
Cambridge, Massachusetts

PREFACE

BENEATH the rhetoric and fanfare of the 1988 presidential campaign lies an important message about the future of democracy. The message is the media.

This is an old message with a new twist. In 1988 the media continue to play a central role—according to some *the* central role—in presidential selection. But for the first time, a dazzling array of new communication technologies—satellites, cable, videocassette recorders, computers—have moved off the showroom shelves and onto the campaign trail. Traditional broadcast media and newspapers continue to dominate political communication, but candidates have learned that they ignore the new media arsenal only at their peril.

In New Hampshire and elsewhere, candidates distributed videocassettes to voters' homes and interest-group headquarters, soliciting support and appealing for funds through a new form of video direct mail. In Iowa, political consultants used speedy microcomputers equipped with communication devices to conduct instant polls of viewer responses to televised debates. This same technology has enabled political insiders to keep abreast of the latest campaign news on a day-to-day basis through nationwide electronic conversations. In several states, campaigns have shown paid political ads and call-in programs on cable television, targeting their messages to key primary and caucus battlegrounds and to specific voter constituencies. Candidates also have discovered how to bypass the national television networks and still cover great distances quickly by creating their own personalized satellite networks, beaming interviews directly to local television stations in carefully selected communities.

While this sudden flurry in the use of new communication technologies in campaigns has yet to be matched in other areas of politics, the impact of the new media has been felt widely, and further transformations are likely to alter, for good or ill, the way we conduct politics generally. Virtually every institution of American government has exploited recent advances in communication to some extent. Organized interest groups have pioneered the use of the new technologies to mobilize their supporters. Both the House of Representatives and the Senate have adjusted to the presence of cable television cameras. And much of the daily work of government would be impossible in the absence of computers or satellite telecommunications.

In contrast, the political impact of the new media on the ordinary citizen is still sketchy and limited. At the receiving end many citizens are the targets of direct mail campaigns. But a more active use of the new media by grassroots organizers still lies in the future. In theory, the new media promise the rebirth of participatory democracy, through the ability of citizens to attend electronic town meetings, to speak as well as be spoken to through television, and to use computers to gain access to remote data. In practice, nonprofit, civic uses of computer and video power are dwarfed by the commercial market in electronic information services, videoconferencing, and the like. This gap between civic and commercial access to the new media, between candidate use and citizen use, is a vexing problem for democracy in the new electronic age.

This book falls into three major parts. In chapters 1 and 2, we introduce both the democratic theory and the new technologies that will occupy us throughout the work. In chapters 3, 4, and 5, we study the implications of the new media for three major political domains: elections, governance, and citizen participation. In chapters 6 and 7, we turn to issues of law and regulatory policy, in a comparative as well as an American perspective. A concluding chapter 8 builds on these three parts of the book to discuss the value choices that lie ahead.

The title of this book makes sudden neighbors of technology and democracy. In actual political practice, of course, coexistence between the new media and democratic ideals is hard to achieve. High-tech enthusiasts complain that old-style democracy makes a fetish of slowness and turns its back on ways to accelerate communication between citizens and government. On the democratic side, many a Jeremiah has responded by railing at the worship of speed and the invasion of privacy that comes from "updating" democracy. On both sides, these lamentations have much to teach us—about uncritical allegiance to the political status quo, on the one hand, or to the so-called communications "revolution," on the other.

Preface

Ultimately, modern telecommunications is neither democracy's devil nor its messiah. The electronic breakthroughs studied in this book *can* be a boon to democracy, if they are devoted to public purposes as well as to private enterprise. As suggested by the title of this book, democratic uses of the new media depend on developing and regulating technology as a *common* wealth of the citizenry. But these technical advances can also hinder democracy, if they are used to magnify the problems of equality and access, of amplified leaders and voiceless audiences, that have plagued mass media politics. Of course, it is far easier to invoke the term "commonwealth" metaphorically than to give democratic substance to the word. Much of this book will be devoted to delivering that substance but a prefatory remark may be helpful here.

The idea of a common wealth or a common good has figured prominently in the history of democratic thought. We can hardly describe, much less justify, democratic politics except by reference to the common good and to the participation of the people in shaping the political life they seek to share.

The classical notion of a common good, however, does not jibe entirely with modern individualism. Freedom of choice—the right of individuals to follow their own conscience and choose their own values—has become central to our understanding of liberty. In a pluralistic society such as ours, there is no orthodox or shared standard of what is morally valuable. Instead, we cherish the very act of having to choose values for ourselves. The task of a free government, in this view, is to preserve freedom of choice and of conscience intact.

But this task can be accomplished only by separating politics from morality—by treating every person's value choices as worthy of equal political respect. In short, democratic politics must be neutral on the question of values, no longer seeking to define a public or common good for citizens but leaving the matter to be resolved by the individual conscience.

In the United States, the protection of individual liberty against state-imposed orthodoxies has attained heroic, even epic proportions. Whether the subject is birth control, religion, or speech, the ideal of freedom of choice and of conscience remains the sovereign ideal. This is the distinctive American contribution to the meaning of liberty, and it is a contribution whose importance cannot be overstated.

Still, there are limits to a politics of individualism and free

xiii

choice. In extreme form, such a politics isolates people and undermines the neighborhoods and communities, the group associations and allegiances that give content and stability to individual choices. In extreme form, such a politics also deprives citizens of a shared identity and diminishes the reach of the common good.

The challenge for democratic thought in the United States is to retrieve the politics of the common good in a way that will honor the lessons we have learned about individual liberty and social diversity. In this task, the image of a commonwealth can be our guide. Citizens of a commonwealth are divided in their aims and aspirations in life; they share no single conception of the good life and conform to no one sovereign moral or religious authority. Nonetheless, they understand themselves to be united into a community with a distinctive political culture and tradition. They accept that their individual ways of life are bound up with the survival and perfection of that political culture, and they treat each other as equal participants in governing the community that is their common wealth. So understood, the commonwealth ideal guards against three dangers that concern us in this book: (1) the corruption of the politics of the common good into a politics of mass conformity; (2) the corruption of the politics of pluralism and diversity into a politics of faction and balkanization; and (3) the corruption of a politics of individualism into a politics of isolation.

The choices we make about the electronic media will greatly influence our success or failure in avoiding these dangers. Used wisely, mass communications is a powerful antidote to the democratic ills of group faction and personal isolation. Across obstacles of time and distance, the mass media make it possible to expand participation in the debates and deliberations, the meetings and assemblies that are the hallmark of democratic politics. Used unwisely, the mass media are themselves the disease. They turn active citizens into passive spectators, lulled by bland and homogeneous messages. They eliminate collective deliberation in favor of soliciting immediate responses from isolated individuals. And they ignore the rich diversity of group life in favor of appeals to an undifferentiated mass audience. Clearly, the new media present us with important choices. Our purpose in writing this book is to bring a concern for democratic values to bear on these choices, which even now are being made in Congress, in administrative agencies, and in corporate offices across the country.

ACKNOWLEDGMENTS

THREE AUTHORS working together on a book over five years compile a long list of intellectual debts. Collectively, we wish to express our gratitude to the Institute of Politics at Harvard's John F. Kennedy School of Government, where the authors spent time in residence while writing this book. The faculty study group on new communications technologies at the Institute, whose members are listed in the Foreword, provided a lively forum for discussing the topics around which this book eventually took shape. We owe a special debt to Professor Joseph S. Nye, Jr., who as chair of the faculty study group gave our discussions both focus and wisdom. Jonathan Moore, the former director of the Institute, conceived this project and was a whirlwind of activity in securing the support a project of this magnitude required. Wendy O'Donnell of the Institute staff was both a valued research assistant and participant in every stage of this study.

We also are indebted to the John and Mary R. Markle Foundation for their generous support. The Foundation is a model of how programs of scholarly assistance can work best. Thanks in particular to Paula Newberg and Larry Slesinger of the Foundation.

Special thanks are due to Stephen Bates, who served as the principal researcher during the initial stages of this project and who collaborated on an earlier study of the new media funded by the Roosevelt Center for American Policy Studies. Research assistance of the highest order also was given to us by Elizabeth Bussierre, Victoria Fabisch, Philip Guentert, Steven Kotran, William Mayer, Andrew Robertson, and Karen Skelton.

Preliminary versions of chapters 1 and 2 were given at an Aspen Institute Conference on Communications Technologies and the Democratic Process in June 1985 at Wye Plantation, Maryland. An earlier version of chapter 3 was delivered at an Aspen Institute Special Executive Seminar, "How Goes the Communications and

Information Revolution?" in August 1987 at Aspen, Colorado. We are indebted to Michael Rice, Director of the Aspen Institute's Program on Communications and Society, both for the invitation to deliver our research in progress and also for the substantive advice that followed. Portions of chapter 4 were presented in February 1987, at a conference on "Representation, Information Technology, and Democratic Values," sponsored by the Office of Technology Assessment of the U.S. Congress. Parts of chapter 8 were discussed before a faculty study group on "News, The Mass Media, and Democratic Values," at the Center for Philosophy and Public Policy of the University of Maryland in December 1986.

A preliminary draft of the entire manuscript was presented at a conference hosted by the Institute of Politics at Harvard in December 1985. In addition to members of our faculty study group, participants included Benjamin Barber, John Florescu, William Greener, Kathleen Jamieson, Thomas Patterson, Michael Rice, Michael Robinson, Michael Schudson, and Frederick Weingarten.

The authors also benefited from the thoughtful comments and criticisms of Amy Gutmann, Mark Hulliung, Robert Klitgaard, Judith Lichtenberg, Susan Moller Okin, Michael Sandel, and Edith Stokey. One colleague in particular, Henry Geller, was an ever-generous source of information about the new media.

Lisa Belsky, David Brittan, Lisa Carisella, Anne Doyle Kenney, and JoAnne Watson helped to bring the manuscript to final form. Paul Golob of Basic Books rescued us from many errors with intelligent and fastidious editing.

Our children were always on our mind and under our feet while writing this book. This is as it should be, when writing a book about the future. After all, it is their generation that will decide how to use the emerging wonders of communication. And it is they who will enrich or impoverish democracy. Their tender years have served to remind us how difficult it is to predict the future. But the trust they have in us as fathers makes it our responsibility to participate as best we can in securing the future of democracy.

Our wives had to contend with the usual havoc that accompanies the writing of a book. They had to do this, moreover, while pursuing their own distinguished and demanding careers. The result was often turmoil but it was turmoil from which we all extracted an important lesson: No amount of new technology can substitute for democracy at home—or elsewhere.

The Electronic Commonwealth

C H A P T E R 1

THE NEW MEDIA
AND DEMOCRATIC
VALUES

THIS IS A BOOK on the political implications of the new media—a term we use to describe those technologies, ranging from the computer to the satellite, that are powerfully changing the way communication takes place in modern society. Our discussion of the new media is at once descriptive and normative. We survey current political uses of the new media and also debate the value choices that lie ahead. In a book about technologies, such a concern for values may seem strange. But nothing in the machines determines whether they will be used to befriend or belittle democracy. Ultimately, the politics of the new media depends on the ends and purposes of those using them.

What are the new media and what makes them novel? The names of the chief symbols of modern telecommunications are well known. There is the satellite and the way in which the orbiting bird liberates communications from obstacles of time and distance. Equally important is the computer and the quantum leap it achieves in the volume of information that can be stored or the speed with which data can be retrieved. In the world of video, there are cable channels and videocassette recorders (VCRs)—two developments among many that have transformed television from a scarce medium into an abundant one. Other new technologies are less well known but potentially just as significant: fiber optics, a technology that transmits voice, pictures, and other data by sending digital bursts of light down thin strands of super-transparent glass; and videotex, a hybrid video-computer service for electronically publishing everything from the daily paper to the *Encyclopaedia Britannica* on the home video monitor.

Some but not all of the new media are *news* media in the traditional sense. For instance, cable television includes news departments and even a national news network of the familiar sort. But other new technologies are used principally by nonnews organizations. One familiar example is the way elected officials use new videorecording techniques to bypass reporters and to feed their own footage to local television stations. Direct mail is another conspicuous political example of how the new media (in this case, computers) are exploited by nonnews organizations. Table 1.1 summarizes the full media tapestry discussed in this book. As the table illustrates, modern media of mass communications extend far beyond those controlled by the organized press. This in itself is a development with far-reaching implications.

Given the pace of technological change, any attempt to provide a timely list of the new media is doomed to short life. The sudden explosion in the VCR/videocassette market is a good example of this difficulty. A decade ago VCRs were mentioned only in passing in surveys of new video technologies; far more attention was lavished on cable television and pay television services. Today the climb in VCR sales "continues to rival the takeoff of television itself in the 1950s."[1]

That is why, rather than discuss the technologies one by one, we present readers with a workable set of generalizations about the cumulative impact of the new media environment as a whole; no single technology is crucial to the generalizations offered. As discussed in detail in chapter 2, six properties in particular are characteristic of the new media:

1. They explode all previous limits on the volume of information that can be exchanged.

TABLE 1.1
The Media

New	Computers
	Satellites
	Cable Television
	Videocassette recorders
	Direct Broadcast Satellite
	Multipoint Distribution Service
	Satellite Master Antennae Television
	Subscription Television
	Low-Power Television
	VHF Drop-in Television
	Videotex
	Teletext
	Lasers
	Fiber Optics
Old	Broadcast Television
	Radio
	Newspapers
	Magazines
	Telephone
	Telegraph
Non-News Media	Direct Mail
	Electronic Mail
	Polling
	Videoconferencing
	Computer Conferencing
	Teleconferencing
	Use of the above technologies (cable, satellites, broadcast television, etc.) for political purposes

2. They make it possible to exchange information without regard, for all practical purposes, to real time and space.
3. They increase the control consumers have over what messages are received and when.
4. They increase the control senders have over which audiences receive which messages.
5. They decentralize control over mass communications.
6. They bring novel two-way or interactive capacities to television.

Looking Ahead: A Communications Revolution?

The consensus is that American society is in the midst of a "communications revolution."[2] The principal evidence of this revolution is that information itself is now the major product of the

American economy.[3] As a consequence of this shift from an industrial to an information economy, all kinds of "future shocks" are predicted. Some of the more common predictions about the new media's revolutionary potential are as follows:

• The Gutenberg empire of print is in its last days, as the new technology of videotex accomplishes the electronic publication of newspapers, books, and encyclopedias on the home television monitor.

• The three commercial television networks will rapidly lose their audience share to cable competitors and to home use of prerecorded videocassettes. This loss of audience share may be so great as to threaten the survival of network television programming as we now know it.

• The survival of movie theaters is also in jeopardy, as Hollywood adjusts to the new distribution patterns wrought by videocassettes and by pay cable services such as Home Box Office (HBO).

• Electronic shopping and banking from the home will increase rapidly in popularity, as computer devices make it more convenient to shop and bank over the telephone or television.

• The traditional place of the free public library in American culture will suffer a decline, as information increasingly becomes available only in data base form and at a price.

• Political campaigning will take on a new look, as candidates become more adroit in using the "narrowcast" capabilities of such new media as cable television and computerized direct mail. The current television campaign requires candidates to "broadcast" one and the same message across an entire metropolitan area. Future campaigns will find candidates tailoring their message to specific audiences selected by computer or to particular audiences watching a Hispanic cable channel or Christian cable network or black entertainment channel.

• Television evangelists will increasingly mobilize their electronic congregations for political purposes, thereby putting potentially divisive religious issues at the center of campaign strategy.

• The rapidity of new polling technology will undermine patience with the cumbersome procedures of representative democracy and shift the political process toward more direct, democratic forms.

Given the power of such devices as computers, satellites, or laser beams, the idea of a communications revolution is bound to have widespread appeal. But there are at least two reasons to remain cautious when predicting the impact of technology. First, history has proved notoriously unkind to past prophecies about technology's future. Samuel Coleridge predicted that the printing press would end peaceful society by bringing literacy to the lower classes;[4] Postmaster John Creswell opined in 1873 that the telegraph and telephone were doing away with written mail;[5] Alexander Graham Bell believed the telephone would be an instrument of mass entertainment;[6] Thomas Edison considered dictation to be the principal use for the phonograph.[7]

The history of television also indicates the folly of prophecy. The first practical demonstration of television in the United States was by American Telephone & Telegraph (AT&T) in 1927; a decade later a leading industry executive was still predicting that "the extremely short distance of transmitting, the manifold sources of interference, and the staggering cost of erecting a transmitter and producing good programs will prove the same practical deterrents from buying a television receiver, just as they have in England."[8] Just as skeptical about television's future was a 1938 *New York Times* report:

Against rapid strides in technique must be set grave doubts as to the commercial success [of television]. . . . Wherever the American promoter turns he faces doubts—doubts about the financial feasibility of connecting transmitting stations on a national scale, doubts about making images talk and sing all the time or only part of the time, doubts about finding enough good program material, doubts about what the public wants. Moreover, an investment is involved that dwarfs anything to which even American capital is accustomed.[9]

In 1939 television was prominently displayed at the World's Fair, the theme of which was "The World of Tomorrow." After witnessing a demonstration of television at the fair, the *New York Times*'s reviewer still concluded that "the problem with television is that people must sit and keep their eyes glued on a screen; the average American family hasn't time for it."[10] In his novel *World's Fair*, E. L. Doctorow satirizes the enterprise of depicting and predicting technology's future. After walking through the RCA pavilion at the 1939 World's Fair and seeing a new invention, "picture radio, or television," Doctorow's characters wander on through

the Town of Tomorrow to "a sample community of modern de-
tached houses, each in its own new yard." The mother of the
novel's narrator becomes incensed. "What's the point of showing
such houses," she said, "when they cost over ten thousand dollars, and no one in the world has the money to buy them?"[11] With
such wrong predictions about the future of housing or television
in the United States, who dares to predict the future of the new
media with assurance?

There is a second and more specific reason to question predictions about a communications revolution. Unless qualified, any
prediction rests on a crude technological determinism; it assumes
that changes in technology by themselves trigger social and political changes. This is naive. Consider the impact of the automobile
on American society. Nothing in the invention of the internal
combustion engine itself determined whether American policy
would center on financing public transportation systems or high-
ways for privately owned automobiles.[12] A similar point can be
made about the open-ended political uses to which the new media
may yet be put. The additional channel capacity now available
through cable television and other pay television services *could* be
used to support a rich offering of public-affairs programming. But
it could also be used to reinforce the traditional dominance of
mass-entertainment programming. Computers, to take another
example, could be used to support publicly financed data services
that help to close the information gap between rich and poor. In
the absence of public financing, computerized data services may
very well increase that gap. Thus, starry-eyed prognostications of
the sort offered by AT&T ("The Information Age will become
universal. People everywhere will participate in a worldwide
telecommunity. They will be able to handle information in any
form—conversation, data, images, text—as easily as they now
make a phone call.")[13] would be laughable, were it not for their
self-serving nature.

One of the gravest ways in which speculation about the future has damaged sober assessment of the new media is by exaggerating both the positive and negative claims about the technology. Typical of the positive claims is the World Future Society's
celebration of "computopia": "Now for the first time in history, a
possible answer to the utopian dilemma is emerging. By applying
new technology and adopting a new perspective, we may at last

be able to achieve a way of life that is personal yet communal, secure yet flexible, practical yet spiritually fulfilling."[14] An important part of the utopia promised by new media buffs is the renaissance of democracy. Best-selling books trumpet the arrival of "teledemocracy"—a new direct democracy where instantaneous public opinion surveys replace the unwieldy processes of eighteenth-century representative democracy.[15] "Public opinion will at last become the law of the land" because the technology now permits government to survey public sentiment on any issue.[16]

Every prediction of utopia is met with a rival warning of doomsday. The new media have been described as "an electronic nightmare," a "serpent lurking in this so-called [technological] paradise."[17] Far from ushering in a golden age of direct democracy, the new media threaten "telefascism" and the computerized invasion of privacy. The VCR in particular is seen as a harbinger of personal isolation, and special-interest programming on cable channels as a step in the direction of faction and social fragmentation.

This rivalry of hyperbole, pro and con, about the new media should alert us to the shortcomings of proselytizing in a discussion of this sort. We remain devout agnostics on the issue of whether the new media constitute a "communications revolution." Our more modest position is one that, we hope, recommends itself to common sense. This is that the transformations in telecommunications over the last decade—those associated principally with the computer, satellite, cable, and VCR—are sufficiently impressive to warrant serious (and early) intellectual inquiry. Whether those transformations ultimately will prove as significant as the transformations brought by radio and television, we do not pretend to know. But it does seem highly unlikely that the new media are just a passing fad. For better or worse, we will have to adjust to a world where more people communicate more often about more things more quickly than ever before. It is possible to argue that the new media's impact on the speed, scale, and volume of communication is only quantitatively different from what came before. But when all twenty-one volumes of the Academic American Encyclopedia can be stored on a single 4.7-inch optical disk;[18] when fiber optics networks can transmit eight thousand telephone calls simultaneously; when communication becomes liberated from all the constraints of space and time that have limited it from the beginning of recorded history—then the quantitative changes carry with them qualitative change as well.

Looking Backward

Throughout American history, mass communications and democratic politics have exerted a profound influence on each other. A brief look backward may therefore serve us better than all of the wisdom in futurology.

In the early days of the American republic, news and politics did not yet reach a mass audience. Newspapers catered to an elite readership, interested primarily in shipping notices, other commercial reports, and the foreign news.[19] Likewise, political parties had not yet developed into organs for mass voter mobilization, and candidates remained drawn from a rather narrowly defined commercial elite.

In the 1830s a more populist, democratic sentiment transformed politics and journalism at the same time. The penny press popularized a new concept of news, geared to the interest of the ordinary person in the "nearby and the everyday," in the local happenings of police, courts, crimes, fire, and the like.[20] Due to advertising and commercial financing, the selling price of the newspaper was kept low. The result was the birth of the modern mass-circulation newspaper.

In the political arena, Jacksonian democracy prompted a parallel set of egalitarian reforms. The populism of the day sparked demands for universal white male suffrage, abolition of the Bank of the United States, and overthrow of the entrenched commercial elite symbolized by the bank. This new economic and political democracy, with its elevation of the common people, fueled the new journalism; and the new journalism, geared to the interests of the common people, fueled the new politics.

Electronic communication was born with the telegraph in 1844. Its speed and reach allowed the entire nation to share the same news at the same time. National news services such as the Associated Press arose to exploit the telegraph's significance for news operations. Along with advances in national transportation, electronic communications thus emerged as a strong force for nation building. At the same time, the monopoly power of Western Union (and AT&T, after the invention of the telephone) led to new anxieties about private corporate power and potential corruptions of democracy through exclusive control over an entire medium of communication.

In the twentieth century the scale-conquering power of the telephone and over-the-air broadcasting has eclipsed the telegraph and solidified the national mass audience for news and politics. Among the more remarkable examples of interplay between media and politics, television in particular has buttressed a long-festering mistrust of political parties in the United States. Instead of communicating with voters indirectly through the channels and patronage of a party boss or ward leader, candidates now typically take to the airwaves to communicate on a one-on-one basis with home voters. They use television to highlight their person, not their party label.

Other examples of the interplay between politics and mass communications can readily be drawn from American history. Indeed, the steady parallel between media development and political development in the United States is striking. Over time, both American politics and American media have shifted from decentralized to centralized structures, from a local to a national audience, from strong to weak partisanship, from heterogeneity to homogeneity, and from governmental to private commercial financing (see table 1.2). The following sections provide brief summaries of these parallel shifts in the life of politics and the media in the United States.

Centralization. Today, ownership of the key mass media in the United States tends to be in the hands of giant corporate conglomerates. Broadcast television is dominated by three commercial networks, cable television by multisystem operators, newspapers and magazines by chain owners, and the news wire services by two (perhaps soon only one) enterprise.

The growth of conglomerate ownership has changed the concept of news in profound ways. Washington and New York have emerged as the news capitals, eclipsing the local scale and

THE ELECTRONIC COMMONWEALTH

TABLE 1.2
Trends in the Media and Politics

Features	Media	Politics
1. *Organizational Structure:* Decentralized to centralized	From community newspapers to conglomerates, wire services, national newspapers, three TV networks. Dominance of Washington and New York.	Power shift from state and local parties to national party. Adoption of national party nomination rules. Decline of convention, rise of primaries. Growing importance of national political consultants (polling, fund raising, media). Dominance of Washington and New York.
2. *Audience Orientation:* Local to national	Growing reliance of public on national television for news and entertainment.	Increasing nationalization of voting patterns. Presidential focus. Voting in midterm elections as referenda on national issues. Growing awareness by public of national public opinion.
3. *Partisanship:* Strong to weak	Decline of party and "cue-giving" press. Rise of objectivity ethic in journalism. Broadcast coverage overwhelmingly nonevaluative.	Decline of party organizations, party loyalty, and party voting. Shift from strongly partisan to "merchandising," centrist campaign style. From caucuses to conventions to primaries for nominations.
4. *Message:* Diversified to uniform	From multinewspaper to single-newspaper cities. Three networks broadcast same content.	From substantial regional variation in each party in the nineteenth and early twentieth centuries to greater ideological homogenization within the parties.
5. *Financial/Resource Base:* Government to party to private sector	From government sponsorship of newspapers, to nineteenth-century party press, to twentieth-century market-oriented press and commercial advertising.	From government patronage and legislative caucuses, to party as the key source of funds and campaign workers, to ad hoc candidate organizations and fund raising from individuals and political action committees.

location of news operations prevalent throughout much of American history. Our most politically influential newspapers, news magazines, and broadcast networks are now all giant corporations with managements that are international in their orientation. Satellite transmission of text is likely to centralize and nationalize the production of newspapers to an even greater degree, as the fledgling national newspaper *USA Today* illustrates.

Not coincidentally, American politics has undergone a paral-

12

lel process of nationalization. The most visible sign of such centralization is the explosive growth of the federal government, and the
shift of basic health and welfare responsibilities from the state to
the national government. The same nationalization of the political
arena is apparent in the life of political parties. In pre–Civil War
elections, the state and local party organizations dominated the
conduct and financing of campaigns. In fact, it was the local party
that typically published its own newspaper and controlled the
flow of news to the party faithful. Hampered by the absence of
national communication or transportation networks, the national
political party remained a weak actor. Today the balance of power
inside political parties is reversed. In all important respects from
raising money to drafting rules for party primaries and conventions to attracting media attention to nominating national candidates, party management has become centralized in the national
committees.

It is difficult to conceive of the nationalization of politics having taken place without the nationalization of news, or vice versa.
After all, the national channels of communication provided by the
mass media are what permit politics to reach a national audience.
Conversely, the democratization of politics throughout the nineteenth century created its own demand for mass circulation of the
news to an expanded electorate.

Mass Audience. The rise of the mass audience has been part
and parcel of the nationalization of politics and communication in
the United States. In essence, modern media have conquered the
problem of scale and freed communications from obstacles of time
and distance. In so doing, mass communications may well be
thwarting the intent of the Founders, who embraced the expansive size of the United States as a central feature of the republic.
Fearful that opportunists might attain high office by pandering to
the masses, they sought to design an indirect democracy that
would elect men of distinguished character and established reputation. One of their principal safeguards was the principle of extended sphere. Holding elections over a large territory had the
advantage of hindering communication between candidate and
constituent, and thus controlled electioneering of the pejorative
sort. Their fear was that candidates of questionable character
could triumph in small districts by practicing the popular arts of
flattery and demagoguery.[21]

But, as the political philosopher Benjamin Barber recently noted, the Madisonian link between large size and democracy "was conceived in an unwired world, one without telephones, computers, or television"[22] (not to mention mass-circulation newspapers). It is no exaggeration to say that the conduct of national elections in the United States has radically altered in response to the mass audience the media make available to candidates. The Founders could hardly have foreseen the strides in communication that have undermined their notion of proper political scale and have permitted candidates to woo voters directly in large districts, even in a district as large as the nation.

Decline of Partisanship. Another trend has been the dampening of partisanship in the press and in politics. As already noted, the press was intensely partisan in tone and content through much of the nineteenth century. Today journalism has become a far more professional occupation, bound by an ethic of objectivity.[23] By contrast to the evaluative, cue-giving style of an earlier day, today's reporter adopts a more narrative approach to the news and believes in the duty to present facts, not values, to the audience. Network television has perfected this nonpartisan, non-editorializing approach to news. In part the networks' avoidance of partisan politics stems from their economic incentive to attract the largest possible mass audience. In part the nonpartisan stance is enforced upon them by legal regulations requiring balanced reporting and equal time to opposing candidates and parties.

Partisanship has been in parallel decline in twentieth-century American politics. As decades of political science research confirms, the strength of party organizations, the loyalty of citizens to parties, and the grip of party labels on voting have seriously eroded over the last fifty years. In the nineteenth century, candidates waged campaigns by rousing the party faithful and mobilizing tight-knit, army-like party organizations. In the twentieth century, candidates downplay partisan messages and party labels, competing instead for swing voters, independents, and ticket splitters. They turn to the mass media and to their own ad hoc campaign organizations, more than to the political party, for publicity and support.

The decline in the partisan behavior of voters and the decline in media partisanship have reinforced one another. The death of the party press stripped party organizations of their early monopoly over the news. No longer beholden to the party for financing, the commercial press popularized a far more independent approach to newsworthiness. Conversely, the rise of the independent voter solidified the growing hold of objective standards on the new journalism. In other words, it is not a question of media change producing political change or vice versa. It is a matter of the interplay of politics and media in the United States.

Homogeneity of Message. Closely related to the rise of a nonpartisan press is the shift toward a more uniform message across the media. Multinewspaper communities are disappearing. When cities had several newspapers (Boston had eight of them in 1948), the papers typically sought to differentiate their products by expressing distinct points of view. In a single-newspaper town, controversial editorials are infrequent, because they may antagonize some segment of the paper's heterogeneous audience. The recent history of FM radio illustrates the same tendency. At first it was thought that FM would offer listeners a variety of alternative programming; today most FM stations broadcast music and news that is indistinguishable from that of their competitors. This uniformity of media messages is most evident on television. The three major networks say and do essentially the same thing day in and day out.

Likewise with American politics. Time has worked to erase many of the regional differences that flavored nineteenth-century culture and politics. "States' rights" is a slogan of a bygone era. The Fourteenth Amendment to the Constitution has long since authorized the federal judiciary to enforce the same understanding of the Bill of Rights against each state. In the world of party politics, until a half-century ago, there remained important regional factions within the national parties. There were southern wings, western wings, and so on. This variation has become muted over time, as each of the parties has become centralized and homogeneous.

Commercialization of Financing. Money, it has been said, is the mother's milk of politics. It is no less a nutrient to the media. Initially the American press had extremely close financial ties with the government, for a time even becoming part of the formal machinery of state. Newspapers were created, sponsored, and controlled by public officials. Because of their narrow circulation base, they could not generate enough revenue to remain financially independent. Before long they became the appendages of political parties and relied on them for the bulk of their financial support. Starting with the penny press of the 1830s, newspapers gradually became privately owned and advertiser-supported. And although alternatives have been considered, it is advertiser financing that sustains most radio and television in the United States. The commercialization of the press reinforced and accelerated some of the trends already mentioned, such as the growth of mass-circulation papers, coverage of daily events of interest to the ordinary reader, and dilution of partisanship and point of view in news reporting.

Politics has followed a similar financial progression, from a system dominated by government patronage and a narrow elected elite (in a legislative caucus), to a system in which the principal monetary resources came from political parties, and then to our current political system, which is highly dependent on the private sector. Today ad hoc candidate organizations raise money from individual donors and political action committees (PACs) that represent corporations, labor unions, and trade associations.

Even this sketchy review of the historical interplay between media and politics in the United States is sufficient to illustrate two of this book's important themes. First, technological determinism is inadequate to describe the way in which new communications devices influence the course of politics. Consider the case of the penny press. It is true that mass circulation of newspapers could not have been achieved without technical improvements in transportation, printing presses, and paper production. But the same communications breakthroughs occurred in England without democratizing the definition of newsworthiness in the same way. The politics of Jacksonian democracy pushed American journalists to pioneer the use of new technologies to report the common people's news.

Today, latter-day technological determinists are busy predicting ways in which the computer will inevitably democratize politics or ways in which it will inevitably foster authoritarian politics. The same warring predictions are made about satellites, video, and the other new media. The problem with these deterministic predictions is not just that some must be wrong if others are right, but, more important, that they all rest on the fallacious assumption that machines have politics. The history of media-politics relations in the United States shows that "what matters is not the technology itself, but the social or economic system in which it is embedded." To find

either virtues or evils in aggregates of steel, plastic, transistors, integrated circuits, and chemicals seems just plain wrong, a way of mystifying human artifices and of avoiding the true sources, the human sources of freedom and oppression, justice and injustice.[24]

Second, the past history of media-politics relations in the United States also rules out what might be called "political determinism." In this view, "technical *things* do not matter at all. Once one has done the detective work necessary to reveal the social origins—power holders behind a particular instance of technological change—one will have explained everything of importance."[25] There are many who fall into the fallacy of believing that the invalidity of technological determinism proves the validity of political determinism. That this is not the case is clear from the impact of television on American politics. The political determinist is certainly right to stress that the politics of television do not flow from any inherent properties in the technology itself, that the power of advertiser financing plays the pivotal role in deciding which programs are broadcast. Still, while television itself does not *cause* any particular political changes, video technology has certainly proved more compatible with some political practices than others. For instance, television made it possible for the first time for millions of Americans to see and hear a *live* speech by the president, without being in the physical presence of the president. This in itself has bred a new sense of familiarity of citizens with the president, a familiarity that presidents exploit in their election campaigns and tenure in office. After all, you cannot televise an entire political party but you can televise an individual candidate. What works best on television is the candidate-centered campaign, with all the attention to personality, individual character, appearance, poise, and demeanor that mark the television campaign. An older campaign strategy, which centered on party label, and endorsement of party bosses, has not translated nearly as well into the television era.

Another influence of television has been on the arena of politics. Television coverage of a presidential candidate's appearances in New Hampshire during primary season means that the audience for the candidate's words is national as well as local. The ability of candidates to retract in California what they say in New Hampshire is diminished, as the campaign has been nationalized from an early date.

Thus, while television does not require any particular kind of politics, it is more congenial to candidate-centered than party-centered campaigns, to national rather than local focus for presidential politics. It has also given politics the wherewithal to concentrate on what is visual and personal in a candidate. This congeniality of television with one set of political practices over another is at times so strong that to choose television as our central medium of mass political communication is to choose a politics as well.

Because political determinism is an incomplete account of how mass communications affects politics, it is necessary to study any new communication technology in and of itself, with an eye toward discerning the qualities that might tilt the technology toward one form of politics over another. Yet because technological determinism is an incomplete account of how mass communications affects politics, it is also necessary to study democratic theory in and of itself, with an eye toward discerning the choices we ought to make in order to put the new technologies to the best democratic use. In the remainder of this chapter, we turn to this study of democratic theory. Our effort will be to clarify the value choices that regulators of the new media will soon have to make.

Democratic Theory and the New Media

What are the opportunities and what are the dangers for democracy in the new age of instant and global communications? In grappling with these questions, we have avoided judging the new media against some master list of democratic values. Of course, essential democratic values do come to mind—freedom of speech and of the press; tolerance; equal treatment of persons; the rights to vote, hold office, and participate in the political process on an equal basis; limited government; constitutionalism; privacy; and due process of law. The problem with any such list is not only the difficulty of justifying why some values are included and others not (why is privacy more essential to democracy than, say, free public education?). The deeper problem is that naming democratic values one by one does not explain how those values cohere into an overall system of democratic government. At this level, the history of politics in the United States betrays fundamental disagreement about what a democracy is. In particular, three competing understandings of democracy have vied for supremacy in American politics. Each understanding argues for different uses and regulations of the press and mass communications.

Plebiscitary Democracy

Why do we commonly believe that democracy is morally superior to other forms of government? One prevalent way of stating the moral case for democracy is to emphasize the sovereignty it bestows upon the people, the freedom it gives as many persons as possible to participate as directly as possible in the affairs of government. But if democracy takes its value from the autonomy we achieve through self-government, then representative government obviously entails a serious compromise with democratic values. For, as democratic realists such as Joseph Schumpeter and Robert Dahl have persuasively documented, it is fiction to claim that the people of the United States possess the power to decide political issues directly. Instead of a system of self-government, representative democracy in practice is an arrangement whereby elites "acquire the power to decide by means of a competitive struggle for the people's vote."[26]

What would it take, then, to give us more and better democracy? It is widely conceded that the sheer size of the modern nation-state made representative, not direct, democracy the only practical choice for the Founders. And yet from Jacksonian democracy to Progressivism to the modern presidential primary, reform movements in the United States have searched for ways to broaden the mass base of American democracy and to tighten the fit between public opinion and public policy. For the Jacksonians, this meant the principle of universal manhood suffrage, at least for white males; for the Progressives, the key was to empower the people to set government policy directly through the holding of plebiscites, referenda, and initiatives; for modern party politics, the hope lies in mass-based primary elections where the people at large, and not party bosses and regulars, nominate candidates for office. In this book, we refer to this first understanding of democracy as plebiscitary democracy. The plebiscite stands as a symbol of those democratic reform movements that seek to empower individuals to do more in government than simply elect representatives to do the governing. Instead, the core ideal is the sovereignty of public opinion in a democracy; and what better way to make the people sovereign than to empower them to function as their own legislature through the holding of plebiscites and referenda?

Plebiscitarians have had only moderate success in changing the official institutions of American government. Over the course of U.S. history, the drift of democracy has certainly been toward a mass-based system; no fewer than seven of the sixteen amendments to the Constitution passed since the Bill of Rights deal with extending the franchise. This drive for universal suffrage now stands formally complete. But no national referendum or initiative procedure has ever been adopted; rates of electoral participation have actually declined in the twentieth century from the more partisan and mobilizing campaign eras of the nineteenth century; and it is only since 1968 that the primary election has decisively replaced the caucus or convention as a method for nominating candidates for office.

Unofficially, plebiscitary democracy finds its greatest triumph in the reliance candidates and elected officials now place on polls and public-opinion surveys. This is not to say that government policy is held captive to the latest poll or that the classical concept of independent representatives has wholly lost its grip on American politics. Nonetheless the technological breakthroughs that allow candidates and officials to know at any particular time what public opinion is on any particular issue have lent considerable support to the plebiscitarian argument that a more direct and participatory democratic process is available than the Founders ever imagined possible.

Of special concern to us here are the distinct uses of mass

communications for which the plebiscitary theory of democracy argues. From the telegraph to the television, the electronic media have already served to conquer many of the problems of scale that once made direct democracy an ideal impossible to practice. Today satellites and computers eliminate the remaining constraints of space and time on communication. Conversations are relayed almost instantly across the globe—and increasingly to the moon and planets beyond. An almost unlimited number of persons can be present electronically at the same place at the same time, exchanging an almost unlimited volume of information. All this adds up, according to some, to the obsolescence of representative government as we now know it and the dawn of a new era of electronically aided direct democracy.[27] Schemes for electronic voting from the home, via telephone or cable television, are touted; computers are to be hooked to television or telephone to tabulate results instantly. Compared to the mass democratic possibilities of such electronic voting, modern elections and representative government are dismissed as parodies of democratic participation.

We, however, take a jaundiced view of plebiscitary democracy and of the uses of the new media for which it argues. Although it speaks to a yearning we share for more participatory forms of democracy, plebiscitary forms of participation—especially in the quickened form contemplated by advocates of electronic voting—contain a characteristic danger. In their concern for speed and numbers, so-called feedback schemes can be rigged to communicate public opinion to government without pause for the public meetings and assemblies, the talk and deliberations that focus an individual's attention on questions of the common good and public interest. The result is to reduce political participation to the passive and private act of registering one's own preconceived opinion on an issue. When public opinion in this crude and unreflective sense becomes the law of the land, then democracy is divorced from any politics of the common good. Politics becomes simply a set of institutional arrangements for expressing and satisfying the interests we hold as private persons. Without benefit of discussion, we record our own interests on the question at hand, and the public interest is simply the aggregate or sum total of these individual interests.

It is in the nature of a plebiscite or poll to collapse democracy into a crudely majoritarian system. But, while one strand of democratic thought obviously requires deference to the will of the majority, another more libertarian strand focuses on protecting individual and minority rights against majority rule. In the United States, this libertarian strand and the rights-based democracy for which it argues runs deep; one has only to think of the central role we give to the Constitution and the Supreme Court in defining a sphere of liberty that lies beyond the encroachments of the majority. The gravest danger in plebiscitary democracy is that its hurry to make public opinion "at last the law of the land"[28] does away with the libertarian strand in our democracy.

We have no doubt that the new media can and will be used to accelerate political debate and to privatize voting in a way that fits with plebiscitary understandings of direct democracy and participation. In Hawaii and elsewhere, experiments with televoting from the home have already been held.[29] But one of our prime purposes in writing this book is to argue that such uses of mass communications are more foe than friend of democratic discourse.

Communitarian Democracy

An alternative understanding of democracy rests the moral superiority of self-government on service to common rather than merely private ends. Democrats of the "common good" tradition are, of course, not hostile to the individual. But here the ambition of democratic politics is to reorient our ends in life; to enlarge the interests of the individual through debate and discourse with others; to enrich the self through the experience of citizenship. In John Dewey's phrase, democracy is "a way of life itself"—not some set of cold procedures for serving the private lives we lead elsewhere. This common way of life is available only to individuals who conceive of themselves as citizens, sharing a common identity and purpose with fellow citizens. Democracy is not a process for allowing a majority to rule over minority interests antagonistically; it is a process of persuasion through which we seek to create and maintain a good life in common.

"Create citizens and you will have everything you need; without them, you will have nothing but debased slaves," Rousseau admonished.[30] But the creation of citizens requires politics to "produce . . . a very remarkable change in man."[31] Without losing autonomy, individuals must gain a capacity for common vision, for seeing things in general.[32] Such commonality of vision is hard for citizens of the modern nation-state, separated by distance as well as background, to achieve. Like the plebiscitarian, the communitarian therefore balks at the watered-down version of democracy accomplished by representative government. Without opportunity to participate directly in government, citizenship is a passive and periodic experience, leaving us strangers, not fellow human beings.

But the communitarian ideal of participation is radically different from the plebiscitarian ideal. In plebiscitary democracy, casting votes on a secret ballot still remains the individual's preferred way of participating in government. Only now a person can vote more quickly, more often—and for issues as well as candidates. For the communitarian, no extension of voting on secret ballots can overcome the alienation between citizen and citizen or sponsor the public debate that alone makes participation in government a course in civic education. What is required is participation in public space—in the meetings and assemblies, the deliberations and persuasions that distinguish the democratic process and make participation in it a transformative lesson in the common good. As one contemporary political theorist expresses the connection between democracy and community:

What "is most significant [about] democracy is the involvement of citizens in the process of determining their own collective identity." A true democratic polity involves a deliberative process, participation with other citizens, a sense of moral responsibility for one's society and the enhancement of individual possibilities through action in, and for, the *res publica*.[33]

A politics of fraternity and community, while not the predominant American experience, has shaped our democracy in powerful ways from the beginning. Throughout the founding period, there ensued a debate between those who viewed democratic politics primarily as a clash among interest groups and those who held to a more classical conception of a common good pursued only by a people with sufficient civic virtue and patriotic spirit to triumph over narrow self-interest and the antagonisms it breeds. This latter conception of politics requires a radical democrat's faith in the virtue of the people. By the time of the Constitutional Convention, that faith was already fragile, and substantial parts of the federal structure—the indirect election of senators, the presidential veto, the life-tenured appointment of federal judges—speak to moderating the average citizen's influence on government.

Still, the communitarian conception was not entirely lost; at the local level, in institutions such as the town meeting or school committee or jury, public forums for participation and deliberation survived. Visiting the United States in the 1830s, Alexis de Tocqueville remarked upon the civic education Americans gained through meaningful self-government at the local level. In France, the Revolution had succeeded in destroying the ranks and classes of the old order and in achieving equality of social condition. But it was the equality of the obscure and powerless: a mass of isolated individuals facing an increasingly centralized state.[34] In the United States, Tocqueville saw a difference. There were vibrant local communities and loyalties that gave individuals genuine opportunities for participation in government and that staved off the dangers of mass society and centralization. About town meetings in particular Tocqueville remarked that they "are to liberty what primary schools are to science; they bring it within the people's reach, they teach men how to use and how to enjoy it. A nation may establish a free government but without municipal institutions it cannot have the spirit of liberty."[35]

Thus, though politics on the scale of the nation-state threatened a centralization of power inconsistent with participatory democracy, the United States had found in the articulated political distinctions of federalism a partial antidote to the problems of scale. State and local governments were to remain a plurality of decentralized powers in their own right, accessible to the participation of the many and supportive of the common allegiances that breed in citizens civic virtue and a common identity.

How can modern mass communications come to support the public forms of participation that inspire the communitarian vision of democracy? Is there an electronic version of the old commonwealth ideal where technology overcomes the obstacles of space and population to the town-meeting model of politics? We have seen that the plebiscitarian counts on the speed and reach of the new media to give public opinion increased legislative power on particular issues. But the communitarian distrusts modern mass communications precisely for such reasons. Politics on an ever more national and centralized scale is hostile to the local involvements that deliver civic education; speed is inimical to the deliberativeness of democratic discourse. What the communitarian looks for in the new media is a way to reverse the centralization of politics and political communication that has been characteristic of television's impact, in particular, on politics. For instance, a conventional broadcasting station has no way to televise a local school board meeting to only those neighborhoods served by the board; because it would have to broadcast the meeting to an entire metropolitan area, the station typically attends to politics at this level only sporadically—when something dramatic or of appeal to a wider audience is at issue.

One of the enticing features of cable television, from the communitarian's point of view, is that its wired technology allows a much more pinpointed or tailored use of television: different programs going to different neighborhoods or regions, with the geographical area variable from program to program. Another enticing feature of the new video age for the communitarian is its two-way or interactive capacity. To date, television has empowered government to speak to citizens far more effectively than it has permitted citizens to talk back to government. But today state-of-the-art hookups of telephones, televisions, and computers can facilitate the electronic equivalent of a town meeting. People can be present to talk with one another at places and times and in numbers previously impossible. If used, for instance, to allow parents to engage school board members in back-and-forth conversation, cable television might come to represent an important breakthrough in television's passivity and have important democratic uses and consequences. Experiments with electronic town meetings—in Reading, Pennsylvania, for instance, between senior citizens and the city council—have already been held, with promising results (see chapter 5).

The communitarian conception of democracy is, in our judgment, fundamentally more attractive than the plebiscitarian conception. But its strength—emphasizing the communal rather than private values served by democracy—is also its characteristic weakness. For there is always the danger that communities will move in a closed direction, enforcing some monolithic set of collective values and shutting their doors to foreigners or outsiders. Not all communities are a common wealth. One virulent, anti-democratic abuse of the communitarian vision is to support extreme nationalistic notions of community. Not only does a nation as a whole rarely form a genuine community; the politics of national identity can be used to expunge the rich plurality of sub-communities to which we more meaningfully belong—ethnic, racial, religious, ideological, occupational, and regional groups to which we owe loyalty and allegiance by virtue of the impact fellows in such groups have on one another's lives.

Antidemocratic invocations of community and national identity have echoed throughout American history—in nativist movements against Catholics; in immigration restrictions and closed-door policies; in defense of segregation as essential to the South's distinctive way of life. Communitarianism with a democratic face rules out such forms of community. What we value in a community—what makes a community just—is the equal respect and treatment of all persons within its midst. Unless a community is premised on equality in this sense, it has no moral claim on the obedience of its members.

In this book, we have taken seriously the classical argument that democracy is more than some procedure for adding up or aggregating the preferences and interests of individuals; that democracy instead speaks to a conception of the common good that can be known only among a people that sees itself not merely as a loosely connected set of private destinies but as a body of citizens embarked on a common way of life. But, because the danger that communitarian arguments can be put to antidemocratic use seems apparent to us, we turn now to a third conception of democracy—pluralism—in hopes of tempering the claims of "the" community with respect for the moral diversity of the many communities among us.

Pluralist Democracy

So many different theories of democracy have been called pluralist that it is hard to give a unified account of what a pluralist thinks democracy is. If there is one essential claim that pluralists agree upon, it would be that the modern democratic process is based on the principle of free competition among groups. Individuals join groups on the basis of some perceived group interest; the democratic process is the clash that results among these group interests—the bargains, compromises, trade-offs, coalitions, and negotiations that take place as each group seeks to put together majority support for its particular and partial interests.

In the pluralist description of interest-group politics, the classical conception of the common good plays no part. "We can only distinguish groups of various types and sizes," Robert Dahl admonishes, "all seeking in various ways to advance their goals, usually at the expense, at least in part, of others."[36] There is neither "a common good or a public interest independent of a compromise of group interests. The governmental process can be seen simply as group warfare."[37] As opposed to a politics of the common good in any strong sense of the term, then, the pluralist describes as democracy those situations in which individuals organize into political groups to fight for the particular interests they hold as individuals:

I and my "interests" become attached to my social segment and organizations; leaders in my organizations in turn seek to increase the strength and salience of my attachments; my public interest becomes identical in my mind with my segmental interest; since what is true of me is true of others, we all passively or actively support the organizational fight on behalf of our particularistic interests.[38]

Pluralism is both an empirical theory, describing how states classified as democracies actually work, and a normative theory, defending free competition among groups as the most just political arrangement that it is possible to achieve. What, then, is the moral virtue of interest-group politics? Some pluralists value interest-group politics for its service to majority rule: the process gives every group an incentive to engage in the bargains and coalitions that alone produce majority support for a particular set of interests. Thus any obstacle to the expression of interests (for instance, restrictions on free speech) or to having interests equally represented or to organizing with others to fight for overlapping interests (for instance, racial prejudice) is rejected by pluralists as destructive of the majoritarian political process.

But it is far more common for pluralists to defend interest-group politics precisely for the contribution it makes to tempering the majoritarian strand in democracy. Here the moral argument in favor of pluralism harks back to *Federalist* No. 10 and to James Madison's fear of faction. Factional conflict among minority interests was bad enough, but even more fearsome was the social conflict likely to result if the majority were powerful enough to rule on the basis of its particular interests to the exclusion of concern for minority interests. If majority rule in democracy was not to be tyrannical in this sense, then the principle of majoritarianism had to be moderated. The United States Constitution embodied many strategies for tempering majority rule—the federal system itself; separation of powers and checks and balances; a Bill of Rights that placed certain matters beyond the power of the majority; an unelected federal judiciary; provisions for a presidential veto; and others. For the pluralist, the result was and is a novel system of government in which there is no single center of sovereign power. Instead,

there must be multiple centers of power, none of which is or can be wholly sovereign. Although the only legitimate sovereign is the people, in the perspective of American pluralism even the people ought never to be an absolute sovereign; consequently no part of the people, such as a majority, ought to be absolutely sovereign.[39]

Here, then, is the moral case for pluralist democracy: it avoids tyranny of the majority, tames political power, and avoids the conflicts between majority and minority that any crude understanding of popular sovereignty would breed. It provides minorities with an opportunity to organize effectively with other minorities to veto objectionable policies; it places a premium on negotiation and bargaining among different interest groups, thereby reducing social conflict to a minimum and allowing for coalitions of ever more overlapping interests to rule. In a famous phrase, Dahl summarized the pluralist norm as "minorities rule," rather than majority rule.[40]

Pluralism carries its own set of recommendations for how mass communications and the new media in particular can best realize democratic values. Given the importance of television as a political medium today, problems of gaining access to the airwaves and the high cost of purchasing broadcast time fit ill with the pluralist model of effective group politics. It is highly unlikely, for instance, that any group can mount an effective national or statewide campaign for a candidate or issue without substantial free or purchased time on television. And yet minority and novel political views are the ones least in the position to attract television attention or to buy promotional time. The range of political programming on television thus tends to be fairly homogeneous—aimed at the tastes and preferences of the widest possible mass audience.

From the pluralist's point of view, what is needed is to break the hold of mass-audience programming on television—to move to a diverse menu of programs aimed at the diversity of groups and interests that constitute a morally pluralistic society such as ours. In this regard, cable television especially captures the pluralist's attention; special-interest programming is already plentiful on cable channels. There are black, Hispanic, Christian, and Jewish cable networks; public-access channels open to local groups or individuals on a first-come, first-served basis; local government channels televising city council meetings, school board sessions, and the like; educational and children's channels. To flip through the cable dial is to tour the pluralism of American life.

Essentially, there are two reasons why the new television age promises a new pluralism. First, the scarcity of conventional broadcasting in any one geographical area has given way to an abundance of video programming via cable, the VCR, the backyard satellite dish, microwave relay, videotex, and other new video delivery systems. Second is the difference between free and subscription television. The advertiser-driven nature of conventional television gives stations an economic incentive to use each programming hour to reach the largest audience (for this is what advertisers pay for). Financed in large part by viewer subscriptions, cable systems and other new pay-television technologies currently lack the same incentive to air mass-audience programming on each and every channel in the system. For instance, if cable operators can add some new segment of the local population to their subscription list by televising opera on one of their 108 channels rather than *I Love Lucy* reruns (which are already available on another of the system's channels), then it makes economic sense for operators to do so. In this way, the abundance of channel capacity and the subscription financing of cable combine to make plurality in television programming *possible*. These, at any rate, are the kinds of arguments about the significance of the new media that a concern for pluralism provokes, and we shall explore the strength of such arguments throughout this book.

If the characteristic danger of plebiscitary democracy is the quickness with which opinions are registered and if the characteristic danger of communitarian democracy is closed and exclusionary communities, what is to beware in pluralist democracies? One problem often pointed out is that pluralism tends to exaggerate the equality of group resources and to hide the extent to which prejudice and poverty preclude certain groups from politicking effectively in the United States. These *are* problems with pluralism, but the problem we have in mind is not simply that pluralism is an ideal difficult to practice; it is that the ideal itself is flawed. The interest-group model of democratic politics starts and concludes on the premise that there are only particular and antagonistic group interests in society, that the "common good" is nothing beyond the result of the clash and competition among such groups. To describe democratic politics in this way is to bless it with partisan animation. But it is also to legitimize a thin view of political life as a game with winners and losers, with the winners owing few obligations to care for the losers. We take the position that politics is more than a market game in this sense, that we are fellow citizens implicated in a common project in a way that imposes obligations of solidarity. These obligations transcend the mere attempt to achieve one's own group interest.

The democratic theory that lies behind this book can be described as a cross between the pluralist and communitarian views —pluralism with a communitarian face, as it were. In line with the communitarian view, we believe that democratic citizenship is never fully reducible to our status as Jews or Christians, blacks or whites, poor or rich. Over and above these particular identifications, we join together to govern our own community, and this act of self-governance imposes on us the obligation to explore and maintain common grounds and common goods. In line with pluralism, we believe that the community we share and seek to defend is neither a closed nor an exclusionary one, but one premised on tolerance and equal respect for the diversity of communal members. Nor is the nation itself the relevant political community for all purposes; a rich and robust democratic life demands support for the plurality of local communities in which the ideals of participation and deliberation—of self-government, in short—can actually be practiced.

The New Media and Democratic Values

The history of mass communications in the United States has not served pluralism with a communitarian face well. The scale-conquering capacity of electronic media, from the telegraph to the television, has led us to communicate on an ever more national, mass basis. And while a national communications network has helped to give us a kind of common culture and to avoid the dangers of faction and fragmentation that have stalked democracies and republics before ours, the common national culture of television has narrowed the range of American values and neglected the local politics—the school board meeting, the selectmen session, the town meeting—that from Tocqueville on has been seen as providing the core civic education of democratic citizens.

How, then, we can seize the opportunity presented by the current changes in the media environment to reorient mass communications toward more robust democratic service is the subject of this book. The electronic commonwealth referred to in this book's title is not a place of gadgets and gimmicks. It is not—at least not yet—the rallying cry for high-tech politics run amuck. Instead, the electronic commonwealth harks back to the old democratic ideal of congregating the people together. The contribution of new communications technologies is not to change or update that ideal. It is simply to use electronics to practice the lost democratic arts.

C H A P T E R 2

WHAT'S NEW ABOUT
THE NEW MEDIA?

THE FUTURE of any technology can be perceived on the horizon
only dimly. That is particularly true of new media technologies.
For one thing, the changes taking place in the communications
industry today are based on no single invention—no Gutenberg
press or telephone—but on new combinations of several recent
innovations. Technologies that have been around for decades—
computers, coaxial cables, telephone lines, satellites, television
sets—are being merged and integrated in new ways so as to create
different methods of gathering, storing, retrieving, and transmitting information. As a consequence, the boundaries between the
media are becoming blurred, if not disappearing altogether.

Yet as significant as these changes might be, they are not
wiping the technology slate clean, and this too obscures our view
of the future. Current transformations in telecommunications—
like earlier transformations in speech, writing, and printing—will
not replace earlier media. Reading and writing did not eliminate

Parts of this chapter, as indicated in the endnotes, were drafted by Stephen Bates.

speech. Nor did television relegate the printing press or the radio to the scrap heap. Each new technology added to the communication options. The same will be true today. Broadcast television, printed newspapers, in-person mail delivery, and movie theaters will not disappear with the arrival of cable, videotex, electronic mail, and videocassette recorders. Thus one cannot simply say that down the road the public will rely on this particular technology or that one. The more complicated truth is that the future menu of media options will be enlarged.

Finally, the speed of change in modern communications makes it difficult to identify the specific items on that menu. Over time, changes in communication have accelerated. Indeed, during the last century more innovations in communications have appeared than in the preceding 360 centuries. Communications analyst Frederick Williams has cleverly illustrated this quickening pace with the following analogy:[1] Imagine that the history of human communications from Cro-Magnon times to the present were squeezed into the twenty-four hours of a single day. We would spend all of the morning hours with very little change. Writing (Egyptian hieroglyphics) would appear as late as 8:40 in the evening, followed by the Phonecian alphabet at 9:28. It is not until 11:38 P.M. that the first Gutenberg Bible would be printed. The pace begins to quicken as the steam press appears at 11:53 P.M., then the telegraph twenty-four seconds later, the telephone at 11:55:02 and the phonograph 2 milliseconds later. The last five minutes, a mere speck of time in the history of human communications, virtually explode with new communication technologies: commercial radio, motion pictures, computers, xerography, transistors, television, satellites, microelectronic circuitry, and all the rest.

Modern communication technologies, then, are advancing at an unprecedented rate. As discussed in chapter 1, which particular new technology will prosper and which will fall by the wayside remains unsettled. But while the precise shape of the future media landscape is obscure, its broad outlines can be discerned. Our strategy, therefore, has been to emphasize the "generic properties" of the new media, the most important features they share in common, particularly the features that contrast with those of current media. Some of these generic properties apply to all of the new media; others are shared by a few of them. Six properties stand out:

1. Greater volume of available information.
2. Faster gathering, retrieving, and transmitting of information.
3. More control over the media by consumers.
4. Greater ability of senders to target their messages to specific audiences.
5. Greater decentralization of the media.
6. Greater interactive capacity.

We examine each of these properties in turn.

Volume: The Greater Flow of Information

Perhaps the most apparent change wrought by new media technology is an increase in the volume of information available to the public. The sheer amount of information, as well as the number and diversity of information conduits, has multiplied rapidly over the past decade or so. In addition to newspapers, magazines, radio, and broadcast television, the communications marketplace is buzzing with new electronic media, chief among them cable, computer, teletext, videotex, VCR, and satellite.

Of course, the new technologies do not conjure new information out of thin air; instead, they greatly expand the ways that consumers gain access to existing information. For example, most of the information that can now be retrieved instantaneously by personal computers and videotex terminals existed long before it was placed in electronic data bases. But it was stored in the basements of public libraries and other out-of-the-way places that were beyond the reach of distant consumers.

Neither is higher consumption a foregone conclusion. True, an expanding supply of information may create demand just as music videocassettes invigorated the popular music market; the growing availability of information on people's favorite subjects might satisfy an unmet demand just as special-interest magazines captured a hidden market. Yet it is equally possible that the individual's overall appetite for information, particularly for public-affairs information, will remain the same.

In any case, the communications menu is fast becoming more plentiful and varied. The word that invariably pops up in discussions on this subject is cornucopia. Surveying the growing abundance of communications choices and the vast amount of information they provide, one futurist concluded: "To an increasing degree we will be able to find out almost everything we want to know about anything whenever we want."[2]

Cable television, to use a particularly good example, has greatly increased the amount of information available to consumers by offering a multitude of channels and thus making possible a multitude of information services. Cable adds to channel capacity by compressing the over-the-air signals into an enclosed medium; this prevents signals at similar frequencies from interfering with one another. The number of channels can therefore grow from the dozen or fewer typical on broadcast television to as many as two hundred. In March 1988, 77 percent of all cable-subscribing households had access to thirty or more channels, 90 percent had access to twenty or more.[3] Future refinements in technology—conversion from coaxial to fiber optic cable—could provide up to a thousand cable channels. In 1983 more than 5,700 cable systems served approximately 39 percent of American television households.[4] By 1988 some 7,800 systems served slightly more than 50 percent of these homes (about 45 million subscribers), with an increase to 60 percent anticipated by 1990.[5]

The cable operation in Irving, Texas (population 100,000), a city with no local broadcast television station of its own, is fairly typical. It has experienced the ups and downs felt throughout the cable industry over the last decade. In terms of the volume of information made available, the Irving cable operation in 1982 came close to being a maximum-capacity system. At that time the system's 107 channels reached subscribers through one of three package deals.[6]

Package One offered thirty channels. Eight carried programming from television stations within a thirty-mile radius. Governmental, educational, and other kinds of community programming "coordinated by the City of Irving" occupied ten more. There were channels originated by the local library, public schools, minorities, youth, women, and local religious organizations. One of the channels was reserved for signed and captioned programming for the hearing-impaired, and four were combined to allow area cable systems to share programs simultaneously. Finally, there was a choice of two premium channels, which carried family films. This package cost $2.95 a month in 1982.

Package Two offered the preceding channels plus fifty-nine others. The emphasis switched from local access to the advertiser-supported satellite program services: superstations, sports and news services, the health network, the national public-affairs network, religious networks, and movies (viewers could subscribe to any of the five premium movie channels). This package cost $6.95 a month.

Package Three offered nine additional services, five of which had interactive capabilities. Included were pay-per-view programs, news and information-retrieval services, interactive college-level and professional training courses, and "enrichment classes" for school-age children. This package cost $9.95 a month.

This bounty stood in stark contrast to the two broadcast channels imported from Dallas-Fort Worth. The cable system in Irving transformed television from an entertainment medium into a powerful information source connected to data banks and a convenient municipal communications network.

By 1988, however, this abundance of channels and services had shrunk from 107 to 54 channels, and from a rich array of interactive services to none. As in other cities, the multi-tiered packages were replaced with a single basic package: 48 channels (which cost $10.95 a month) along with five premium movie channels and one regional sports network (each of which cost an additional $9.45 a month). Although there are far fewer options in 1988 than in 1982, the current 54 channels still represent a larger menu than the eleven broadcast stations now imported from Dallas-Fort Worth.[7]

Nationwide the cable industry is experiencing growing pains. Although cable is available to some 82 percent of the 89 million U.S. homes with television sets, only about 62 percent of those households subscribe.[8] The growth spurt that sent cable's "audience penetration" from 13 percent in 1975 to 35 percent in 1982 has given way to more modest expansion. Having encountered serious political and economic hurdles, many of the largest cities in the country have only recently been wired. Moreover, some of the current cable systems, installed before the 1970s, have limited channel capacity—twelve or fewer channels. The unrealistic expectations and glowing promises of cable's initial phase have collided with reality. Euphoria has given way to sober reassessment and revised timetables.

Nonetheless, cable continues to spread across the country and, despite the recent slowdown, to grow faster than many experts expected. It is still true that cable commands primacy among the new telecommunications technologies.

Yet other new media promise to increase the volume of available information as well. Teletext is a one-way technology that delivers textual and graphic information to TV screens or computer monitors. Teletext receives data from satellite, radio, or (most commonly) TV signals (broadcast or cable). Teletext cycles its information, repeating the full data base over and over. By punching a number on a decoder, viewers can retrieve hundreds of "pages" of information, including news headlines, weather reports, sports scores, videogames, stock prices, and local livestock auction bids. The user who tunes in just after the desired information has gone by must wait for it to cycle through again. During one TV station's evening newscast (which contained a mere six hundred words), the anchor periodically urged viewers to "see page 18" of the teletext for more information on a given story.[9] The number of teletext subscribers in the country at this time is probably less than 75,000. Both CBS and NBC have begun transmitting teletext signals (news, sports, weather, travel information, and advertising) over their networks, but few decoders are in use to unscramble the signals.

A more powerful, and more costly, technology is videotex, a two-way link between the television set and a central computer. In theory, it can hold an infinite number of information "pages" by connecting the user directly to the data base via telephone or interactive cable. Users can retrieve precisely the information they want. One proposed system offers 75,000 pages; in contrast, a typical Sunday paper contains about 300 pages of text. Videotex screens can display words, numbers, and sophisticated color graphics. For the cost of a videotex terminal, a monthly subscription fee, and telephone charges, one can retrieve real estate listings, library catalogs, newspaper stories, and "almost anything else that can be printed,"[10] as well as conduct a variety of transactions (banking, shopping, and so on) from home. Videotex-based "electronic newspapers" offer the user virtually as much, or as little, information on a story as he or she wants. They begin with headlines but can provide more information, far exceeding what appears in a printed newspaper, depending on the user's interest.

Several videotex-based information searching services have been launched—including the Dow Jones News/Retrieval Service, CompuServe, the Source, and Nexis—which virtually eliminate the barriers of distance and time in the retrieval of news information. A score of major city newspapers, including the *Washington Post* and the *Boston Globe*, signed on with the national videotex services that were conducting pilot projects to test the feasibility of electronic publishing, the transmission of the information contained in the daily newspapers to people's homes. In all, over one hundred newspapers and a number of other organizations have had videotex operations in progress or on the drawing board. Various consulting firms forecast that anywhere from 7 to 25 percent of U.S. households will be using teletext or videotex by 1990.[11]

One giant videotex project on the drawing board is "Trintex," a joint venture of IBM and Sears. CBS had been involved in the early stages of planning but pulled out in 1986. Trintex is scheduled to begin operation in 1988. Another new videotex service is Covidea, a cooperative venture of Bank of America, Chemical Bank, AT&T and Time, Inc. Covidea offers a wide range of electronic information but specializes in banking services.

For all its promise, videotex has yet to achieve commercial success. In 1983 Knight-Ridder launched its pioneer electronic newspaper (Viewtron) in southern Florida. Times-Mirror followed with its Gateway service in 1984. By 1986, both newspaper companies had halted their videotex experiments. The demand for the greater volume of general news information just was not there.

At the heart of the expanded volume of information and the proliferation of communication sources lies the communications satellite. Virtually all of the traditional media (radio, broadcast TV, the newspaper wire services, and the telephone) and many of the new technologies, particularly cable, have come to rely heavily on satellites.

Signals are beamed from a transmission station on the ground to a satellite 22,300 miles above the earth, where they are received and amplified by any one of a satellite's twenty-four transponders, devices that retransmit the signal. Each transponder can handle one video signal or one thousand telephone signals at a time, many more than a copper telephone wire can handle. The rebroadcast signal is picked up by an earth station, usually a radar dish.

With their twenty-four-channel capacity, satellites have fulfilled cable's promise, transforming it from an ingenious solution to TV reception problems in rural areas to a way of providing more TV signals nationwide. The technology has spawned about forty national satellite networks, including Home Box Office (HBO), the Cable News Network (CNN), Music Television (MTV), and the Cable-Satellite Public Affairs Network (C-SPAN).

In addition to serving as the handmaiden of media such as broadcast and cable TV, satellites are becoming a new medium in their own right. A direct broadcast satellite (DBS) can beam television programs directly to individual homes equipped with relatively small and inexpensive receiving dishes, thus bypassing local broadcasters or cable operators entirely. DBS holds particular appeal in areas too sparsely populated to justify wiring for cable. Thus far, high capital start-up expenses, the limited supply of costly programming, and intense competition from other technologies have retarded this new medium's progress.

The cornucopia of new media technologies includes not just cable, teletext, videotex, and satellites but also a wide assortment of exotic delivery systems and consumer services.

Several over-the-air technologies are already giving viewers a greater choice in television programming. The oldest of them, subscription television (STV) uses a conventional over-the-air television channel (usually UHF) to send a scrambled signal that can be unscrambled with a special receiver on the subscriber's TV set. Because STV has so far been limited to a single-channel service, it has had a hard time competing with multichannel cable systems. Although it is the oldest of the new pay TV services, STV seems unlikely to survive. It has been outdated not only by cable, DBS, and home VCRs but also by a new generation of subscription video services. These include microwave distribution service, low-power television, and VHF drop-ins.

Multipoint distribution service (MDS) is sometimes known as wireless cable. It delivers TV signals to the home using line-of-sight microwave in the ultra-high-frequency band of the electromagnetic spectrum. A special converter is necessary to convert the signal to VHF. Since 1983 the FCC has reallocated microwave channels from educational to commercial MDS use. The result has been multichannel MDS operations (MMDS). A certain number of microwave channels are still reserved for educational use; this programming goes by the name "instructional television fixed service" (ITFS).

Low-power television (LPTV) consists of broadcast television stations licensed to cover a relatively small geographic area (ten to fifteen miles in radius); it may be well suited for local programming or special-interest networks. VHF drop-ins are weak local stations that can be sandwiched between two existing VHF stations without causing frequency interference. Satellite Master Antenna Television (SMATV) is the equivalent of a miniature cable system, receiving programs via satellite and distributing them to a hotel, apartment building, or housing complex.

Still other new video services include home video equipment —particularly videocassette recorders, which are selling at a breakneck pace, and videodiscs, which have not been very popular so far; laser optical disks, which may become an ideal visual-information storage medium; personal computers equipped with communication devices (modems and special software) that enable the user to tap into computerized data bases or communicate with other users through "electronic mail"; and teleconferencing, which permits people in distant cities to confer with one another via satellite.

All these new technologies form the "second stage" of TV. The effect will be to augment, not to replace, broadcast television. As political scientist Ithiel de Sola Pool once noted:

Men did not stop speaking when they learned how to write; they did not stop writing by hand when they learned how to type; they did not stop reading when broadcasting came along. More often, however, all that a new medium does to an old one is to slow its rate of growth; more books are published than ever before, but less than would be if newspapers, magazines and broadcasts did not preempt so much of readers' time. So when we talk loosely of a possible "decline" of one medium with the growth of another, we most likely refer to only a relative decline.[12]

It is estimated, for example, that those who now have cable TV in their homes do about 30 percent of their viewing on cable channels. Thus, while cable may slowly eat away at the networks' share of the audience, the networks will remain the dominant media force for years to come. But this dominant force may take on a somewhat different face. New media often transform their predecessors. Although network television did not kill the radio industry as many predicted it would in the 1950s, the radio medium that is alive and well and stronger than ever today is not the mass medium of thirty years ago; it is a specialized medium that appeals to specific, fragmented audiences.

Finally, while the new media will substantially expand the total amount of information available to the public, the increase might vary from one kind of information to another. Will the new media increase television time for news and public affairs as well as for entertainment? For the past thirty years or so, the viewing audience that has tuned in around the dinner hour has had little option but to watch the national and local news. What will happen as the evening news competes with a wide range of attractive alternative programs on independent VHF stations and cable—including sports, current movies, and special-interest shows? Although the general appetite for public-affairs information is not great, newspapers provide a summary of the day's political events for everyone, regardless of their particular interests. What will happen if electronic publishing becomes widespread, allowing people to construct their own newspapers at home to suit their tastes? Will the volume of public-affairs information decline relative to other kinds of information? Newspaper readers and television viewers consume much of their news information inadvertently; a headline catches their eye, or a news bulletin interrupts their football game. An abundance of cable channels and electronic newspapers might sharply reduce such media "browsing."

Similarly, the relative volume of local, national, and international news may change with the growth of the new media. Studies of both print and broadcast media point to an increase in local news and a corresponding decline in national and international news in recent years.[13] In fact, somewhat surprisingly, local news has emerged as a profit maker. Some of the new media, such as cable and LPTV, might strengthen this trend toward localism, while others, such as direct broadcast satellites, might encourage more national and international coverage. The effect of the new media on the volume of different kinds of information—entertainment or news, local versus national news—depends in large measure on the impact of other inherent properties to be discussed—particularly the increasing control of senders and receivers.

Speed: "The Annihilation of Time and Space"

A second capability shared by all the new media is their acceleration of gathering, transmitting, and retrieving information.

Colonial newspapers got their stories by mail or by word of mouth. Most news in colonial papers concerned European affairs, which took from two to six weeks to reach London and an additional four to eight weeks to arrive in America. Originally, then, the news was not "new" at all. Instead, information was recorded as a historical account of a day's events long after it had occurred. In the 1830s, the penny press gave news a sense of timeliness; with large advertising revenues, newspapers could spend unprecedented sums for gathering news from all over the country in "speedy fashion," and their mass public appeal encouraged a new emphasis on current and sensational news.[14]

The age of rapid and regular news transmission ushered in by the telegraph, which for the first time separated communication from transportation, came to full maturity with telephone, radio, and television. "News" grew into its name. "The awesome fact of instantaneous communication provided cause enough for intense speculation," writes one media historian. "No future possibilities seemed as dazzling as present reality."[15]

The increased speed at which information will travel with new media technologies will probably alter the character of news yet again. Transmission is being accelerated through the combination of several technologies, principally satellites and computers, and this trend could continue to the point where "new" will be at once ubiquitous and ephemeral.

Satellite technology is facilitating the emergence of national newspapers, such as *USA Today*. Information is relayed via satellite to regional production centers where a conventional newspaper can be printed for local distribution. The *Wall Street Journal* also uses satellites for facsimile transmission of its text to regional production centers.

The Associated Press also has used satellite transmission to deliver what it calls "AP NewsPower 1200," a high-speed programmable news service for radio. The new system prints copy at a rate of 1,200 words per minute, thirty-three times faster than the old radio teletype technology.[16] The system is programmable, so radio stations can easily select exactly which news subjects they want to pull from the wires. Because the news is targeted to individual radio stations, the time-consuming task of sorting through reams of extraneous printed stories is eliminated. And because the system operates through computers, stories can be typed on location into portable computer terminals, circuited instantly to a base for editing, and then transmitted via satellite throughout the country. For the fast-breaking and "top of the hour" reports in which radio news has long specialized, the increased speed can mean making deadlines not previously attempted.

The Associated Press has experimented with another new system that combines high-speed computers with graphics software to enable the faster delivery of more sophisticated graphics for news stories. Traditionally, newspaper art departments took from three to eight hours to produce a single graphic; the new system takes thirty minutes or less. A similar system called News Plus is a graphics-enhanced automated news service for cable TV aimed at replacing the "newspaper on a roller" characteristic of teletext and videotex. It is designed specifically for television viewers who want quick updates.[17] Cable's broad bandwidth, which gives more room to send more data per minute than telephone wires, is well adapted to the sudden and occasionally very high rate of computer data transmission.[18] Here again, the addition of new technology to the old might alter the qualitative characteristics of news.

Over-the-air videoconferencing, portable telecommunications, and broadband telephones accelerate the flow of information by increasing the speed with which people are connected. Videoconferencing could become the vehicle by which communication substantially replaces transportation, less than two centuries after communication ceased to be a by-product of transportation. Electronic meetings are becoming a popular way to conduct business between offices separated by great distances. For example, in 1982 hundreds of reporters in thirty cities simultaneously attended a live-via-satellite news conference during the Tylenol poisoning case. Businesses, universities, unions, and political candidates have used videoconferencing for instructional, organizational, and fund-raising events.

The new media accelerate not only the transmission of the news but also its collection. Reporters for newspapers, television, magazines, and radio can file stories from portable "bureaus in a phone booth." Using a tape recorder and a briefcase-size computer terminal, they can send copy or voice reports to station-based computers over the telephone.

As with targeted news to radio stations, videotex lets users expeditiously select specific information while avoiding extraneous data. Computer-based videotex and teletext condense information, making it easy to access, interpret, and use. For example, congressional offices can easily tap into preselected data bases such as the Selective Dissemination of Information, the Congressional Research Services' Issue Briefs, the *Federal Register*, or the *Congressional Record*.

New technology already has streamlined mail service in the Congress. Physical portage of mail is becoming anachronistic in congressional offices, where electronic mail systems operated by microcomputers handle the writing, sorting, sending, and receiving of mail. Political scientist Michael Robinson has observed:

Today's Senate office is a spaceship of electronic communications systems. . . . The modern Senate mail system (Communications Management Systems, or CMS) produces up to forty letters per hour on each in-office computer terminal. CMS letters appear personalized and individually typed, of course, although they emerge mass produced from the multimemory bank of the central processing unit. . . .[19]

New technologies can reduce distribution time from hours or days to seconds or minutes, making distance irrelevant. For example, Senator Edward Kennedy's Washington office receives about one thousand pieces of mail per day. The letters are opened and read by staff members, who then use computers to code, answer, and address responses usually the same day, or in "no less than a week."[20] The response time in a noncomputerized office could be several weeks. (In one pilot project, one House office linked itself directly to its constituents who owned home computers.)[21]

An unmistakable property then of new telecommunications technologies—cable, videotex, satellites, computers, and the rest —is that (separately and in combination) they let journalists, politicians, and citizens send and receive information much faster than ever before. Eventually our concern will be to understand how this increased speed might affect the way politics is practiced in the United States. We can easily anticipate some of the points to consider.

The impact of news depends fundamentally on its timeliness. Old news usually commands little attention, and thereby exerts little influence. This is aptly illustrated by the media's coverage of the voting that took place on March 9 during the 1984 presidential primaries, on what was called Super Tuesday. Walter Mondale won two southern states while Gary Hart captured one New England and one southern state. The results of the primaries and caucuses that took place that day in the West were not available in time for the evening deadlines of the next day's eastern newspapers. Therefore, the results were not prominently reflected in the papers' morning editions and the day's balloting was widely described as a "draw," although Hart had scored a clean sweep of the western states. The interpretation probably would have been different if the state of the art had permitted the late results to be incorporated into the next day's stories.

Generally speaking, broadcast television has collapsed the interval between real-world events and news reports about them. The new media promise to shrink this lag further. The instantaneous quality of the new media will further compress the time that political leaders have to respond to events. This will emphasize even more the constancy of media scrutiny. It will magnify the costs of mistakes, gaffes, and disappointing performances. Some might bemoan this trend even as others applaud it. What some regard as time for careful deliberation, negotiation, and reflection, others see as time spent dissembling, stalling, and wiggling away from issues. Broadcast television, the telephone, and the computer have reduced the time between events and the registration, through polls, of the public's response. The new media will shrink that time even further through "instant" polls on interactive cable. In chapter 5 we will consider at length ways in which the speed of the new media may increase direct citizen participation in our democracy.

Weighing the effects of faster information transmission calls to mind the question that once was posed with regard to the invention of the telegraph: "What might [these new technologies], 'annihilator of time and space,' augur for thought, politics, commerce, the press, and the moral life?"[22]

Receiver Control: The Democratization of Information

Another generic property of new communications technology is the greater control it grants users over the information they encounter. First, by expanding the number of media, the new technologies let the user select more freely among available information. Second, the VCR in particular allows viewers to program their own television sets, either by shifting the time of broadcast programs or by viewing rented or purchased videocassettes. This has been heralded as a "shift in sovereignty to the consumer."[23] The traditional hegemony of the senders—network executives, producers, editors, or publishers—is increasingly eroded as the receiver exercises more discretion.

In recent years people have seemed to want something other than conventional network programming—not simply more but also different kinds of media. Greater volume of information and number of conduits inherently offer more options, and thus control is in part defined by the fact that the public has a wider menu from which to choose. In the 1980s consumers can exercise more control than ever before over their media diet.

Increasing user control derives not only from the growing variety of media sources; it also reflects greater direct public access to the messages' origins. The spread of personal computers, word processors, videotex, low-power television (LPTV), home video equipment, and public-access cable channels gives the public more discretion over media content, and even allows the public to create entirely new kinds of information. Consumers become producers. "The historical gap in broadcasting between the oligopoly of transmission and the democracy of reception may thus be drastically reduced."[24]

A trend toward local-user control is suggested by the use of LPTV. In 1982 the Federal Communications Commission (FCC) adopted new LPTV rules aimed at providing "the general public and minorities with more diversity in television programming and station ownership."[25] Among other things, these rules encouraged small towns and neighborhood groups to apply for licenses. By 1983 more than twelve thousand applications were filed. In early 1987, 383 LPTV stations were operating, primarily in small-town America.[26]

Similarly, public-access channels on cable television provide another potential "instrument of empowerment."[27] Public-access channels offer a forum for television programming free of charge for community members. They provide an outlet for local expression, with programs produced by groups ranging from political radicals to the Boy Scouts. Some cable systems also provide channels for educational and government access that televise such events as school board meetings, student productions, and information on city services. Public-access channels usually obtain a franchise guarantee that rules out any content control by the cable operator.[28]

When Sony introduced their videocassette recorder, they coined the phrase "time shifting." VCR owners are no longer prisoners to network television time schedules, nor are they confined by network programming. Each VCR owner becomes a "network program executive" theoretically able to record a program, store the cassette, and watch it when he or she wants. (We have already seen an analogous shift in our society in the change from trains to automobiles as the dominant means of personal transportation. With the advent of the low-cost automobile, suddenly we could travel on our own schedule and as our moods suited us.) And both VCR and cable's push-button tuning make it possible for the user to easily skip over taped commercials, which raises the question of what will happen to TV's role as a marketing tool. Finally, as cassette recorders proliferated, a film rental market has developed, generating estimated annual revenues of $3.3 billion in 1986.[29]

The net result has been an explosive growth in the number of videocassette recorders. By 1986, fully 40 percent of all television households owned VCRs, and while the rate of growth is slowing, in 1987 the industry was expected to ship an additional 14 to 15 million units in the United States.[30]

The most observable shift in user control comes with teletext and videotex, video hardware that is linked to computer-controlled information systems. With these media, "the sovereignty over the text moves from the suppliers of information to the controller of technology."[31] Teletext allows viewers to select exactly what news they care about and to ignore extraneous information. Rather than viewing a whole newspaper's worth of news, viewers can choose from among its specialized sections.

Videotex takes teletext a level beyond content control, to content creation. Combined with interactive capabilities, videotex transforms passive newscopy into an electronic newspaper specifically crafted to user preference. In addition to selectively tailoring news, users may supplement the news with graphs, charts, definitions, clarifications, colors, and audio effects.

The public's increasing control over the media represents, according to media analyst Anthony Smith, "the key to the nature of the information society into which industrial society is now evolving."[32] An alternative view holds that the new media may not universally increase the user's control over the information received. In this view, effective control over the *content* of what one receives is as or more important than simply the *volume* of choice. In fact, one can well imagine a situation in which a viewer has a huge array of choices, but so little information about them that he in fact has less control over his experience than was the case in the more restricted environment of the old media. An apt analogy may be to ask who has more control, a person entering a large, anonymous cafeteria with hundreds of selections, or a person going to his favorite diner with a limited menu that he knows by heart.[33]

This line of thought has led us to distinguish between three types of user control. First, *mediated user control* describes a situation where the user can choose among several options although the options have been determined by someone else and the user has little prior knowledge of the content of each. This is analogous to a consumer buying food in a large cafeteria. Another example might be a shopper in a bargain basement. There is an abundance of choice, but until the shopper sorts through the goods there is no way of knowing whether he will find what he is looking for. A second type of user control might be called *informed selection.* Here the user knows something about the product he is buying, or has some assurance that he will be satisfied with the product. One can imagine the consumer going into a fine clothing store with a limited selection of brand-name goods and a liberal returns policy. The consumer knows something about the brand he is looking for, and the store's return policy assures the consumer of quality. Therefore, while the options are more limited in number than in the first case, the user retains a greater sense of control over his environment because he has better information on which to base his decision. Finally, in an *interactive environment*, the user can directly affect the options. Purchasing a custom-tailored suit or working with an architect to design one's dream house are examples of how interaction with the sender increases the user's control.

Targeting: From Broadcasting to Narrowcasting

The new media also increase the capacity of those who send messages to determine who will get what information. Cable television in particular has been thought of as the video equivalent of the corner newsstand. Like the diverse array of daily newspapers and special-interest magazines, cable is seen as providing a wide assortment of programs tailored to particular, narrow audiences. The technology permits the sender to aim messages with some precision at identifiable market segments. This is commonly referred to as narrowcasting as opposed to broadcasting.

The new technologies make it technically possible and economically viable to send video messages to relatively small groups of people. As James C. Emery, then president of the Interuniversity Communications Council, has noted:

Applications of technology to date have been largely confined to lowering the cost and reducing the time lag in the mass dissemination of information. Relatively little has been done to increase the discrimination of a channel so that a message will reach a more selected audience or will encourage feed-back from them. However, some of the new technological developments, such as microcomputers, information storage, and computer-linked information systems, can possibly overcome these limitations.[34]

Targeting has long been a staple of election campaigns, and the methods of targeting have become increasingly refined. "By narrowing the channels of campaign communication, politicians seek to direct what they believe to be effective appeals to the precise audience that will be most influenced by it."[35] Politicians use new advances in computers to select and assimilate data about individuals in order to produce a detailed profile delimiting particular groups of voters. The process begins "with the registrar's list of all 165,000 voters in the district. Then you look at Democrats or Democratic households, then you want households in which someone is over 65. Then you say, 'O.K., give me all those who are Jewish renters.' Now you're down to a pretty small number, but they're a powerful segment."[36]

Because computer technology allows campaigns to identify specific groups of voters, it facilitates direct-mail appeals. Computers can generate mailing lists and personalize letters with the recipient's name. For example:

Responding to a liberalization of the [California] state law governing absentee ballots, the [Republican] party sent each party registrant in the state an application for an absentee ballot, with his or her name and address already printed on the relevant lines. All the recipients had to do was sign the form and drop it in the mail; those who did so could then vote from their homes, and take more time to plow through the enormously complex ballot.[37]

As the cost of these services decline, more and more candidates have adopted such methods. High-speed laser printers allow rapid production of personally targeted mail within a single mass mailing. But the user must be willing to be targeted; this is the catch. People must open their mail and read it. Technology has not yet overcome the public's prerogative to receive or reject information.

Traditionally, political elites have set the communication agenda, deciding which issues should be addressed to what people and by whom. With the advent of effective targeting, however, candidates can hire polling firms to obtain information about voters' concerns and thereby circumvent party leaders. As political scientist Gerald Benjamin writes, "By means of TV, polling and computer-based mail, candidates can enter into a direct relationship with citizens, bypassing the mediating institution of the party."[38]

Similarly, cable stations allow candidates to leap over the costly quagmire associated with network television bureaucracies and to target selected viewers. For example, satellite master antenna television (SMATV), "a 'mini' cable system on private property," is a bypassing technology through which campaigns can target small communities. Since SMATV is excluded from federal and municipal regulations, it is a simple and cheap medium for targeting. The largest single SMATV system is located in the Bronx in a thirty-five-building, fifteen-hundred–unit apartment complex that houses six thousand people. For $9.00 per month, every unit will receive SMATV. Promoted properly, this reservoir of people living in a community bound by one common (and inexpensive) communications system lends itself to targeted promotions and programs as well as repeated direct mail.

Cable television targeting, a video form of direct mail, is already possible, and the potential is there for even finer segmentation in the future. Currently, advertisements or programs can be targeted by showing them in certain cities or towns (that is, certain cable franchises) and not others. For example, in the hotly contested 1982 race for the fourth congressional district in Massachusetts, Barney Frank ran paid political ads and appeared in person on cable in the New Bedford–Fall River area. Success in these particular communities was crucial to Frank's campaign. Programming content addressed the particular concerns of residents in those communities. Frank's campaign put ads in the local newspaper to notify and urge people to watch these shows on cable.

Cable's potential for narrowcasting especially excites political admen.[39] Previously, TV advertising has been an extravagance—albeit sometimes a necessary one—for most congressional campaigns. Congressional candidates from New York, for example, must advertise on TV stations whose signal reaches well beyond their districts. Statewide candidates in New Hampshire and New Jersey frequently have had to advertise on neighboring Boston or New York stations, reaching millions of people they do not want to, and paying for it. But advertising on local cable systems reaches the franchise's edge and no farther—a substantial benefit for political campaigns for local or district office.

Narrowcasting also offers interesting potential uses to larger-scale campaigns. Presidential candidates will be able to customize television spots for a given state or even city, a capability heretofore limited mainly to radio advertising. Further, national campaigns will be able to place special ads on nationwide cable or satellite networks. Thus a candidate could argue for national health legislation on the health network, support affirmative action on the black network, and oppose government regulation on the business network. As Richard M. Neustadt, a pioneer in commercial and political uses of satellite technology, has noted, "The art of saying different things to different people is hardly new, but the advent of narrowcasting and electronic mail will make it easier to do and harder to catch."[40]

Another method of targeting has been the exclusive preserve of incumbent officeholders. One study found that nearly half of Capitol Hill press offices produce cable programs, and that many more plan to do so when major cities in their districts are wired.[41] Members of Congress and the Senate have recorded messages that are essentially video newsletters and sent them to their local cable stations to be shown in their home district or state once or twice a month. Cable systems hungry for programming gratefully air such video reports. Other legislators have sent copies of their congressional floor speeches recorded by C-SPAN. Several senators have held "cable town meetings" in which they spend an hour chatting with constituents, a small number of whom join them in the cable studio and a much larger number who watch their cable channel at home and call in questions.[42] Legislators are increasingly using the new media in order to bypass the sometimes cynical, often disinterested press, giving incumbents "an unparalleled advantage over challengers at election time."[43] As one congressman put it: "I am not only a newsmaker, but a newsman—perhaps the most widely read journalist in my district. I have a radio show, a television program, and a news column with a circulation larger than that of most of the weekly newspapers in my district."[44]

Such techniques are also being used in election campaigns. Videocassettes are used to train staff in basic campaign operations, as newsletters for campaign coordinators, and for fundraisers.

What's New About the New Media?

Especially noteworthy during the early stages of the 1988 presidential nomination race has been the use of satellite technology to send video press releases, interviews, and campaign biographies directly to local television stations. The new media technologies thus allow campaigns to bypass the national networks and to target their messages at key early battlegrounds like Iowa and New Hampshire.

Political campaigners and public officials are not the only ones to see the potential uses of narrowcasting. Interest groups have already begun to experiment with the targeting potential of the new media. Indeed, Common Cause president Fred Wertheimer has said that for interest groups the new technologies represent "the battleground of the future."[45] This battleground is scrutinized in chapter 4.

No one has yet constructed a "switched cable system" in which messages can be targeted to particular homes and not to others. It might seem that the same technology now used to send certain programs to cable's pay-per-view customers and restrict them from other households could be used to deliver targeted messages. In fact, pay-per-view programs are now transmitted to an entire cable area, but operators have pulled a switch so that only certain people receive the message, which is scrambled for others. The technology is available that will permit the targeting of specific homes: fiber optics. Fiber optic cables have a much greater capacity and are much more efficient than current coaxial cables or conventional phone lines. However, the fiber optic industry is still in its infancy.

Eventually, more sophisticated cable systems will offer powerful narrowcasting capabilities. Messages could be tailor-made for particular neighborhoods, perhaps augmented with appearances by local luminaries. It will be possible to send particular advertisements (or other programming) to individual homes. Thus special ads could appeal to professional people, others to people living alone, still others to people who did not vote in the last election. In this, cablecasting will truly come to resemble a combination of phone banks and direct mail.

A similar shift from mass to targeted appeals has occurred with other media. Examples are the shift from mass, wide-angle magazines (*Life, Look, McClure's*) to special-interest publications and from network radio to independent stations catering to segmented audiences (so-called "boutique" radio). Although the new media technologies create the potential for a parallel shift in the video world, it is no foregone conclusion that this shift will occur, or at least not soon. At present, the vision of abundant specialized cable channels is giving way to a limited number of channels aimed at mass audiences. This reflects the difficulty of turning a profit when the audience is small and when faced with the high cost of high-quality programming.

Opinion is sharply divided on the value of narrowcasting. Some hail targeting as a sign of a healthy pluralism that will create a greater diversity of speakers and content. Others fear that targeting will foster factions in the body politic, as the public comes to know more and more about less and less. Targeted appeals will accentuate focus and depth at the expense of variety and breadth. The effects of narrowcasting on democratic politics will occupy us throughout this book.

Decentralization: The Question of Ownership and Control

Whether the new media will be more centralized than their predecessors is one of the most controversial questions surrounding these new technologies. In part, this dispute turns on which specific developments one chooses to look at: some aspects of the new media are highly centralized, others are significantly decentralized. In addition, much of the discussion about decentralization has been confused by failing to draw a distinction between ownership and control. Consider, for example, the case of videotex. When some analysts claim that the new media are highly centralized, what they have in mind is the question of who will own these new videotex services. Clearly, this is an important issue. But an equally valid question is: who decides which specific stories or messages each user will receive? In many cases, as we will see, ownership of the new media remains highly concentrated while control of decision making has shifted in a more decentralized direction.

What's New About the New Media?

Much of broadcasting and publishing in the United States today is in the hands of a few media giants. No question is more important about the new media than whether the established conglomerates will extend their dominion into the new media colonies. Some media analysts—including Alvin Toffler, John Naisbitt, and Ithiel de Sola Pool—believe that the new technologies foster a shift from the last three decades of centralized network television back to the more segmented and localized media more characteristic of the American press historically. Naisbitt cites decentralization of corporations, including media corporations, as one of the ten "megatrends" of our era. Pool notes that the high degree of media centralization characteristic of television is an exception to the prevailing historical patterns.

Communications through the ages has generally been directed toward individuals or small groups.[46] Conversation fits this mold. So does all the writing up to the Gutenberg watershed, and much beyond it. It remained for the penny press of the nineteenth century to create the first true mass medium; previous newspapers had been little more than newsletters, aimed at businesses. Combined with the wire services, the penny press created a data base shared by a significant proportion of the American public. Radio, film, and especially television extended and enriched this pool of common information. With the telegraph and television came centralized national control over news content and procedures.

"The dominance of mass media lasted a century and a half," Pool notes. "This was a unique period in human history, in which media reached the whole society. The new media in some ways restore the normal state of affairs."[47]

If there is to be a shift toward more decentralized media, satellites may hold the key. As one analyst put it, satellites are a "democratic technology."[48] The effective trademark rights ABC, CBS, and NBC hold over the term *network* have disappeared with the explosive growth of satellite-linked networks. Not only has satellite transmission made modern cable economically viable, but it also has reduced network control of broadcast television by feeding programming directly to stations, bypassing the Big Three giants. According to media analyst Les Brown:

Satellite transmission has created instant networks among the independents.

Indeed, satellites are rapidly turning the entire program-syndication field into a form of networking, which could eventually erode the affiliate structure that supports the three majors. During the 1960's radio stations found it economically advantageous to disaffiliate from the networks, except for hourly news; and TV stations in this decade may well decide to go it alone should the satellite make it more profitable to do so.[49]

The satellite has been a major factor in the challenge to AT&T's dominance of the long-distance telephone market as competitors substitute satellite transmission for phone lines. Direct broadcast satellites also decentralize communication by beaming signals directly to homes, avoiding traditional delivery systems. Finally, satellite-based videoconferencing permits people to communicate face to face over long distances.

The growth of alternative information sources may thus erode the hegemony of the three giant broadcast television networks. To some extent, this is already happening. The three broadcast networks now compete with syndicated programming carried on networks of independent stations, satellite cable networks, and other subscription television networks. The broadcast network share of the prime-time television audience was down to 71 percent in 1987.

But as we will be at pains to point out throughout this book, the established media giants are doing quite well in acquiring ownership of the new media, especially cable television and the home video market. These giants include: ABC, CBS, NBC, RCA, Time Inc., Warner Communications, Times Mirror, Westinghouse, Cox Communications, Columbia Pictures, Storer Communications, Viacom, Oak Industries, Taft Broadcasting, Tribune Company, and Turner Broadcasting. Time Inc., for example, may be associated in the public mind with print journalism, yet in 1986 its video division overtook publishing as the company's largest source of operating income. Time's cable system, American Television and Communications, is the second largest in the country; its cable service, Home Box Office, is the largest and most profitable cable network; and it is now engaged in a joint venture videotex service (Covidea). There is thus much truth in Benjamin Barber's assertion: "Even as the audience is broken into splinters, those who control it become fewer and more monopolistic."[50] We will study the process of media conglomeration in detail in chapter 8.

But if ownership is still highly concentrated, operational control over the content and delivery of media messages appears to be moving in the direction of greater decentralization. Take, for example, the invention of the minicamera. "Minicams" have significantly simplified the logistics, lowered the costs, and reduced the time of filming. They require much smaller crews, usually only one to three people. When combined with satellites, this gadgetry has revolutionized news gathering by local stations. During the 1984 Democratic and Republican national nominating conventions, for example, many local stations were able to dethrone national networks by using minicams and satellite transmission. Convention news, which in the past had always been filtered through the eyes of network anchormen, was seen in 1984 from the perspective of reporters from more than four hundred local stations who fed their coverage directly to local markets. During evening prime-time hours, local stations often broke away from network coverage to show their own reports. News coverage has become decentralized between elections as well. In the last few years, the Washington press corps has swelled with the addition of local television reporters.

It is not hard to imagine how these developments might affect news coverage, especially if the national networks have a different point of view from regional and local stations. Decisions on news content will be less routinely prescribed in Washington and New York. The new technologies loosen the grip of central editorial control within media organizations.

Perhaps the ultimate image of decentralized media is that of solitary individuals at home with their videotex terminals creating personal, electronic newspapers. Although major experiments with electronic newspapers by Knight-Ridder and Times Mirror have flopped, they did permit individuals to serve as their own newspaper editors, using computer technology to select items of interest from a large menu of offerings.

By giving consumers more control over what they watch, and by allowing senders to target their audiences more efficiently, the new media thus permit us to decentralize decisions over media content, and create a more fluid relationship between users and senders of information. The new decentralized media let information flow between consumers and an expanded range of producers (citizens with a gripe, candidates with a plea for votes, public officials with a message for constituents, interest-group leaders with an ax to grind) without the intervention of the professional press. Not only can the public construct its own daily newspaper without an editor's judgment of what is important news, but it can learn the day's baseball scores or stock quotes without thumbing through a sheaf of printed paper. Citizen activists and political leaders can make their cases on public-access channels. Political party and interest-group leaders can beam their messages directly to audiences from their own cable or satellite networks.

The new technologies create, in a sense, "unmediated" media. For much of American history, sending or retrieving information on a mass scale required large media institutions like newspapers or television networks. New technology enables users to contact the audience directly. Curiously, this development recalls the media that existed during the infancy of the republic, when newspapers were created, sponsored, and controlled by political leaders; Jefferson had his paper, and so did Hamilton.

Two-Way Video: From Passive to Interactive Television

None of these generic properties of the new media is unique to the current era. The volume and speed of transmitting information has increased steadily over time. For many years special-interest magazines and specialized local radio have allowed senders to target their messages. These trends, plus the proliferation of topical sections in newspapers, have given the consumer an ever richer menu of information options and, hence, greater control. And, apart from the last three decades, the media in the United States has been mostly decentralized and localized.

But interactive capacity is something new. Of all the properties of new communications technology, the capacity for interaction between sender and consumer sharply distinguishes the new media from the old. Traditional media have offered crude forms of "interaction," such as letters to the editor and radio call-in shows. But two-way cable and telephone lines make television truly interactive, allowing a genuine two-way conversation. The user can affect what information he or she receives. Interactivity, in effect, blurs the distinction between user and sender control.

One of the most important applications of interactive media is electronic publishing.[51] Although existing electronic newspapers have yet to capture any substantial viewership, videotex enthusiasts continue to predict the death of news-on-paper. Newsprint prices have tripled since 1950,[52] fuel prices have skyrocketed, and labor costs (for typesetters, printers, and deliverers) have increased dramatically. In all, 80 percent of newspaper dollar outlays go into production and distribution costs; reducing that share could result in lower prices for consumers or advertisers, in more frequent editions, or in more money for editorial content.[53] And, once the paper is delivered, the average consumer reads only one-tenth of its content.[54]

Videotex and teletext receivers currently cost around $1,000. Mass production should drop the cost to around $200 to $300. Beyond the cost of the receiver or adapter, teletext probably will be free to consumers, paid for through advertising (movie theaters will advertise on the film-time page, and so on). Videotex probably will continue to be financed mainly through user charges, based on the amount of time connected to the system, on the particular information accessed, or on some combination of the two. Spending half an hour on a videotex system now costs around $10, a fee that keeps videotex from being competitive with the twenty-five-cent newspaper as a way to learn the day's events.[55] In 1982 technology expert Ben Compaine estimated that within ten years, the cost of spending half an hour on a videotex system would be roughly equal to the cost of buying a newspaper (assuming, reasonably, that videotex costs continued to fall and newspaper production and delivery costs continued to rise).[56] But so far the market has not borne out this prediction.

The book (or newspaper) is not perfect, but it is a workable compromise between many ideals. It is, as media analyst Bruce Owen notes, durable, compact, portable, and cheap, "but not as durable as stone, and not as cheap as talk." To replace the printed page, writes Owen, teletext and videotex must "produce a substitute that has these qualities in a superior combination."[57] This has not yet occurred.

One of the chief technological advances of cable television over broadcasting has been the two-way nature of some cable systems. The earliest interactive cable system was QUBE in Columbus, Ohio, introduced by Warner Amex in 1977 and now aborted. Among other services, QUBE offered instant political polls. Viewers frequently were asked to express opinions on various issues, by way of small keyboards. During a discussion about gays, for example, this statement flashed on the screen: "I have a friend, relative, or acquaintance who I know is homosexual." Viewers keyed the yes or no button on their consoles, and seconds later the results flashed on the screen (65 percent yes, 35 percent no). QUBE polled subscribers following presidential speeches, asking them to rate the president's effectiveness. Using the interactive capacity, residents of a small Columbus suburb participated electronically in a meeting of their local planning commission. They were able to vote with members on local zoning, housing codes, and proposed highway construction. They were also able to participate in debate over the air.

The potential for interactive television has received massive attention, favorable and unfavorable. It has been held forth as "our electronic town meeting and village green,"[58] as a mechanism by which "public opinion will become the law of the land."[59] Others have seen in it the threat of demagoguery, mob rule, and class-based government: "Clearly, any instant referendum scheme is so destructive as to be inconceivable."[60] The truth is probably that interactive TV is likely to be neither as good nor as bad as its notices claim. However, the debate is sufficiently heated and its implications sufficiently important to warrant considerable attention. In chapter 5 we will study in detail the impact of interactive television on citizen participation. But a brief comment here will be helpful.

The appeal of "teledemocracy" is simple. According to its proponents, officials need never again claim ignorance about what constituents want. American government could move from the compromise of representative democracy toward the ideal of direct democracy. And as individuals gain a greater voice in government, their sense of efficacy—and their rate of participation—would also increase. Yet there are problems with this vision.

Several are methodological problems. At least in the short term, interactive TV will not be universal. Where it is offered—which is so far quite a limited number of cities—interactive capability generally costs the consumer a fee in addition to basic cable service. Moreover, as noted earlier, on the average only three-fifths of the households passed by cable currently sign up for it. Due to the costs of cable and interactive programming, unless some sort of public subsidy is established, the voting public on interactive systems will be a skewed, upper-class sample of the full citizenry. Beyond that, for results to be accurate, the voting must go on for at least a day. Quickie referenda may be biased by the fact that the audience at any particular point in the day is not representative of the public as a whole. Further, some mechanism must be established to ensure that each citizen has one and only one vote. Currently each household gets a vote on QUBE—be it a single apartment dweller, five-member family, or fifteen-member commune. But if each household had, say, as many votes as residents, what would ensure that the multiple votes were not coming in at the initiative of one viewer?

The power to pose the questions, of course, is a substantial one. The people controlling the interactive capacity, former FCC Chairman Charles Ferris has noted, "can wield incredible political power by which questions they choose to ask and how the questions are framed."[61]

Advocates of teledemocracy often assume a much greater interest in politics than currently exists among citizens. The public's appetite for politics is modest at best. The era of widespread political participation is long gone; other forms of entertainment have replaced politics as a recreational activity. As sociologist Daniel Bell points out, "There is the common assumption that we're all wise solons, just waiting for the opportunity to participate. It just isn't so."[62] In fact, participation rates in teledemocracy projects have been low, between 12 and 20 percent.[63] Conversely, some worry that teledemocracy might pose a danger if its electronic voting schemes ever arouse intense political interest. As Pool notes, "If citizens are brought, by effective personal participation, to the point of caring very deeply about political outcomes, then there had better not be too many important decisions, for every time one is made there are losers as well as winners."[64]

More fundamentally, teledemocracy could alter the political system in ways that might not be wholly salutary. Our current system of representative democracy is viewed by advocates of teledemocracy as a poor, but (until now) necessary, substitute for direct democracy; now, they claim, the new technologies make possible what has always been desirable. Yet representative democracy by its very nature gives the political system a stability that might otherwise be lacking, a stability that teledemocrats would no doubt decry as lumbering slowness and resistance to change. For better or worse, the U.S. political system places a premium on deliberation, deliberation often removed from the swift currents of public opinion. The authors of the *Federalist Papers*, for example, warned against "unqualified compliance with every sudden breeze of passion." Bargaining, negotiation, and compromise do not occur easily in full public view, nor do they occur speedily.

Interactive TV might make decision making substantially more open, public, and volatile. Writes Pool, "War could be declared on Monday, cancelled on Tuesday, and declared again on Wednesday, depending not only on which demagogue was most effective but also on who happened to be home and was not tired of politics from last night's session."[65]

Expertise is related to speed. Even today's divisive referenda usually direct the government to perform some general function —to cut taxes, say—without specifying precisely how it ought to be carried out. Descriptions of teledemocracy often imply that referenda have a much greater specificity. The notion of an electronic town meeting suggests that the citizenry would rule directly, at least in broad parameters, and that raises the issue of expertise. Congressmen and senators now devote full time to governing (albeit not to legislating); moreover, they have large staffs and sophisticated research agencies to help them. "You don't have to be an expert to know what you want," a Washington state experiment in limited teledemocracy trumpeted,[66] but you may have to be an expert to get it adopted and get the details right in so complex and interdependent a nation as ours.

In chapter 5 we will suggest ways in which the electronic town meeting model can be enriched to avoid many of these problems of expertise. We will explore ways in which the new media can indeed support an electronic commonwealth characterized by direct citizen participation. But it must always be kept in mind that today the average voter is not an expert on even a small percentage of public policy questions. The "rational voter," political scientist V. O. Key discovered, exerts principally a naysaying, thumbs-down power when he or she is dissatisfied, by voting against the incumbent without investigating the specific policy alternatives; when satisfied, he or she may vote for the incumbent regardless of the alternatives.[67] While this falls short of the ideals of democratic self-government, it is an effective mechanism of accountability for citizens faced with a multitude of other duties and interests. If so, society might err in presenting more decisions, particularly more specific ones, to the unprepared voter. Moving toward a more direct form of democracy cannot take place in the absence of a full-scale campaign of civic education. The ability of the media to deliver such a course in civic education will also concern us in chapter 5.

Complete self-government via interactive television raises many thorny problems. But full-scale teledemocracy is something of a straw man, one advocated by few but the most wild-eyed futurists. More restrained and more realistic applications of the interactive technology to politics are possible. Interactive capabilities can be used to guide political discussions along, not merely to compile public opinions. Interactive systems could be oriented more to public relations than to legislation. And, as discussed earlier, their use in electronic publishing holds enormous potential.

Despite the excitement about interactive television, it remains but a possibility for the future. Only a small number of homes have two-way cable today. Most cities want it, but rising costs have led cable operators to postpone installation. Industry predictions vary widely as to the future of two-way videotex. Its public acceptability is no foregone conclusion. Warner Communications has canceled all interactive programming for QUBE. As political scientist Russell Neuman has noted, "From the study of the flow of audiences from one program to the next in network prime time television we know that there is a substantial segment of the audience which seems reluctant to exercise even the minimally interactive potential of broadcast television—changing the channel."[68]

If interactive media do become a reality, they may have to await the installation of optic fibers—those thin, flexible glass fibers that can carry virtually every kind of signal (telephone, radio, cable, data, and so on), including interactive video, more cheaply and with higher quality than coaxial cable or current telephone wires. Their widespread use is probably ten to twenty years away.

Summary: Some Questions About the New Media and Politics

We cannot say which of the particular new media technologies will flourish and which will fail. But we can predict with a measure of confidence that the new media, in contrast with traditional means of mass communication, will display these six generic properties: expanded volume of information, increased speed of transmission, greater consumer control over the media, increased capacity of senders to target messages, technological forces of decentralization vying with economic patterns of conglomeration, and more interactive communication.

What will media, with these properties, mean for our political life? Will the proliferation of options in the new media (mostly nonpolitical ones) and the public's limited appetite for politics and public affairs lead to a less politically informed public than we now have? Will the decentralized media draw the citizen's attention away from national politics in favor of local affairs? Will the new media discourage media "browsing" and limit occasions for citizens to pick up political information inadvertently?

Will the expanded ability of users to select messages, and of senders to target them, encourage the "articulation" of interests at the expense of the "aggregation" of interests? Can we expect the pool of common knowledge to shrink, precipitating an erosion of national consensus? Will we witness the balkanization of public opinion into narrow "issue publics" as citizens come to know more about fewer subjects? Or will the interactive capacity of the new media (in the form of teledemocracy) foster expressions of majority will that submerge minority sentiment? Which will it be, a tyranny of minorities or a tyranny of the majority?

Current news programs that are broadcast to large and heterogeneous audiences generally avoid expressing a point of view. Will news programs on more abundant channels of the new media adopt a different, and indeed more traditional, style of reporting that conveys more partisan or interpretive cues? Will the greater ability of citizens, politicians, interest groups, and public officials to produce and transmit messages over the new media result in more direct, unmediated political communication? Will the influence of the professional press decline?

Will the new technologies sharpen inequities in access to the media? Will the gap widen between those who can afford the skills and hardware associated with the new media and those who cannot? If so, will this create class and generational cleavages between a traditional and a new media culture, and a consequent hardening of political power differentials?

Will the increased speed and immediacy of media transmissions provoke more—and more specific—demands on government, and a growing impatience with the slow, deliberative process of democratic decision making?

Will the new media accelerate broadcast television's tendency to "privatize" politics? If so, will engaging in politics from the privacy of one's home undercut a conciliatory and compromising perspective? Will it encourage splintering and polarization? These and related questions are the subject of the rest of this study.

Throughout American history, communications technology and the dominant style of politics have undergone parallel evolutions. We expect the correlation to continue and anticipate that the answers to these questions about the technology of communications will deeply color the politics of our future.

CHAPTER 3

ELECTIONS AND THE MEDIA: PAST, PRESENT, AND FUTURE

IF THE FOUNDERS could see the way we conduct elections, they would be shocked. They would never have predicted universal suffrage, active participation by political parties and the public in the selection of nominees, or presidential candidates out in the hustings appealing directly to the people for votes.

Neither could they have foreseen the emergence of technology capable of bringing campaign coverage and political advertising to mass audiences. Indeed, the evolution of the electoral system has been closely linked to changes in communication technology, and the history of U.S. elections strikingly parallels the history of media.

As noted in chapter 1, communications technologies have always shaped our politics. In America's earliest days the scarcity and relatively high cost of newspapers helped promote an elite government in which political influence was confined to a small group of notables. In the first two decades of the nineteenth century, social transformations merged with technological advances to create mass-readership newspapers, which aided the emergence of mass political parties. Late in the century, the appearance of opinion magazines nurtured policy-oriented interest groups that gave voice to the middle-class Progressive reform movement. The advent of electronic journalism in the twentieth century has enabled public officials to build personal followings that are independent of party structures, a hallmark of contemporary government and politics.

Does media technology really affect politics? Imagine what might have happened if the Lincoln-Douglas debates, which lasted three hours, had been tailored to the constraints of television—or if the Reagan-Mondale debates, which were judged largely on appearances, had been accessible only through newspaper transcripts.

Which is the cause here, and which the effect? Do communications technologies necessitate a certain kind of politics? Or does a particular style of politics and political culture dictate which technologies will be developed and how they will be utilized? The relationship, in our opinion, works in both directions.

As an example, consider the complicated interaction between television and the presidential nomination system. In the first place, television coverage of the 1968 Democratic convention helped to create the perception in many people's minds that the nomination system needed reforming—and thus led to the creation of the first Democratic party reform commission (the McGovern-Fraser Commission). The party reforms, in turn, enhanced the importance of television. By diminishing the role of party leaders, and opening up the delegate selection process to any Democrat who wanted to participate, the new system necessarily gave great power to those who provided information and interpretation to the mass electorate—the media in general and television in particular. One can also say, however, that television enhanced the role of primaries by publicizing their results as the authentic voice of "the people," thus giving them greater legitimacy.

A similarly tangled story could be told about other forms of communication and styles of politics. Under such circumstances, it is clearly misleading to claim the primacy of one over the other.

It is equally important to avoid the trap of technological determinism. While we believe that there are strong links between
television and the current nominating system, we reject the notion
that that system was inevitable, given recent changes in communications technologies. The system is also the product of numerous
explicit decisions taken over the last twenty years by party reform
commissions, state and national legislators, candidates, consultants, and media elites. Part of the purpose of this book is to make
clear that our politics is not simply the prisoner of technology—
and that depending on our vision of democracy, we can make
decisions that will enhance the values we care about most.

Has the politics-media linkage run its course? If not, how
might the introduction of new media technologies alter the landscape of political campaigns?

The very nature of campaigns makes these questions difficult
to answer. Campaigns are highly secretive, notoriously disorgan-
ized, and short-lived. Because they are obsessed with the present,
they tend to preclude careful recording of day-to-day behavior.
Campaigns share some of these characteristics with other organizations that engage in sporadic, intense competition—organizations such as armies and athletic teams (which not coincidentally
supply much of the imagery of electoral life). But campaigns are
far more ephemeral than military forces and sports teams; the
latter usually do not disband after a contest is won or lost.

The task of anticipating and analyzing the impact of emerging
media on elections can be made easier by an examination of the
old media. We will turn first to the longstanding and intricately
woven connection between the media and elections in the United
States.

The Past: From Statesmen to Politicians to Personalities

The history of democratic practice and thought, we have
argued, can be understood as a debate between three competing
visions of democracy: plebiscitary, pluralist, and communitarian
democracy. Without ignoring the differences in vision, it is possi-

ble to array the three democratic theories along a continuum. At the plebiscitary end, democracy is valued as a means for satisfying the interests of individual citizens; the public interest is conceived as the sum of individual preferences. This conception of democracy owes a debt to the populist streak in American political culture and to the demand for a tighter fit between public policy and public opinion. Farther along the continuum lies a second democratic ideal, pluralism, which follows more in the tradition of Tocqueville, viewing democracy as fostering a diverse, competitive group life. The democratic process involves bargaining and compromise among interest groups, political parties, voluntary associations, and ascriptive identifications. At the far end of the continuum is communitarian democracy, the vision of a democracy that serves common goals rather than private ends or narrow group purposes. Rousseau is a principal architect and defender of this ideal. Communitarian democracy calls for more than just the registering of individual preferences through representative institutions. It calls upon citizens to participate directly in governing, to deliberate among themselves and exchange views, and to exercise public-spiritedness.

Throughout American history, the individualist ethic of democracy has set the underlying tone of elections. Voting is seen as fundamentally a personal act. This is a country devoted, at least in principle, to popular sovereignty and, increasingly, to political equality. Each citizen's vote counts the same, and popular preferences are determined by a tally of individual votes. Thus, elections—in which everyone gets one vote—fit most squarely with the individualist, plebiscitarian vision of democracy.

Within the electoral domain, nevertheless, elements of the other two types of democracy have coexisted with individualism. In fact, the interplay of media and elections in the United States has evolved through three periods—roughly corresponding to the eighteenth, nineteenth, and twentieth centuries—and in each period one of the three types of democracy found its strongest expression. Communitarian democracy had its heyday in the eighteenth century; pluralist democracy in the nineteenth; and individualist or plebiscitary democracy in the the twentieth. Naturally, there are no clean breaks between the three periods. Still, the differences among them are strong enough to suggest that one brand of democracy held sway in each of the three eras.

Not only were elections in each century influenced by different democratic ideals, but the shift from one type of democracy to the next coincided with changes in the media. Each century displayed a distinctive media culture that sustained a particular set of democratic institutions. Tracing the media-election linkage from the eighteenth to the twentieth century will help us understand how the new media and their inherent properties might help or hinder the expression of different democratic values in the twenty-first century.

The Eighteenth Century: Civic Virtue and Democracy

At the time of the Constitutional Convention, America's statesmen were precariously poised between two political worlds. On the rise was a politics we take for granted today—a politics at home with the material and acquisitive desires of human nature, at home with self-interested and partisan behavior. On the wane was an older, more austere vision of life in a republic, in which democracy depended on civic virtue, on the ability of citizens to serve the common good rather than private ends. This vision also stipulated that democratic politics depended on the preservation of the moral character of citizenship against the corruptions of modern commercial life.[1]

Even as it waned, this older tradition of republican politics still exerted its power over the eighteenth-century American mind. From colonial times until the 1820s, the prevailing view was that the virtuous should lead. A republic needed statesmen who embodied civic virtue, who had the character and judgment necessary to apprehend the common good and not just to act as brokers among competing interests. Washington and even Hamilton and Jefferson saw themselves as such disinterested statesmen, always partly above representing one group of partisan interests against another. Washington's Farewell Address was not only a powerful lament for the passing of the age of republican virtue but also a stern warning against the rise of party politics.

Clearly, this view of politics was elitist and hardly mass democratic in our sense of the term. This helps explain how the constitutional clause guaranteeing a "republican form of government" to each state (Article IV, section 4) could coexist with a host of state restrictions on the right to vote, including property and literacy qualifications, as well as the obvious racial and gender exclusions. These restrictions limited the voting electorate in 1800 to less than 10 percent of the adult population. Indeed, the Founders displayed a remarkable distrust of direct popular elections and of the kind of person likely to be elected to office through such popularity contests. Their preference was for an indirect electoral process in which "a few respected electors, state by state, sift . . . the merits of the worthiest eligibles . . . like a church council naming a new pastor, or a faculty bestowing a professorship." [2]

This distrust of direct popular elections was embodied in many of the institutions adopted during the eighteenth century: the Electoral College, the selection of senators by state legislatures, the choice of governors by legislatures in some states, the nomination of candidates by legislative caucuses, and the adoption of restrictive property qualifications for voting. Equally noteworthy is the absence of any mention of political parties in the Constitution.

The Founders' distaste for mass democracy was reflected most clearly in the method of presidential selection that they adopted in 1787.[3] They hoped to limit the influence of personal popularity in presidential selection yet still attract highly regarded candidates. But how should men of merit and good character be chosen?

Their solution made use of a substitute for merit: established reputation. An institutional arrangement thought to favor this was the "principle of the extended sphere." In allowing a presidential election to cover the largest possible district—the whole nation—the Founders hoped to discourage local favorites and to foster candidates of "continental" reputation. An auxiliary precaution was indirect selection through the Electoral College. It was assumed that the contest for electors would be much less likely to stir public opinion than the selection of the president. And because the people would not choose the president directly, the candidates would have less reason to curry popular favor.[4]

The Founders objected to pluralist democracy largely because they distrusted parties, which they associated with sedition. Even in the 1790s, when incipient parties were first formed, few leaders advocated "party" as a good, and most remained hostile to the conception that parties represented legitimate opposition.

They never entertained the idea of two political parties contending peacefully against each other, bargaining and compromising, in mutual tolerance and forbearance. Even the leaders who somewhat haphazardly and incompletely invented parties—as necessary evils—did not see themselves as party builders.

Not surprisingly, then, the "first party system" (from the 1790s to the 1820s) was not a real party system by today's standards. Parties were nascent, transitional structures that "reached backward into eighteenth century political culture as much as [they] forecast the shape of future politics."[5] Until the 1820s partisan activity took place only in some states some of the time. It was often difficult to pinpoint a leader's partisan identity in the 1790s and early 1800s, and shifts between parties were frequent.[6] After 1800 the Federalists disappeared in some states, and by 1816 Federalists and Republicans no longer divided the nation into rival factions. From 1802 to 1822 the Republicans won three-quarters of all contests for presidential electors and congressmen (even excluding the unopposed presidential election of 1820) and four-fifths of all senatorial contests.[7] The Virginia dynasty of Jefferson, Madison, and Monroe governed the country for twenty-four years, each succeeding the other without much difficulty, as the "party" system gave way to the nonpartisan "Era of Good Feelings." True, the same generation produced political professionals like Aaron Burr and DeWitt Clinton, who lived for the pursuit of office. But they inspired distrust and contempt even among their allies.

In the early 1800s men in the executive and legislative branches alike bitterly condemned parties and disparaged the bargaining, competition, compromise, and power-seeking intrinsic to pluralist politics. Indeed, they saw the possession of power as unleashing men's aggressive instincts, and considered it antisocial.

Thus from the 1790s through the 1820s it was not mass or pluralist democracy but the older politics of republican virtue that most shaped the activities of the small cadre of political leaders. Eighteenth-century democracy revolved around talk and deliberation, mostly face to face. In the span of thirty-three years, delegates from the colonies or the states convened in no less than seven assemblies to discuss and debate the issues of the day: the Albany Congress, the Stamp Act Congress, the First Continental

Congress, the Second Continental Congress, the convention to establish the Articles of Confederation, the Annapolis Convention, and the Constitutional Convention. Both before and after 1776 state legislatures served as arenas for political deliberation and as training grounds for political leadership. Institutions like the Virginia House of Burgesses or the Massachusetts General Court were crucibles for democratic citizenship. Indeed, during this time, as historian Gordon Wood notes, "the American [state] legislatures, in particular the lower houses of the assemblies, were no longer to be merely adjuncts or checks to magisterial power, but were in fact to be the government. . . ."[8] This was the age of the legislative caucus, a forum where like-minded men could debate who should be tapped to run for office.

Life outside the chamber encouraged political discussion as well. National legislators formed close-knit peer groups; when they arrived in Washington, they would join boardinghouse fraternities where they lived, took their meals, and spent most of their leisure time talking among themselves.[9]

The focal point of democratic politics in the seventeenth and eighteenth centuries was local. James Madison remarked that the "spirit of locality" was the foundation of eighteenth-century American political culture.[10] The town, not the individual, was the basic unit of political representation. Local political decisions were made through discussion and consensus rather than through interest-group conflict. And neither the revolutionary ideology nor the establishment of a more centralized national government drew Americans away from their informal, communal, and essentially oral brand of politics. For decades after 1789, public affairs were placed primarily in the hands of leaders whose authority was grounded in their local status.[11] Localism and communalism carried over to the Washington community as well. Geographic origin determined which boardinghouse a congressman lived in. In fact, certain boardinghouses were regarded as the "property" of certain regions from one Congress to the next. Apparently congressmen looked to their messmates for policy guidance as much as for companionship; congressional voting correlated highly with the boardinghouse residences of legislators. The boardinghouses thus operated as informal caucuses and reinforced the sense of attachment to the local community.[12]

Clearly many aspects of communitarian democracy were evident in the years before 1830. However, we should not exaggerate the extent and depth of that kind of democracy in the new nation. The moral aversion of congressmen to politics, their stark pessimism about the possibilities of political community, and the absence of fraternal or cooperative impulses beyond regional ties underscore the limited potential of communitarian democracy. The traditional view among historians has been that early American values were rooted in Lockean liberalism, an ethic that glorified the pursuit of individual material interest and factional advantage.[13] Historian John Diggins, for example, argues that the classical idea of virtue as a subordination of private interests to the public good was "an idea whose time had come and gone by 1787, when the Constitution was framed."[14] The language of virtue may have persisted in political discourse, says Diggins, but that was mere rhetoric.

Historians debate the exact timing of the erosion of civic virtue as a republican norm.[15] Unquestionably, there was a shift over time from a politics of the common good to a politics of group interests. In social science parlance, this shift reflected the transition from "community," with its emphasis on personal, face-to-face relationships within a limited geographic area, to "society," which emphasizes impersonal, mass relationships through which organizations coordinate activities over broad geographic areas.

Nevertheless, in the half century after the revolution, national electoral politics displayed significant aspects of communitarian democracy, certainly more so than in later years. Communitarian democracy owed its brief existence to the limited geographic scale of politics, the small circle of homogeneous leaders, an ideology among political leaders that subordinated private ambition to the common good, a rare consensus on key political issues, the impressive expertise of political leaders on most issues of the day, and the embryonic state of representative institutions, including parties. Communitarian democracy was also fostered by the communications media at the time.

In colonial, revolutionary, and early republican America, the press shared two crucial traits with politics: small scale and elite orientation. Numerically speaking, newspapers flourished in colonial America long before they caught on in England; by 1730 seven newspapers were being published regularly in four colonies, and by 1800 there were over 180.[16] Yet circulation was quite small and was largely restricted to the affluent. At the time of the Stamp Act in 1765, only 5 percent of white families in the colonies received a newspaper weekly. By the end of the century the average circulation for dailies (which accounted for only around 10 percent of all papers), weeklies, and semiweeklies was no more than seven hundred readers.[17]

Readership was limited for three principal reasons. First, newspapers leaned heavily toward trade or commercial news. In 1800, roughly 80 percent of dailies were mainly commercial, and newspapers on the whole contained little political or human-interest information that might appeal to a wide audience.[18] Furthermore, what political news there was focused on high-level government policy. In fact, the dominant political topic of the day was foreign affairs, especially news from England. Second, papers were expensive, because they could not be sold economically by the copy but only by annual subscription. This expense meant that "only people with strong commercial interests or members of the advantaged classes could regularly afford to buy their own newspapers."[19]

Finally, because of its small, upper-class readership, the early press displayed a literary style and tone that discouraged mass consumption. Until the last decade of the eighteenth century, newspapers bolstered the deferential attitudes and "above the fray" respectability that marked first-generation American politics. Even harsh denunciations of leading politicians, which became common in newspapers after 1790, were clothed in a lofty, sophisticated verbiage inaccessible to most of the public. As political scientist Richard Rubin points out, "Much of the political dialogue, particularly between opposing politicians, was still carried on in a fairly cultivated style, usually veiling direct personal attacks with a veneer of literary reference."[20] The charges and countercharges hurled between the Federalists and the Republicans, especially between Hamilton and Jefferson, were expressed in scholarly metaphor and snide allusions. Take the following invective from Hamilton's paper, the *Gazette of the United States.* The paper noted that Jefferson's real character would be revealed

when the visor of Stoicism is plucked from the brow of the epicurean; when the plain garb of Quaker simplicity is stripped from the concealed voluptuary; when Caesar coyly refusing the proffered diadem, is seen to be Caesar rejecting the trappings by grasping the substance of imperial domination.[21]

Political leaders were writing "more for other leaders" than for the public at large. Newspapers served well the needs of the well-educated, upper-crust leaders who dominated politics in the new nation. All in all, the small-scale and elite-oriented press was well suited to the small-scale and elite-oriented politics of the time.

An elite-oriented press was also encouraged by the financial structure of these early presses: they relied on government patronage for much of their financial support. As one historian has noted:

It was the needs of the colonial government that supported printers in the beginning. Everywhere [presses] owed their establishment to government subsidy. The bulk of what issued from the presses was government work: statutes and the votes and proceedings of colonial assemblies.[22]

Newspapers supported by government and controlled by political notables served to bolster a citizenship democracy limited in scope but intense in belief. These papers were essentially interoffice memos full of "political talk," which circulated among a cadre of politically attentive and active citizens.

In the late eighteenth century, newspapers became part of the formal machinery of government. When Congress established the State Department in 1789, it also authorized the Secretary of State to designate at least three newspapers as the official heralds of new laws and resolutions. This provision gradually spawned a system through which federal officeholders rewarded their allies in the press with money and prestige.[23]

Financially strapped because of their small circulation, newspapers often turned to the government for sponsorship. After 1789, many newspapers were created, supported, and controlled by political leaders. When Washington was president, for example, Alexander Hamilton and the Federalists created the *Gazette of the United States* to promulgate their views. In retaliation, Thomas Jefferson and the Republican Party started the *National Gazette*. Jefferson is remembered for having said "Were it left for me to decide whether we should have a government without newspapers or newspapers without a government, I should not hesitate a moment to prefer the latter."[24] But he did not have to choose; in his day the government and the press were virtually one.

Yet it is important to distinguish between these "partisan" papers and their successors, the "party" papers of the nineteenth century. Because they were designed for an elite audience, the newspapers of the 1790s to the 1820s could debate political ideas, often in fancy language. In contrast, the Jacksonian party sheets, which were aimed at a mass audience, did not so much expound principles as trumpet catchwords and slogans meant to arouse the party faithful.

The early press further strengthened deliberative democracy through its slowness in gathering and reporting the news. By today's standards, transportation moved at a snail's pace, and breakthroughs like the steam-driven cylinder press and the telegraph would not appear until the nineteenth century. In addition, the press was far more reluctant than it is now to tread where it was not wanted. The contrast between the immediacy and intrusiveness of contemporary media and the slowness and deference of the eighteenth-century press is aptly illustrated by the press coverage of the Constitutional Convention of 1787: there simply was none. The framers of the Constitution conducted their business—which extended over four months—in secret, with little objection from the press. James Madison thought that secrecy was essential "in order to secure unbiassed discussion within doors, and to prevent misconceptions & misconstructions without." Later he said that if the delegates had been working in public they might never have compromised enough to produce the Constitution. In secret debate "the minds of the members were changing and much was to be gained by a yielding and accommodating spirit."[25]

In the current age of speedy electronic communication, the idea of keeping such an important event under wraps for four months seems highly foreign. Commenting on the subject of lawmaking in the age of television, House Minority Leader Bob Michel said:

Few words uttered on the floor are left unrecorded or unreported. In this environment there is less chance—and, yes, less desire—to sit down and work our problems out in a bipartisan fashion. There are fewer opportunities to work a compromise, to deliberate, to "come together" (which after all, the definition of Congress is—a "coming together") prior to the members' being locked into positions or forced into partisan exchanges by the swiftness of mass communication. There isn't enough wiggle room.[26]

Unquestionably, the ample "wiggle room" granted by the press in the eighteenth century helped political leaders engage in the deliberation and bargaining so crucial to the prevailing norms of democracy. Who knows what might have happened to the many compromises reached during the Constitutional Convention if the press had been present and able to file news reports swiftly! And who knows how the presidential elections of 1800 and 1824, both of which were thrown into the House, might have turned out under the glare of media spotlights!

One final point on the role that the press played in fostering republican virtue in the eighteenth century. Although newspapers were more popular in the United States than in England, much of political discourse at the time took place orally and face to face. Although newspaper circulation was low, copies were passed from hand to hand and often read aloud in taverns, coffeehouses, and other public places. Newspapers were often treated like handbills and public forums. Media consumption often took place in a social or group setting, one that generated discussion. It was rare for individuals to be sitting alone privately consuming the news.

The Nineteenth Century: Pluralist Democracy

By the third decade of the nineteenth century, politics had assumed a different character. Pluralist or group-based democracy found its truest expression in U.S. elections.

The eighteenth century had its share of political rivalries and quarrels. But most of those disputes revolved around the policy differences among national statesmen. Political conflict in the nineteenth century, on the other hand, was dominated by deep social cleavages. The main divisions were between ethnocultural or religious groups: Protestants versus Catholics, liturgical denominations versus pietistic ones, native Americans versus immigrants, Yankees versus the Irish. The political parties of this era were "political churches."[27] Not only were the mass followings of the parties rooted in ethnic or religious divisions, but political and religious groups were organized similarly. Discussing his plans for local party organizations, a Whig politician in 1840 wrote:

The model of my primary local association is the Christian Church. The officers, the exercises, the exhortations, the singing, the weekly meetings, the enrollment of members, the contributions, and all are to be on the primitive apostolic model as presented in the Congregational churches of New England. Then I want itinerant lecturers, political preachers going about in regular circuits, next spring and summer, on the Methodist plan. . . . Each of all the hundreds of thousands of members of these associations will also make a weekly contribution of one cent to the great cause of our "church militant."[28]

Political combat also grew out of strongly felt sectional or regional differences—north versus south, east versus west, urban versus rural—as well as economic ones—farmers versus industrialists, working class versus middle class. These many group rivalries spawned a wide variety of political parties and social movements, including Democrats, Whigs, Republicans, Free Soilers, Populists, Greenbacks, Prohibitionists, and Progressives.

During the nineteenth century a genuine party system was established, replacing the embryonic one of the early republican era. In 1824 Andrew Jackson initiated a new era in American politics by seeking "the support not only of political elites but also of the mass electorate. . . ." As a fiercely partisan candidate, Jackson expanded the scope of the battle for the presidency beyond the narrow confines of the national legislative leaders of the congressional caucus to the citizenry outside Washington.[29] Electoral politics rapidly became intensely partisan.

The second generation of American political leaders did not believe that the quest for unity among parties—so common in the previous century—was appropriate. Nor were they anchored in the deferential politics of the past. As Rubin has noted:

With Jackson, a new generation of political leaders had entered the political arena. The first professional party politicians, their ideas, attitudes, and organizational skills played the most critical role in changing how the electoral game was played. These new organizers of elections were not generally men of wealth or aristocratic background. No political positions had been offered them out of deference to their high economic or social positions. They were not "notables" in their local communities to whom opportunities for office flowed as a normal result of the deferential attitudes ordinary people directed at political leadership.[30]

To mobilize mass followings, they built political parties that flourished. "In America," Lord Bryce observed near the end of the nineteenth century, "the great moving forces are the parties. The government counts for less than in Europe, the parties count for more."[31] Fervent partisanship and strong party organization introduced a new style of politics into election campaigns. Mass rallies, torchlight parades, brass bands, long oratory, and campaign songs became standard fare. The Lincoln-Douglas debates of the 1858 senatorial campaign in Illinois, for example, attracted crowds of 25,000 cheering, jeering partisans. Noisy parades punctuated the proceedings as the candidates spoke for three hours.

A military metaphor seems most appropriate for describing nineteenth-century campaigns, for

the candidates and their managers thought in military terms. The election was conceived as a great battle pitting the strength of two opposing armies and genius of their generals, with the spoils of victory being patronage and the seats of power. The parties were army-like organizations, tightly knit, disciplined, united.[32]

This was the epitome of group politics. Elections hinged on which party could most fully mobilize its partisan supporters. The task was to raise the morale and whip up the enthusiasm of the troops. Elections were rituals of group solidarity.

As in the previous century, the press helped to foster the dominant style of politics. Wide-circulation, mass-based newspapers replaced the small, elite-oriented press. Papers dropped the cultivated verbiage and lofty tone of an earlier day, and adopted vernacular language more accessible to ordinary citizens. Several breakthroughs in print technology (faster presses, better paper and ink) and transportation that reduced the high cost of newspaper production and delivery permitted less expensive newspapers, and this too widened newspaper circulation.

The penetration of the new press was phenomenal. Between 1800 and 1833 the number of papers increased from about two hundred to twelve hundred, a more rapid growth than at any time anywhere.[33] The United States became the greatest newspaper-reading country in the world. Only two decades later the number of newspapers had doubled, and the number of daily papers had tripled.[34] The period not only witnessed a flood of papers, but a flood of political papers. Whereas most eighteenth-century newspapers were trade-oriented journals, by the 1830s most papers were concerned more with politics than with commerce. Mercantile papers continued to prosper, but politics was paramount in most newspapers. "Gazettes and journals are now chiefly filled with political essays," wrote printer Isaiah Thomas in

1810. Editors took sides in partisan controversy, as they "lived by and for political groups."[35]

Newspapers served as the principal weapons in the intense group conflicts and partisan battles of the age. In those days the ardent partisanship of American journalism was its most notable quality. Most newspapers were appendages and propaganda organs for political parties, nurturing the growth of party organizations and cultivating devoted mass followings. Neutral or independent papers were an anomaly. In fact, the 1850 census listed only 5 percent of newspapers as "neutral" or "independent."[36] "The distinction between the press and the party nearly vanished. It is fair to say that the most important editors in this period were actually politicians wielding newspapers."[37]

These editor-politicians were not expounders of general principles and policies. They were manipulators of group loyalties and allegiances, who used catchwords and slogans to fortify and arouse the party faithful. Many of these editors became leaders of state and local party organizations. Thurlow Weed, for example, published the *Albany Evening Journal* and used it to organize the Whig party in New York. Scores of campaign newspapers, published strictly for electioneering, sprang up throughout the nation. One of the most successful was Horace Greeley's *Log Cabin*, which was devoted to perfecting the image of William Henry Harrison.

The partisan press was not the only mode of communication in the nineteenth century. The inexpensive "penny press," which emphasized human-interest stories and scandals rather than politics, developed alongside highly partisan papers. However, through the Civil War the party press dominated American journalism. Thereafter the penny press began to take hold. Even then, however, party newspapers did not disappear. In the post–Civil War years, for example, an extremely partisan Populist press located mostly in the South and the West became a major arm of electoral mobilization for the People's party. By the 1880s and 1890s, however, changes in the press became so pervasive that they ushered in a third, and wholly different, type of electoral politics.

The Twentieth Century: Plebiscitary Democracy

Several media changes that had been underway throughout the nineteenth century converged in its final two decades. Technological improvements allowed wider circulation and speedier reporting, and this encouraged the publishing of real "news" instead of the expressing of points of view. The telegraph broke political leaders' monopoly control over the flow of information. Because the wire services hoped to sell their reports to as many papers as possible, they courted clients in both political parties. This naturally muted the partisan bias of news stories. Newspapers discovered that they could make more money through advertising than through politics. Before long they became dependent on advertising revenue. The competition for ads required high circulation, another reason why papers began to appeal to both Democratic and Republican readers. Journalist-entrepreneurs replaced editor-politicians at the helms of newspapers. An ideology of "independence" from political parties appeared, and eventually a professional ethic of objectivity developed.[38] Ultimately, the prominence of political news diminished, as did the party's voice in shaping the news.

Toward the end of the century newspapermen wrote about the emergence of a press free from party domination. In 1872 Whitelaw Reid, Horace Greeley's successor as editor of the *New York Tribune*, proclaimed:

Independent journalism! that is the watchword of the future in the profession. An end of concealments because it would hurt the party; an end of one-sided expositions . . . ; an end of assaults that are not believed fully just but must be made because the exigency of party warfare demands them; an end of slanders that are known to be slanders . . . of hesitation to print the news because it may hurt the party . . . of doctoring the reports of public opinion . . . of half truths . . . that is the end which to every perplexed, conscientious journalist a new and beneficent Declaration of Independence affords.[39]

A majority of newspapers remained closely affiliated with political parties. But by 1880 one-fourth of the country's newspapers were independent of party control, and by 1890 that proportion had reached about one-third. By 1940 the number of independent papers grew to nearly half of the total, and only a quarter had outright partisan ties.[40] And of course it was the press itself that led the reform assault against local party machines around the turn of the century. Political leaders like Theodore Roosevelt and Woodrow Wilson used newspapers as a counterforce against party organizations to establish their own direct links with the public.

It was not until the middle of the twentieth century, however, that these shifts—toward a wider, more heterogeneous audience; toward a highly commercialized, market-oriented, advertiser-driven media; toward an audience viewed as individual customers instead of tightly knit social and political groups; toward more objective, less evaluative news stories; toward a press independent of political partisanship; toward more human interest and fewer political stories—emerged full-blown. The most distinctive features of twentieth-century communications emerged only with the arrival of broadcast media, especially television.

Rarely has a technological innovation spread as rapidly as television did. In 1946 only seven thousand American households had television sets. By 1952 there were 19 million, and by 1960 the number of homes with sets reached 45 million.[41] Today virtually every American home has at least one television set, which is tuned in, on average, more than seven hours each day.

With television leading the way, the communications technologies of the era of plebiscitary democracy have five important properties that stand out for their crucial impact on American elections.

First, television has been an intrinsically *personalizing* medium. It communicates privately to people's homes, establishing a "seemingly intimate" relationship between the communicator and individual viewers.[42] Television also personalizes the content of its messages. That is, it focuses the viewer's attention on the personal qualities of political figures. Even in fairly issue-oriented forums like candidate debates, television viewers focus overwhelmingly on the style, personality, and "image" of the candidates. This privatizing quality of television is plainly evident in modern campaigns, where public rallies and speeches have given way to the televised appearance of candidates speaking directly to individual voters in the privacy of their homes.

But long before the growth of television, this personalized quality had already appeared in radio, the first broadcast medium. In his final radio address of the 1928 campaign, Al Smith observed: "Tonight I am not surrounded by thousands of people in a great hall and I am going to take this opportunity to talk intimately to my radio audience alone, as though I were sitting with you in your own home and personally discussing with you the decision that you are to make tomorrow.''[43]

The broadcast media of radio and television have also created the first truly *national* mass media. Unlike newspapers, most television messages are not directed primarily at specific local audiences. Instead, network television is aimed at a huge national audience. Related to this is the fact that the networks are highly centralized organizations.

This nationalization of the media is fairly recent. Throughout most of our history we have had a localized, segmented, and decentralized press. This nationalized media has helped to democratize elections by allowing direct rather than mediated communication between candidates and voters. This is most evident in primary elections, where news coverage and the ability of candidates to solicit votes directly via television are key.

Television has accentuated the trend toward a *commercial* media. The earliest radio stations were not advertiser-supported, and there was consideration given at the outset to noncommercial alternatives, including public financing or a common carrier status. However, the commercial model prevailed. Television networks compete fiercely for shares of the same audience so as to attract advertising dollars. Market imperatives have fostered uniform programming across the three networks and dictated limited airtime for news.

The history of the mass media in the United States thus records an almost total triumph of commercialization—the dominance of private ownership and advertiser financing. The triumph is more complete here than in any other Western democracy. In other countries state ownership and state financing are dominant. Accordingly, the United States is distinct among democracies in permitting political candidates to purchase advertising time on television. Most democracies—including Britain, France, Germany, and Italy—deny candidates this opportunity.

Television has accelerated the *speed* and the *immediacy* of news reporting. Not only does the public get information more quickly than before, but it gets it simultaneously. Politicians and candidates find it difficult to avoid the glare of the media spotlight; they are subject to intense and sustained scrutiny. Television is an inherently intrusive medium that makes the private more public, and the public more exposed than ever before.

Finally, television has intensified the trend toward a *less partisan* and less evaluative press. Faced with a vast, heterogeneous audience and federal regulations demanding fair and balanced coverage, television strives for a narrative rather than a cue-giving tone. The networks have achieved an impressively nonpartisan, nonideological, nonevaluative coverage. Occasionally the news is interpretive, critical, or even prejudicial. Yet, given the partisan and ideological leanings of the newscasters themselves, it is surprising how little personal political bias infiltrates the news. To the extent that there is bias, it is a negative attitude toward politicians and politics as a whole.[44]

Transformations in the media since the end of the nineteenth century—including the movement toward a more commercial, nonpartisan, national, personalized, and immediate press—have been accompanied by equally profound changes in electioneering. These political changes are attributable to a wide variety of causes, including long-term social and demographic trends (rising education), governmental changes (the establishment of the civil service), and amended election rules (adoption of direct primaries). More than anything else, however, the media have nurtured the strongly individualist culture of twentieth-century democracy.

At the turn of the century, electoral politics, like the press, started becoming more centralized organizationally, more national in scale, less partisan in tone, financially more dependent on the private sector, and oriented more toward individuals than to social groups. Campaigns became less of an armylike effort to whip up morale and more of an attempt to seduce the voters. The new emphasis was on the voter who might be swayed by intelligent argument. The voters were seen as customers, and the two parties began competing for the same customers. More than before, politicians were seen as products who had to be packaged attractively.

The *New York Herald* spotted this transformation during the 1892 campaign, noting "the exceptional calmness" and "an unprecedented absence of noisy demonstrations, popular excitement and that high pressure enthusiasm which used to find vent in brass bands, drum and trumpet fanfarenade, boisterous parades by day and torchlight processionals by night, vociferous hurrahs, campaign songs, barbecues and what not." The campaign, according to the *Herald,* "indicates the dawn of a new era in American politics."[45]

It would take several decades for this new era of politics to unfold completely. But already in the 1890s campaigns were conducted on merchandizing principles, with heavy emphasis on mass-media advertising and a downplaying of party slogans and symbols. The candidates tailored their appeals to partisan waivers, independents, and potential switchers. Not coincidentally, state after state discarded party ballots in favor of secret balloting procedures for the first time. Historian Richard Jensen aptly described the shift from nineteenth- to twentieth-century politics as a shift "from the battlefield to the marketplace."[46]

These changes proceeded gradually, accelerating suddenly only after 1960. The general trends set in motion at the turn of the century—the shift from groups and parties to individual voters and from a mobilizing to a merchandizing style—have continued. But they have been heightened so much in the past three decades that today's electoral system bears almost no resemblance in its specific details to the one that existed on the eve of the 1960 election.

Among the most important factors that set the current electoral era apart from its predecessors are the greatly altered roles of six actors and resources:

Political Parties. The strength of political parties has declined significantly over the past three decades. Regardless of how one measures partisanship—by personal party identification within the electorate, by partisan defection rates of voters, by party discipline in Congress, or by the vitality of party machinery—massive evidence attests to the weakened condition of the parties in the United States. In the nineteenth century the distinguishing characteristic of American parties was decentralization—they revolved around state and local party organizations. In recent years parties have become more nationalized and centralized as the authority of state and local party apparatuses has waned. Both party atrophy and nationalization can be traced in large measure to the growing importance of direct primaries, which loosened the parties' hold over their main source of power: the ability to grant or deny prospective candidates access to the ballot. The eclipse of political parties has given rise to candidate-centered campaigns for president as well as for lower-level offices. Also, zealous single-issue groups have benefited from the void left by weakened political parties.

Interest Groups. Whether or not the total volume of interest-group activity has increased is unclear. Though it has become fashionable in recent years to claim that organized groups are more powerful than ever before and have stalemated government, interest groups have long been an important feature of American politics; histories of the early twentieth century, for example, show that groups also played a significant role in policy formation during the Progressive Era. Moreover, if the influence of interest groups has increased in recent years, we suspect that the most important reason has been the decline of political parties.

But the apparent flurry of interest-group activity has overshadowed an equally important development: the declining role of group identifications in individual voting decisions. If political parties can no longer deliver their supporters at the polls, neither, it appears, can most interest groups. In 1984, for example, women's groups and labor unions both made highly publicized endorsements of Walter Mondale—and then watched a majority of their members vote for Ronald Reagan. Similarly, in 1980, a large number of conservative fundamentalist preachers endorsed Reagan, but a plurality of fundamentalists voted for Jimmy Carter. The power of contemporary interest groups stems largely from their capacity to raise money and to carry on direct lobbying. When they enter the polling booths, voters increasingly behave like atomized individuals, with group affiliations having progressively less influence on their decisions.

Campaign Technology. Accompanying the erosion of party organizations and the rise of candidate-centered campaigns is the professionalization of elections—the growing importance of political consultants. Campaigns turn more and more to the sophisticated services of these technical specialists: television advertising (prepackaged thirty- and sixty-second political spots), public-opinion polling, direct mail, and voter targeting. Such technologies let campaigns bypass party leaders and elected officials in their communications with voters.

Money. Faced with costly technologies, especially expensive television time, campaign costs have soared. Under a series of laws enacted by Congress in the 1970s to regulate how money is raised and spent in elections, the influence of any single contributor has diminished. However, a law designed to reduce the weight of money in elections has actually increased the time spent on fund raising since donations must now be raised in relatively small amounts. Incumbents and challengers engage in never-ending solicitations. The voices of organized interests have been amplified with the proliferation of political action committees (PACs), the fastest growing source of money in congressional and senatorial campaigns. Candidates rely increasingly on fund-raising experts, direct-mail appeals, sources of money outside their home districts or states, and their own personal funds. Consequently, the raising and spending of money is now dominated by individual candidate organizations on the one hand and PACs and independent expenditure committees on the other. This has further hamstrung political parties, because neither candidates nor PACs rely heavily on political parties and both are often downright antagonistic to them.

Electoral Competition. The current electoral system fosters little incumbent security at the top of the ticket but great security at the bottom. In the last three decades only two presidents have been elected to a second term. In fact, incumbents and seasoned politicians find it difficult these days to capture their party's nomination, while "outsider" candidates—mavericks, insurgents, weak partisans, and even party newcomers—have fared well. In elections to the House of Representatives, on the other hand, more than nine out of every ten incumbents who seek reelection are returned to Congress, after running in races that have become less and less competitive over the last twenty years.

Media Power. The news media, especially television, have assumed a commanding role in elections. As the power of traditional intermediary institutions—parties and interest groups—has declined, voters still need someone to give them cues and help interpret the world around them. The media have become that crucial link between the candidates and the voters. Television reporters have become the scorekeepers who set expectations and define the standards of victory and defeat. The necessity for candidates to get television coverage and the magnified risks of making mistakes on the air have inspired the use of pseudo or staged media events. Also, since 1960, televised candidate debates have become a staple of presidential and subpresidential campaigns.

Elections and the Media: Past, Present, and Future

Is there a single thread shared in common by these key features of twentieth-century elections? Over the years, and especially over the last thirty, American politics has assumed an increasingly *individualist* cast. The rich diversity of intermediary groups that once stood between the candidates and the voters has withered, resulting in a politics characterized by outsider candidates and an atomized electorate. The system is also individualist in a legal sense: it defends the rights of ambitious entrepreneurs to sell consulting services and of private citizens to financially reward their favorite candidates. And unlike other Western democracies, it has left the ownership and control of television largely in private hands.

While mass electronic media have furthered considerably the goals of an individualist, plebiscitary-type democracy, they have fit very poorly with our other models of democracy. Television has not served the more communitarian needs of democracy. Its national scale of communication is too large for community-oriented programs or for citizens and local civic groups to have access to the airwaves. Such a national and passive medium is not well suited for communitarian democracy, which depends on deliberation, talk, and direct participation.

The electronic media also have not fit well with the pluralist needs of democracy. By and large the electoral process has moved away from group forms of participation, such as party conventions and caucuses, to more direct, individual forms of participation where all voters have a say in the selection of party nominees and where candidates beam messages to voters on a one-to-one basis. Television journalists themselves have promoted an individualist type of democracy, portraying primaries as the only legitimate way to nominate candidates.[47]

The decline of political parties represents the most serious loss for a pluralist type of democracy. Not only has television accelerated the long-term trend toward party decline, but it has assumed many of the functions once performed by political parties. Television reporters evaluate and test candidates—assessing how well they are doing and setting benchmarks for success and failure. In effect, the media have supplanted political parties as the main connecting rods between candidates and voters, providing citizens with their only real information during the campaign.

Privatizing, commercializing, and nationalizing have penetrated other aspects of American elections as well. Current campaign finance laws force candidates to create elaborate fundraising operations to appeal directly to private individuals, who constitute more than two-thirds of campaign donors. As with the commercialization of the media, the commercialization of campaign financing sets the United States apart from other democracies. Private expenditures for partisan purposes are either forbidden or strictly curtailed in other nations. Most other democracies have long had limits on the use of private funds in elections. Fund raising in the United States also has acquired a national flavor as more and more candidates raise more and more funds outside their home districts or states. Candidates find themselves seeking funds nationwide from individuals and groups that share their positions on issues, and from national rather than state or local parties.

The growing influence of political consultants in elections reflects the same three trends. The technical experts who run campaigns are private entrepreneurs, unattached to permanent organizations like political parties. "We organize a campaign as an independent business," observed one of the first consultants in this field. "And we start a new business every two years, with a new organization, new people, a new board of directors. We have experts. Our writers are good writers, our TV script people are good; we decide on strategy and tactics ourselves."[48] Of course, their high-priced services feed the growing commercialization of American elections. As for nationalization, most political consultants do not have local roots but roam the country from nationally based firms, usually applying similar techniques and messages in different settings. The technical services they sell—polling, direct mail, targeting, and paid ads—are a key source of individualist democracy because they establish the direct pipeline between campaigns and voters.

All told, most every aspect of twentieth-century electoral politics serves the individualist ideal. The net result is a system which might be called "electronic plebiscitary democracy."

The most striking feature of the system of electronic plebiscitary democracy is direct, continuous, highly intense communication between Presidents (and would-be Presidents) at one end, and scores of millions of people at the other. The politicians reach the people via television; the people reach the politicians via polls. In this relationship, the politicians act almost solely in their capacity as popular leaders and scarcely at all in their capacity as party officials or government managers. The people act almost solely in their capacity as atomized individual television-watchers, and scarcely at all in their capacity as citizens of states and communities or members of political parties or other voluntary associations.[49]

The Present: Current Uses of the New Media

If important changes in the organization and technology of the press have gone hand in hand with changes in election campaigns, then we might expect similar changes from the growth of the new media. How are the new media—cable, videotex, satellites, and the rest—currently being used in election campaigns? And what larger changes in the nature of campaigns appear to be emerging as a result?

We have argued that because it is impossible to predict with confidence which particular technologies will endure and which will fade, it is useful to think about the media future in terms of underlying "generic properties" that the technologies share in common and that are likely to alter the future profile of the media. Accordingly, our discussion of the use of new media in elections is organized around the six generic properties already discussed. Each example is listed under the technological property that seems most pivotal to the new campaign application although, obviously, many of the applications depend on a combination of properties.

Volume

The increased volume of campaign information that the new media make available, both to voters and to campaign staffs, has sparked some of the most dramatic, and increasingly common, uses of the new technologies in elections.

During the 1984 presidential campaign, the Republican National Committee committed $1.1 million to the formation of an opposition research group (ORG). The principal task of ORG was to collect, analyze, and prepare for fast and easy retrieval as much data as possible on the various Democratic presidential contenders. In this way, the party hoped that party and campaign officials at all levels would be able to effectively rebut any assaults put forward by the Democrats, and mount their own attacks with the most accurate information possible.

The project, according to Michael J. Bayer and Joseph Rodota, who headed the Republican effort, began in the early weeks of the primaries. Readers familiar with the candidates sifted through thousands of documents looking for useful quotes by or about the various Democrats. These pieces of data were then entered into the Republican National Committee's mainframe computer,

according to a hierarchical, issue-oriented dictionary with a total of over 600 individual categories. The process was evolutionary. As Democratic candidates dropped from the race, day-to-day collection and analysis of materials pertaining to that candidate were terminated and staff resources shifted to the remaining candidates. Eventually, of course, only Walter Mondale remained.[50]

By the time it was clear that Mondale would be Reagan's opponent, the data on him had grown to "approximately 75,000 items, including 45,000 quotes documenting the complete career of Walter Mondale—easily the largest collection of opposition materials on a political candidate ever assembled. . . . During the height of the [general election] campaign, the entire database was updated every 24 hours."[51] Almost as quickly as Mondale made a statement or issued a press release, the material was entered into the ORG system.

Bayer and Rodota acknowledge, however, that such a massive quantity of information is useful to a campaign only if two barriers can be overcome: it must be easily accessible to campaign workers who have little or no computer training, and there must be a way to communicate the information rapidly to workers in field offices, not just to those at the national headquarters. The ORG system successfully addressed both of these problems.

First, the structure of the reference dictionary on Mondale was such that "anyone with 15 minutes of training could use [it] to conduct basic or advanced research."[52] Special staff members were needed only briefly to train workers to utilize the system.

More important, ORG overcame the second obstacle by intercon-
necting geographically disparate microcomputers nationwide:

An electronic communications system was developed to link 50 state party
headquarters, 50 state campaign headquarters, and spokesmen in all 208
ADIs [areas of dominant influence—broadcast rating markets] with Opposition research, the Republican National Committee and Reagan-Bush '84
headquarters. Party and campaign spokesmen had instant access to up-to-
the-minute talking points, issue papers, and draft speeches for use in discussions with local media. The database itself was accessible to key campaign
and party officials—even aboard Air Force One and Air Force Two.[53]

The information was used directly by the candidates and
their aides, and ORG distributed portions of the data to selected
reporters and columnists around the country in a book titled *Vice
President Malaise: 20 Years of Walter Mondale.*[54] The Democrats
could not match the volume of information that was almost instantly accessible to the Republican campaign.

In 1986 the fruits of Republican intelligence gathering became
available to all party candidates for the House through the Republican Information Network. Any candidate with a modem-
equipped computer could search a data base containing the latest
news available on the opposing campaign. Republican challengers
could examine—and thus exploit—the entire voting record of a
Democratic incumbent dating to 1974, much as Reagan could have
ensured that any Mondale misstep would resurface through the
efforts of the earlier ORG. The volume and speed of contemporary
"opposition research" are possible only with the new computer
and telecommunications technologies.

New technologies—computers attached to high-speed
printers—have vastly expanded the volume of "direct mail" that
can be sent to voters. Roger Craver of the political consulting firm
Craver, Mathews, and Smith has noted: "It would be virtually
impossible to have the system we have today without the sophisticated technology . . . Before—in the mid-'60s—we would load a
station wagon and go to a typist, who got out 500 letters a day. We
then used addressograph plates and stamped envelopes. Now we
can send out a million pieces of mail in 12 hours."[55] A particular
boon to the direct-mail business has been the combination of
computer-list and word-processing systems on the one hand with

the high-quality laser printer on the other, which can handle between seven thousand and twelve thousand letters per hour,[56] virtually ensuring that any amount of mail a candidate wants to send can be sent in a timely fashion.

One particular use of laser printing technology helped a candidate win statewide election by permitting an increase in the volume of election information. In 1982 California gubernatorial candidate George Deukmejian used laser printers to mail one million absentee ballot applications, along with preaddressed return envelopes. Because of the liberal absentee voting laws in California, individuals were required only to mark the application and return it by mail. They did not have to prove absence from home. The effort was immensely successful for Deukmejian. Of the million applications mailed, 400,000 were returned to the Board of Elections, and Deukmejian won the election by 113,000 votes. The percentage of absentee ballots filed, 6.5 percent of the total vote cast, was more than twice the proportion in 1976.

The amount of news coverage of elections has expanded with the arrival of the new media. The advent of twenty-four-hour cable news, for example, has spurred the networks to increase their news programming. In some instances the new media outlets have maintained the volume of news coverage that would have otherwise declined without them. Beginning in 1960, each of the networks have broadcast gavel-to-gavel coverage of the national party nominating conventions. In 1984, however, only two cable networks, CNN and C-SPAN, carried the conventions in their entirety. This was not merely a shift from broadcast to cable coverage. The networks were planning to drop full convention coverage several years ago, proposing that the Public Broadcasting Service (PBS) pick it up. PBS decided not to. Were it not for the cable channels, full coverage would not have been available.

C-SPAN also provides previously unavailable coverage of floor action in the House of Representatives and the Senate. The cameras have permitted some members of Congress to bypass traditional party roles and seniority and gain visibility and recognition directly from exposure to the nation's voters.

Finally, information taken from cable television—especially C-SPAN—has found its way into traditional broadcast media, thus expanding the total supply of political news. In 1982, for example, House Minority Leader Robert Michel faced a more challenging reelection contest than originally predicted when a taped statement he had made on the floor of the House regarding Social Security was recorded from C-SPAN and inserted into his opponent's commercials. (It is interesting to note that while Michel's opponent could use the video clip of his floor speech, Michel himself could not retaliate by using C-SPAN coverage in his own ads. House rules permit members to purchase copies of the videofeed from the House floor but restrict their use to nonpolitical and noncommercial purposes. The House rules, of course, do not apply to nonincumbent challengers.)

Speed

The new technologies accelerate the gathering, processing, and transmitting of information. Speed obviously goes hand in hand with volume. If you can transmit information more quickly, you can use the same resources to transmit more information. But speed is not just the handmaiden of volume. The "global village" wrought by ordinary television was traversed only by a one-way street, however fast. But with the speed of new technologies like electronic mail comes the "global conference," which draws political decision makers together across time and space in a conversation that pierces the isolation in which political opinions were formed and acted upon in the past.

In 1984 the American Federation of State, County, and Municipal Employees used satellite broadcasting to help Walter Mondale in his quest for the Democratic nomination. With the aid of a satellite hookup, they held a teleconference with their field operatives in New Hampshire and the five early-March "Super Tuesday" primary states. The link with the field operatives was two-way, permitting them to converse with workers who could not spare the time to travel back to Washington.[57]

Republican field organizers in the 1984 Reagan campaign used microcomputers to speed up campaign decision making. As one Republican official described it: "When the [campaign] plane landed at one stop, you would get to a telephone and download your messages [from the headquarters computer to your microcomputer]. In the plane en route to the next city you could read and analyze the electronic mail. And at the next stop, you were prepared to upload the answer, instructions, or strategy to another location."[58]

This ability to collapse communicating time addresses one of the stickiest problems in campaigns, especially presidential campaigns: how to maintain a communications link among headquarters, the field staff, and the candidate "on the road." As primaries begin to cluster around fewer dates, both the candidates and their staffs find it necessary to maintain a presence in more than one place at a time. Bruce Babbitt and his speechwriter collaborated on a revision of the announcement of his 1988 candidacy for the Democratic presidential nomination the day before he delivered it—with Babbitt in Phoenix and the writer in Washington, both connected by computers.

Advances in the speed of telecommunications also have influenced election news coverage. During the 1980 presidential campaign ABC News stirred some controversy by conducting "instant polls." Immediately after the televised Carter-Reagan debate, ABC provided viewers with two "900" telephone numbers they could call to record who they thought had won the debate. Each call cost the respondent fifty cents. Not surprisingly, some enthusiastic partisans set up phone banks to "stuff the ballot box" and put their candidate over the top. What was new about this technology was the fact that the AT&T computers could process the millions of votes registered by telephone almost instantly, with the results available a few hours later.

Due to the controversy surrounding this project—viewers who responded to the instant poll were not a representative sample of the whole electorate and the immediacy of the results served to accentuate the media's focus on the horse-race quality of the debate—ABC News dropped this weapon from their campaign arsenal. Continuing strides in technology, however, point toward the possibility of less biased uses of such techniques in the future. For example, computers can be programmed to accept only one vote from each telephone number, thereby hampering organized telephone banks. Further, the networks can choose to provide callers with "800" numbers for free telephone service. On the other hand, the new technologies are making polling (real polling) itself so much faster, as discussed later, that the need for such instant news "polls" may fade rapidly.

As long as the methodological problems persist, the networks will be reluctant to use these call-in polls. But behind the scenes political operatives continue the quest for the instant response. As the 1988 Democratic presidential candidates debated publicly in Houston, a selected sample of Iowa party members were treated to a special screening. In the hands of each was a dial, connected to a computer, which when rotated transmitted their relative satisfaction with what was being said at that precise moment. Technicians monitored the audience response with a display of what one observer likened to "a patient's vital signs in an intensive care unit."[59] With instantaneous feedback like this, the temptation to parse out the response to every hand gesture is irresistible for those entrusted with the job of crafting the perfect candidate.

Perhaps even more significant to the 1988 campaign is that analysts are now responding instantly to one another. Political consultants Douglas Bailey and Roger Carver have created a service called Hotline, whose daily report offers a smorgasbord of campaign news when downloaded by computer. Hotline is not so much a wire service as an electronic "conversation" among pols in the know: it is written by and for insiders, the analysts and commentators who make opinion as well as report it. The candidates themselves are allowed to contribute their say, providing a forum for twenty-four-hour responses to the salvos of opponents. Trail-weary reporters no longer need venture forth among the voters to cover a campaign that is now fought across their computer screens. Their stories in turn are plugged into Hotline in exchange for a discount on their subscription fee, their opinions fueling the opinions of others. As Walter Robinson of the *Boston Globe* has noted, "you can be [one of the boys] on the bus without ever getting on the bus."[60] Whether or not it may be important to get off the bus occasionally to stretch your legs is another matter.

Receiver Control

The new communications technologies grant users greater control over the information they wish to receive. For political campaigns, this is a decidedly mixed blessing. Since most voters have little interest in politics, it is likely that many of them will use their greater control to tune out political messages, particularly candidate advertising. This will make it harder for campaigns to get their messages out to the electorate. On the positive side, however, expanded user control will allow highly specific issue publics to acquire more information about how candidates will deal with their particular concerns.

The growing use of computer data banks in political campaigns is the best example of this latter application. Legi-Tech (which will be discussed further in chapter 4) is a computer software program that has been used to track legislation filed in the New York State Capitol. The program has an electoral application as well. Using Legi-Tech, voters and campaigns can access a "contribution tracking model" that lists all the money contributed to legislative and statewide candidates as well as spending by lobbyists in the state. The software organizes these financial contributions and lobbyist expenditures not only by the candidate who received them but also by donor, and it can further classify donors into interest-group categories (banking, labor, horse racing/gambling, and so on). The key to its value is that it enables users to select what information they want and to manipulate that information into useful categories. This flexibility makes Legi-Tech expensive: the entire service costs between $175 and $550 per month. Therefore it is not likely to be used by individual voters at this time. However, lobbyists, interest groups, candidates, and journalists are currently Legi-Tech clients.[61]

Targeting

Most of the new communications technologies allow senders to aim their messages more narrowly to identifiable groups and individuals. Gone are the days when national or statewide campaigns had to rely on "leaflet drops" to reach voters. Computers allied with polling and direct-mail techniques enable campaigns to send fund-raising letters to those most likely to contribute and specialized background information to voters with specific issue concerns. Cable television with its town-by-town franchises allows candidates to target messages within the political boundaries of a small area. Even videocassette recorders enable candidates to appear on the screens of only those selected television sets they wish to reach.

As briefly noted in chapter 2, one of the best examples of the use of cable television for narrowcasting purposes occurred in the Barney Frank–Margaret Heckler congressional race in 1982. Legislative redistricting had thrown two popular Massachusetts incumbents into the same district. The Frank campaign believed that in order to win they had to do well in the city of Fall River. The city was wired for cable, and Frank's media consultant, John Florescu, urged the campaign to exploit it. He explains:

We were down 2–1 and needed media exposure. Boston TV was too expensive. So we designed a 30-minute show to be shown on the local cable system. It included panelists from the various demographic groups. That gave us an instant credibility and built up an audience for us. Using local people enhanced the program instead of relying on some slick promotion.[62]

The campaign spent only $6,000 to produce the three shows specially designed for the Fall River audience, and the air time was even cheaper. Florescu points out that $1,000 cannot buy any spot time on broadcast television, and only thirty radio spots; but it can buy fifty thirty-second cable TV ads in prime time. To drum up viewership, the Frank campaign advertised the cable shows through radio and newspaper ads and door-to-door leaflets.

Barney Frank is not the only Massachusetts politician who has used cable television in a campaign. Michael Dukakis used cable in his 1982 bid to regain the governorship. The Massachusetts Democratic party currently holds party caucuses and a convention prior to the statewide primary for selecting candidates. Prior to the local caucuses, Dukakis placed spot ads on cable systems in seventeen cities and towns urging his supporters to attend the party meetings. The spots were run with usual public-affairs programming so as to reach the desired audience. Each ad was tailored to a particular locale, and included a local telephone number that viewers could call for rides to the caucuses or for baby-sitting services.

In 1988 cable television became an integral part of advertising strategy for the first time in a presidential race. Despite some reservations about the efficiency of cable advertising, many political consultants began recommending cable as a key campaign weapon. For example, seven of the thirteen major party candidates ran political spots on cable television (especially on the Cable News Network) in Iowa and New Hampshire.

Cable played a prominent role in the early stages of the Dukakis presidential campaign, not only as a means to air paid political ads but also to target selected geographical areas and voter constituencies with live, self-produced television shows. The Dukakis campaign sponsored several hour-long teleconferences during which the candidate answered questions called in by cable viewers. Buying time on public-access cable channels in Iowa, Minnesota, South Dakota, Florida, Maryland, Texas, Illinois, Nebraska, and North Dakota, the campaign not only targeted its shows geographically but also aimed its coverage at particular voter groups. On one show Dukakis answered questions from senior citizens; on another he responded to college students.

Assessing the targeting potential of cable in the early days of the 1988 presidential race, and looking ahead to future congressional and gubernatorial contests, one media consultant concluded that "cable is going to dramatically change the way this business works." [63]

In this age of the "permanent campaign," incumbents are always looking toward the next election. Thus many of the uses of the new media by officials in government discussed in chapter 4 are an integral part of the electoral context as well. The new technologies permit elected officials to target messages to their local constituencies. In New Jersey, for example, U.S. Senators Frank Lautenberg and Bill Bradley, as well as Governor Thomas Kean, have used that state's Cable Television Network for monthly public-affairs shows.[64] These shows were part of the channel's regular programming, and consequently the officials did not pay to have them aired. Such programming would not be possible without a new technology capable of directing messages to New Jersey alone, because the state has only one local television station. (New Jersey is served primarily by broadcast stations in New York and Philadelphia.)

Another example of how campaigns have exploited the targeting potential of the new media is in testing political ads. Cable audiences are ideally suited to be testing grounds for ads that will run on broadcast television. While they are not the total audience, they are sufficiently large to get a meaningful reaction. Furthermore, ads can be shown to selected communities with different demographic and political profiles in order to enhance the analysis of voter reaction. Connecticut Governor William O'Neill did just this in his 1982 campaign. Videotape ads designed for local broadcast stations were first pretested on seven cable stations in the southern part of the state.[65] The O'Neill campaign held fund-raising parties at various homes where the participants watched the ads on cable channels and gave immediate feedback on how effective they thought they were.

Closely following the penetration of cable television into the American home has been the videocassette recorder. The potential uses of VCRs in election campaigns seem limitless. Even if campaign messages remain the same, enormous cost savings over traditional broadcast-oriented strategies are possible. For example, in 1984 Democratic presidential candidate Walter Mondale sponsored a television program that was broadcast on CBS one evening when Mondale fund-raising parties were being held throughout the country. Simply by distributing videocassettes to homes with VCRs, the Mondale campaign could have reached the same fundraising parties (with a program indistinguishable from the one beamed from CBS studios in New York) at a tiny fraction of the broadcast cost. Furthermore, this approach would add the feature of exclusivity—only those who attended the fund-raising parties and contributed to the campaign would be able to view the program. Jack Kemp pursued a similar strategy in his 1987 New Hampshire effort when he held 103 home video parties across the state, each featuring the same eight-minute tape.

But like the increased speed of contemporary political communication, the increased quantity afforded by new technology effects other qualitative changes as well. Videotapes are the new direct mail, the cutting edge in targeted communication. Specific messages can be aimed at specific groups compiled household by household. In November 1987 Bruce Babbitt sent uncommitted New Hampshire Democrats a video pastiche of his best quotes from debates and commercials.

The videotapes also present the candidate's image (literally) with an immediacy that direct mail obviously cannot match. In an age in which voters, taking their cues from campaign coverage, are overtly concerned with style as well as substance, this opportunity for the would-be president to perform in living rooms everywhere is invaluable. Often considered stiff in his public appearances, Babbitt benefited from his relaxed performance in the carefully edited spots. Labor organizations like the AFL-CIO have requested videos from the Democratic candidates; the tapes will reveal not only the positions of the candidates on issues of interest to labor but also their capacity for waging a successful televised campaign.

Decentralization

The increasingly decentralized control of media messages enables politicians to contact voters more directly, by allowing them to bypass traditional media organizations. At first it was the parties who mustered the resources to afford their own candidates the vehicles to speak directly to the electorate without relying on regular news coverage. But the latest technology in producing and broadcasting television programming has further decentralized the 1988 presidential campaign: the candidates themselves now have access individually to relatively cheap yet sophisticated means of reaching the electronic audience.

This decentralization began when satellites—in the hands of the party and not the networks—first found their way into Democratic campaigning. The Democratic National Committee (DNC) provides a satellite videotape service for Democratic members of Congress to transmit tapes to their home districts for use by local television stations. According to one account:

The DNC reserves 10 minutes each working day of the Westar IV satellite and then makes the time available to Democratic members of Congress. Normally, a member is interviewed by a reporter or delivers a statement, and the proceedings are videotaped in the House recording studio. The tapes are then sent to [a satellite feeding service] on Capitol Hill, where they are edited and "uplinked" to Westar IV. Interested local TV stations, notified in advance, can tune to the satellite and pull down the feed at the prescribed time. It may then be inserted as part of a newscast. TV stations like the system because they can exercise editorial control over the tape. "The networks do the same thing; we simply use the same technology," said the DNC's [Deputy Press Secretary Terry] Michael.[66]

With the advent of more portable equipment, lower costs, and increased flexibility in the amounts of time that can be purchased, candidates no longer need the parties to broker their satellite access. Gary Hart presaged this development in his 1984 presidential campaign. Hart rented transponder time on a satellite so that the announcement of his candidacy for the Democratic nomination could be beamed directly to local news stations wishing to pick it up rather than being mediated through the national networks.

The 1988 presidential contenders have sought this control throughout the entire campaign, and a breakthrough in broadcast technology has made it possible. Transmitters have been miniaturized to the extent that they can fit into a small truck or the candidate's airplane. It is no longer necessary to make elaborate plans for blockbuster media events involving the party and all of its candidates in order to pool expenses for the exposure. Richard Gephardt and Jack Kemp agreed to split the cost of satellite time —only $11,000—to televise their two-man debate. Bruce Babbitt and Pete du Pont, as well as Michael Dukakis and Gephardt, staged similar mini-debates. These debates—sometimes followed by live interviews conducted by local reporters—were fed directly to television stations across the country.

Columnist Tom Wicker has noted that these satellite debates bypass not only the networks and the parties but also the "eye-glazing cattle shows that such sponsors inevitably produce."[67] In the name of objectivity all candidates must be included in traditional debates, all camera angles controlled, and all exchanges carefully moderated by the equivalent of a Swiss neutral observer. The result often is less than inspired, hardly meriting the label "debate" and the fierce contest of values it implies.

The 1988 presidential candidates exploited this same technology to create their own individual networks. Faced with the daunting challenge of waging a three-week campaign in twenty states for the March 8 ("Super Tuesday") primaries, many of the candidates "conquered time and space" by beaming satellite messages to voters.

In-person "retail" politics common in the Iowa caucuses and the New Hampshire primary ill suited a battleground stretching across twenty states and 90 million people. The vast territory of Super Tuesday even tested the limits of airport-hopping "tarmac" campaigns. Nor could the candidates simply rely on the "wholesale" politics of broadcast television. Paid advertising on the national networks was not cost-effective in a campaign restricted to twenty states, and the cost of running ads on local affiliate stations in 170 media markets was astronomical.

Free media exposure on local news broadcasts was an essential ingredient of campaign strategy for Super Tuesday, for the candidates could not depend heavily on national network coverage. Moreover, in many areas the local news programs draw higher ratings than their network counterparts, and the locals offer much more news programming during the course of the day than the networks do. The new media—especially satellite technology—enabled some candidates to get substantial news coverage over a wide array of states. For example, Richard Gephardt used a satellite hookup to answer questions in a hotel room in Kansas City from television stations in Yakima, Wash.; Washington, N.C.; Casper, Wyo.; West Palm Beach, Fla.; Washington, D.C.; and Spokane, Wash. A week earlier, sitting in an Austin, Texas, television studio, he gave five-minute "exclusive" interviews, in turn, to local stations in El Paso and Lubbock, Tex.; Presque Isle, Me.; Lake Charles, La.; Augusta, Ga.; and Tulsa, Okla. Gephardt was able to construct this decentralized and personalized satellite network from Austin for only two thousand dollars.[68] The new satellite technology not only allowed him and the other candidates to bypass the normal routes for gaining access to broadcast television, but it also allowed them to target their messages to specific communities.

A similar decentralization has taken place in media production. Since 1978 Republicans have provided their candidates with what the Republican Congressional Campaign Committee refers to as "a full-service political advertising operation" to assist party members in all phases of media production. The Committee provides technicians who videotape "actualities" (radio or television tapes of members in action) that are then fed by satellite to local TV stations much as the DNC does.

But just as technological advances have allowed the parties to circumvent the networks, further advances have reduced the candidates' reliance on the technical expertise of the parties. Videotape editing facilities and camera crews are now available for hire across the country. As a result, television commercials can be used for a timely counterpunch as exigencies require. In the 1986 Senate race in Florida, Republican incumbent Paula Hawkins claimed in a commercial that she had met with Chinese leader Deng Xiaoping. Within hours, her opponent, Governor Bob Graham, broadcast a political ad juxtaposing clips of Hawkins's original claim with admissions by her aides that the claim was false.

Elections and the Media: Past, Present, and Future

Cable also has been used to bypass traditional broadcast media operations. In 1984 incumbent State Senator Vincent Piro was running for reelection in Somerville, Massachusetts. After he defeated challenger Sal Albano in the primary, it was widely thought he was assured of victory in the general election. Between the primary and the general election, however, Piro stood trial on a charge of accepting a bribe. The trial ended in a hung jury and Piro continued his campaign. Albano's supporters were outraged, and Albano decided to run a write-in campaign in the general election. The night before the election, Albano supporters staged a reenactment of portions of the trial on Somerville's public-access cable channel. The next day Albano defeated Piro. It is estimated that only about 25 percent of the 14,000 cable subscribers in Somerville saw the show. However, the news media, both print and broadcast, covered the cable event, and consequently many more voters in the area were reminded of the trial. Cable gave the Albano campaign both more publicity and a more direct link to the voters the night before the election than it could have hoped to achieve in any other fashion with its limited resources.

Interactivity

The interactive capacity of media technologies is genuinely new. More than any other property of the new technologies, it has provoked lively, and even heated, debate about the changes the new media may bring to politics. Thus far, however, interactivity has been one of the least utilized features of the new technologies, mostly because of its expense and partly because it requires the greatest adjustment in television viewing habits.

Several of the examples discussed earlier, such as two-way videoconferencing, have relied on interactivity. Interactive technology is also making inroads into campaign polling. The development of computer-assisted telephone interviewing (CATI) permits telephone polling to be tailored to respondents' answers. The interviewer sits in front of a computer terminal and the questions appear on the video screen. The respondents' answers are entered directly into the computer. Based on the answers already entered, new questions appear on the screen that apply directly to the particular respondent. Thus young respondents from the urban Northeast who like Ronald Reagan are asked certain questions, while other respondents are asked a different set of questions. Answers affect questions in a genuine two-way flow across the wires. Inappropriate questions are skipped and a much greater depth of information is obtained. In this way the survey questionnaire is transformed from a blunt instrument into a sharp, finely tuned one.

CATI systems will improve election polling not only because of their interactive capacity, but also because of their speed in data processing. The data are entered immediately into the computer as the interviewing proceeds. The results are available as soon as the interviewing is completed. Timely public-opinion data is an enormous asset in a fast-moving campaign.[69]

Overall, the current uses of the new media technologies in election campaigns have been quite varied. All of the key properties of the new media have been exploited in some fashion or another, certain ones more than others. Prior to 1988, however, relatively few campaigns had adopted the new technologies. In addition to the usual hurdles to greater use of the new media—insufficient audience penetration, meager data on the characteristics and viewing habits of the new media audience, limited number of cable channels—candidates are reluctant to take risks and therefore have been loath to adopt new approaches until they have met with wide acceptance.

Nineteen eighty-eight appears to have been a take-off year for the use of the new media by political campaigns. Several of the presidential aspirants have successfully incorporated the new technologies—satellites, cable, and videocassettes—into their communications repertoires.

The Future: The Near Term and the Twenty-first Century

While to this date the effects of the new media on campaigns have been limited, the potential effects are enormous. The mere proliferation across more campaigns of the types of activities currently in use will create a tremor in the world of electioneering.

And, indeed, the most likely change in the near future is just that—the spread of these applications to more campaigns. Beyond that, the inventory of current usage hints at some potential uses of new media that have not yet been tried.

Some candidates, such as Barney Frank, have already used the new media to aim televised appeals to local community audiences. But such targeting is primitive compared to the potential uses of the new technologies. The development of videotex along with home computers and fiber optics may soon enable campaigns to target advertising on a home-by-home basis, addressing the specific issues that the voters in each household find most interesting. Voter targeting will then truly be a video form of direct mail. A campaign could send a political ad showing the candidate talking to a union official if the head of the household were a union member; and next door, the campaign could send an ad showing the candidate wandering through a forest talking about the detrimental effects of pollution if someone in that home were very concerned about the environment.

Another potential use of the new technologies applies less to campaigns than to voters. As noted earlier, the enhanced receiver control of the new media might grant voters greater access to information that could help them make their voting choices. Voters with personal computers in their homes might gain access to data bases that could provide summaries about a candidate's issue stances or record. One media consultant has envisioned a world in which the voter will be able to watch "a half-hour filmed biography of the candidate, [and] he or she will also be able to superimpose [over the picture] such information as the candidate's voting record, financial disclosure, or positions on major issues."[70] A less ambitious version of this—which may be more relevant to voters with insufficient time or interest to become acquainted with the candidates and issues in each local, state, and federal election—imagines citizens being able to ask a limited set of questions of particular concern to them: what are the candidates' stands on issues they care most about, their main sources of funding, or who has endorsed them.

Cable television might also play a role in increasing voter information during campaigns. Take, for example, candidate debates. For national and statewide offices, such debates are often carried on television. However, local stations have not wanted to devote air time to local contests because they are relevant only to a limited audience. Cable is a logical answer to the local coverage problem. With its multiplicity of channels, including public-access ones, cable is an ideal vehicle for candidate debates for mayoral, city council, school board, and state legislative elections.

In speaking about the current and potential uses of the new media in elections, it is worth repeating a point emphasized in chapter 2. The arrival of the new media will not mean the disappearance of the old. Rarely, if ever, have new forms of communication replaced traditional ones. When the new media are used in election campaigns, they will be an addition to the existing media options. Candidates and voters will continue to use newspapers, magazines, radio, and broadcast television. Russell Neuman has suggested several reasons why this is so. The public likes to scan headlines, photographs, and graphics on paper and will not give up that habit easily. Readers and viewers also depend on the editorial and filtering functions of journalists, which will be lost in some applications of the new media. And the broad stroke of broadcast coverage appeals to many people ("We don't want the sense that our neighbors heard the whole news and we heard only half of it.")[71] Even if the new media penetrate deeply into election campaigns, the old media will survive alongside.

The impact of new media technologies on elections, in any event, will not be felt fully for ten or fifteen years, so it is the twenty-first century that is our point of reference. The twenty-first century has been the stuff of science fiction for so long that it connotes someone else's distant future. But we now are closer to that century than to the year 1975. As we gaze toward that horizon, oriented by our understanding of the historical coupling of the media and elections and the variety of current uses of new technologies in campaigns, we shall suggest several likely and important consequences of the new media for the electoral system. As before, these consequences will be organized according to the six underlying properties of the new technologies. Some of the consequences are listed under more than one property, others under only the most pivotal one, although arguably they all rest upon a combination of properties. Our conclusions are summarized schematically in table 3.1.

Specifically, we offer the following predictions:

The new media may actually foster an electorate that is less

TABLE 3.1

Electoral Consequences of the New Media

Generic Properties of the New Media	Likely Consequences
Increased . . .	
Volume	• An electorate that is less informed about political issues. • Further advantage to legislative incumbents.
Speed	• The risk and consequences of candidate mistakes on the media are magnified; greater use of pseudo media events. • Fewer opportunities for deliberation, bargaining, compromise, and secrecy in electoral institutions; continuing pressure for mass, democratic processes (e.g., direct primaries).
Receiver Control	• Less informed electorate (a smaller inadvertent audience). • Greater attention to local politics (at the expense of national and international affairs). • Less central editorial control by the press in campaigns. • Less political information that is broadly shared by the public.
Decentralization	• Declining hegemony of the three major networks and the national newspapers. • Agendas and content of election coverage less routinely prescribed in New York and Washington. • More national election stories given local spin on the news. • Continuing trend toward candidate-centered campaigns.
Targeting	• Greater attention by public to local politics (due to geographic narrowcasting). • Increased use of television in congressional and local campaigns. • More effective political advertising. • Enhanced power of political consultants; continued decline of political parties; centralization of internal campaign organization. • Shrinking pool of common knowledge in the public. • Greater emphasis on ideological and issue-oriented politics; pressure for factionalization and against coalitions. • Public opinion interpreted more frequently in group terms. • More expression of point of view in election news coverage and paid advertising.
Interactivity	• Use of electronic plebiscites: instant polls, instant referenda, voting from home.

informed about politics and government. This may seem counter-intuitive, given the new media's promise of more abundant information. Yet both greater volume and greater receiver control might ultimately reduce the public's contact with public affairs. Americans' interest in and knowledge of politics, especially electoral politics, is low compared to that of citizens in other democracies. This limited appetite for politics combined with a larger media menu is likely to produce less consumption of political news. The proliferation of media options, especially entertainment ones, will be stiff competition for news programs. Although the absolute quantity of news programming might increase, the abundance of mass-entertainment programs will cause the relative share of news to shrink. Furthermore, because many people now get their political news inadvertently (for example, watching an entire news program while waiting for the sports or weather report, or glancing at the political headlines while turning to a newspaper's food section), greater receiver control will let a public that is generally uninterested in politics miss or avoid public affairs altogether.

The arrival of the new media will not diminish or reverse the long-term trend toward the electoral security of congressional incumbents. If anything, the advantages that incumbents enjoy over challengers will increase. Legislators already are exploiting the expanding volume of new media and the enhanced ability to aim messages at hometown constituencies. The media resources and public relations facilities available to incumbents in Washington are impressive. Cable, satellite transmission, electronic mail delivery, videoconferencing, and so on are fast becoming part of the incumbents' repertoire of techniques for maintaining contact with constituents during the full-time "campaign" between elections.

Incumbents also enjoy an important financial advantage. The only way that challengers can compete effectively against incumbents and possibly unseat them is to spend substantial sums to create name recognition in the district. Indeed, the marginal utility of spending by challengers is far greater than spending by incumbents. Inevitably, challengers are caught in the vicious circle of needing money in order to compete but needing to convince contributors that they are competitive in order to raise money.

Campaign costs have outpaced the inflation rate, mostly due

to zooming media costs, especially television time. The new media probably will exacerbate the problem for challengers by further escalating the cost of waging campaigns. Although the cost of air time on the new media is lower than on broadcast television, production costs remain high. Besides, as mentioned, the new techniques surely will not displace older ones; they will add new costs to traditional expenses of reaching voters. As will be discussed, the new media make it cost effective to use television for the first time in many districts. If challengers hope to keep pace with incumbents, they must raise more money. All but the most well-heeled and well-known challengers will find themselves further disadvantaged.

It is no wonder that politicians today seek refuge in staged media events, "debates" with formats that prevent debating, canned political ads, and infrequent news conferences. The speed of television reporting has compressed the time that candidates and public officials have to respond to events and has made slips of the tongue much more dangerous than in the pre-electronic age. By accelerating even more the speed of gathering and transmitting information, the new media will magnify the risk of mistakes even further.

The speed of the new media also will accentuate the pressures against deliberation, bargaining, and secrecy in electoral arenas. Earlier we quoted Republican Minority Leader Michel's comments about the lack of "wiggle room" created by C-SPAN. The cameras do not grant legislators the time to "come together" slowly and deliberately, according to Michel. The speed of news gathering and the immediacy of news reporting demands that politics be open and public.

It is no accident that the last presidential nominating convention to go beyond the first ballot was in 1952, the year that conventions began to be televised nationally. The deliberative quality of the convention conflicts not only with the entertainment needs of television but also with television's preference for events that are open, fast-moving, and full of action. As political columnist David Broder has noted, television's need for a neat and fast-paced show altered the character of the conventions: "Favorite-son nominations, lengthy caucuses of uncommitted delegates, prolonged speech-making, and many other devices used by organized factions to force a bargaining process with others in the party coalition were swept aside."[72] Conversely, the television networks have persistently favored primaries—which are open and fast-paced, and thus serve the needs of that medium—to caucuses and conventions as the legitimate way to select party nominees. New media that permit even speedier and more timely transmission will weigh even more heavily against bargaining and secrecy and add additional pressure for open, democratic processes like direct primaries.

In the early days of the nation the focal point of politics—electoral and nonelectoral—was local. The unprecedented growth of the federal government and the rise of a truly national media over the last fifty years has changed this. However, the new media may bring a renaissance of localism to American politics. Both receiver control and sender targeting should promote more attention to local politics, at the expense of national and international affairs. Newspaper marketing surveys regularly indicate the public's stronger taste for local news over national and international news. Accordingly, newspapers have increased their state and local coverage compared to national and international stories. User data from the Knight-Ridder "electronic newspaper" (the Viewtron videotex service) showed that those with the option of creating their own newspaper have preferred local news to national and foreign news.

Critics often cite a related point as evidence that the new technologies will undermine the political stability and consensus necessary for democracy. Greater user control and sender targeting will, they contend, "balkanize" the public into narrowly defined groups communicating among themselves and not with non–group members. Richard Salant, the former president of CBS News, expressed the concern this way:

The danger, it seems to me, is that our supposedly indivisible nation might be transformed into a nation of tribes [by the new media]. Yet a successfully functioning democracy depends on a common data base for its people. Some of the new technologies threaten that common data base. Smaller and smaller groups may come to know more and more about less and less.[73]

One might take issue with this view either on the facts—questioning how much information actually is held in common by citizens, and how much of that information is political in content —or on the values—asking how essential this common knowledge is for national unity and effective governance, and whether it may represent instead a bland uniformity that smothers diversity. That is a debate to be joined in chapter 8. For now, let us simply acknowledge that the national media—broadcast radio and television, the wire services, national newspapers—have been one important source of our common civic culture, one that promotes a shared political vocabulary and agenda and in some respects a homogenization of opinion. To the extent that the new media segment the audience geographically and functionally more than it is divided today, that pool of common knowledge and common perspective will be reduced.

Some of the most significant electoral consequences of the new media will come from the shift toward a more decentralized media industry. Greater receiver control holds open the possibility of "unmediated media"—the creation and delivery of political messages that do not require the user to go through large media institutions. The decentralization of the news business also promises to challenge the hegemony of the few media giants who have exercised strong editorial control over election coverage during the last three decades.

A preview of the migration of power from New York and Washington to the hinterlands took place during the 1984 Democratic and Republican national nominating conventions. As noted in chapter 2, some four hundred local stations sent live coverage directly back to their markets, largely due to two new technologies: minicameras and satellites. These local stations frequently broke away from network coverage during prime-time hours to show their own reports. For the first time a significant amount of convention coverage was not filtered through the eyes of the national network anchormen. More often than not, the local stations translated the national convention news into local terms, emphasizing local news angles.

One final example of the localizing effects of the new media deserves special emphasis because it might be the first noticeable effect of the new media on elections. The use of television in most congressional and other local races should increase dramatically. Currently, congressional political boundaries and media market boundaries do not coincide. In some districts, one media market serves twenty or more congressional districts, and advertising on one station requires that candidates waste most of their budgets on voters in other districts. An extreme version of this exists in states without local television stations. A candidate running in New Hampshire must advertise on Boston television, and until recently, one running in New Jersey had to use New York or Philadelphia stations. In other districts, primarily in rural areas, one congressional district is served by several media markets, often out-of-state ones, each of which serves several districts. Consequently, although more than six of every ten congressional campaign dollars are spent for advertising, no more than one in four goes to television advertising. It is simply an extravagance. In many districts television coverage and paid television advertising are nonexistent. Cable franchises and congressional boundaries are much more congruent. As a result, the least efficient areas for political advertising may become the most efficient.

What is true for congressional races is even more true for other local races: mayoral, city council, school board, and state legislative campaigns. We would expect more of these local campaigns to use television, particularly free television. For example, the new media should prove to be an ideal forum for local candidate debates. Congressional candidates often debate each other, but the relevant district is so small a part of the local TV market that the debates usually are not broadcast. The same barrier prevents coverage of lower-level offices as well. Local communities and neighborhoods frequently get excited about elections for school board or city council because officials on these bodies make decisions that touch citizens' lives very directly—schooling, police and fire protection, sanitation. Cable television offers a convenient and inexpensive way to keep voters abreast and engaged in these contests.

The ability to target messages to smaller, more homogeneous audiences over the new media might be a boon to political admen. "Video direct mail" may actually prove to be more effective than current mass advertising. The conventional wisdom among political scientists is that televised political ads have limited impact. Political messages on TV are a surprisingly blunt and ineffective weapon for changing people's attitudes. That is because the messages are filtered through a number of buffers that limit their potential effects—including the audience's group memberships and existing predispositions—and because they must contend with a Catch-22: those who pay attention to political advertising generally have already made up their minds, while those who have not made up their minds—the people whom the campaign hopes to persuade—tend to pay little attention to political ads.

Narrowcasting may create a form of advertising that can convert voters more effectively. Voters can be converted by friends and families. Perhaps carefully targeted messages will ultimately be more closely akin to a conversation with a friend than to a current TV ad. Some direct mail has already moved in this direction by including in the letter computer-recalled information, such as the voter's first name and hometown. One can imagine computer-generated mail far more specific, referring to the voter's job, neighborhood, income, and ideology, and linking the candidate to the voter through one or more such factors. TV advertising could be similar via cable, featuring, say, a prominent local attorney endorsing a particular candidate or an ad addressed only to attorneys in town. Furthermore, by combining polling with the new media, technologies may ultimately permit campaigns to send political ads to voters identified as potentially persuadable.

Converting voters, however, is but one purpose of political advertising. Television seems to fare better at stimulating or fortifying people who have already made up their minds. Even if targeted ads on the new media fail to convert voters, they may prove to be even more effective than broadcasting at reinforcing voters. Currently, the reinforcing potential of political ads on television is diluted by the need to broadcast the message to a large and heterogeneous audience. Some voters might be offended by very pointed messages and perhaps even countermobilized against a candidate. As one political consultant candidly put it, "With targetted communications, you don't have to waffle so much, as you do on television."[74]

If public opinion is organized, as many political scientists claim, into fragmented "issue publics"—groups of people very concerned about particular political subjects and much less concerned about others—then narrowcasts to carefully defined groups of people who share a particular concern should serve campaigns well. The advocacy approach of preaching to the converted is, of course, precisely the strategy of the "electronic church," the most effective narrowcasters on television today. To the extent that the new media encourage candidates to appeal to issue publics, then the mobilization of narrow-gauge factions within each party will be strengthened and the building of broad electoral coalitions will be impaired.

The capacity to deliver customized messages to narrow and specified audiences, messages that are better keyed to the voters' interests, raises another possibility. The new media might create pressures for more ideological and issue-oriented elections. In addition to a heavy emphasis on candidate images, U.S. election campaigns revolve around three kinds of issues: "apple pie" issues (such as peace, prosperity, and honesty, which all candidates try to be identified with); performance issues (candidates claiming credit or, more often, criticizing the past records of their opponents); and substantive policy issues (those that have different ideological sides such as for or against abortion, hawk or dove on nuclear weapons, liberal or conservative on busing). Apple pie and performance issues have dominated American elections. However, the new media's targeting potential raises the possibility that the balance might shift a bit more toward substantive policy issues.

The new media might lead not only to more pointed political ads but to the adoption of more "point of view" in news reporting. If the prophecy of narrowcasting comes true, and cable subscribers can select from among one hundred or more channels, then we might expect news coverage to acquire a more partisan tone. This would mark a return to the more evaluative, cue-giving style of the nineteenth-century press. News reports would then resemble sports writing: stories that report what happened in a game while letting personal impressions slip into the narration, including the reporter's rooting for the home team.

How are the new media likely to affect the relative strength of candidates, consultants, PACs, and parties as they jockey for supremacy in campaigns? The advent of television in campaigns actually began at party initiative in 1952, but eventually candidate organizations have grown more and more independent of parties. Parties are once again trying to jump on the technology bandwagon. The parties have begun to behave like super-PACs, paying for or supplying campaign technology to candidates. Some observers believe that the new technologies will resuscitate political parties, as they become repositories of technical expertise and services.

Frankly, that seems doubtful. Although the national parties, particularly the Republicans, have tried to become major service organizations, they have no monopoly over key services—advertising, direct mail, polling, or fund raising. "Why should [candidates] choose to give up their independence and control of their message to parties?"[75] If anything, the properties of the new technologies —including decentralization and greater user control—will strengthen the trend toward candidate-centered campaigns and strengthen the hand of technical experts as political parties move into further eclipse. Inside campaigns the ability to rapidly assess and coordinate new sources of information will be at a premium, and this will foster an increasing centralization of campaign organization.

Up to now, the electoral application of new interactive media, two-way communications, has been as disappointing as it has been controversial. Participation in instant polls and instant voting has been very low, and Warner Amex has dropped the most ambitious interactive experiment, its QUBE system.

Still, it is too soon to dismiss the future of interactive plebiscites. Historically, the American public has pushed steadily and persistently for an expanded participatory role in politics. The demand for popular voice in elections appeared earlier and has proceeded further in this country than in any other. What reason is there to believe that this democratizing spirit has subsided and will not be mobilized in the service of electronic plebiscites? Once the costs and logistics of that technology become more attractive, the pressure for voting from home, for example, probably will be irresistible. The pressure for instant polling might be equally strong. For the past fifty years or so, Americans have been fascinated with public-opinion polls. They are more eager than the citizens of most democracies to register their views ("send them a message").

Let us conclude this discussion of the electoral consequences of the new technologies with one consequence that is perhaps more speculative than those discussed earlier: the new technologies will likely alter the way we think about elections.

When party organizations were healthier institutions, the party apparatus was the principal technology that politicians used for discovering what the electorate had on its mind. Candidates and elected officials relied on precinct workers to put their ears to the ground to gauge public sentiment. In those days, the interpretation of public opinion had a decidedly *group* cast to it. That is, public opinion was understood as the views of geographic and social groups—southerners, easterners, upstate voters, downstate voters, Italians, Irish, the wealthy, the poor. Interestingly, the voting theories of academics mirrored this same group perspective. Political scientists conceived of politics as a clash among groups and of voting as based on group associations and identities (religion, ethnicity, occupation, and so on).

In the mid-twentieth century a new technology replaced the precinct worker: the public-opinion survey. This technology carried with it the notion that opinions of large populations could be inferred from small samples. With the arrival of polling, the group-based interpretation of politics gave way to a much more micro interpretation. Politics was seen through the prism of polls as the aggregation of many individuals, not the collection of component subgroups. Accordingly, voting theories acquired a psychological cast. The heavy emphasis was on individual attitudes—individual perceptions, values, and identifications. Social groups were assigned a secondary role and nearly disappeared from view.[76]

This shift in thinking from groups to individuals contributed to the growing nationalization of American politics. Ironically, polling's emphasis on the individual helped make national opinion matter more. Polling permitted the measurement of the nation as a whole, through the addition of individual opinions. Before polls, a reading on national opinion required a mosaic of evidence on smaller blocs of voters. But this shift did not simply reflect the introduction of a new measuring device. The distinction between the pre- and the post-polling eras might be likened to the difference between the direct election of the president and Electoral College selection. With polls, the opinion of an individual voter in Kansas counted equally for the first time with the views of someone in New York.

We are now about to enter the third stage in the evolution of public-opinion technology. Like its predecessors, this one will likely change the way politicians and academics think about politics. New and more sophisticated ways of collecting and analyzing polling data permit pollsters to ask special questions tailor-made for particular types of respondents, to interview larger samples more efficiently, and to fine tune their analyses. This new technology probably will revive a more group and segmented interpretation of politics, albeit a more sophisticated version of what constitutes groups than the traditional categories of Irish, southerners, and poor. Political scientists undoubtedly will incorporate this conception of the public into their theories of voting behavior. Whether political practitioners and analysts think about the electorate in group or individual terms is of signal importance to the strategies they pursue and the messages they convey.

New Media and Elections: Choosing a Democratic Future

Different properties of the new media drive the electoral system toward different democratic ideals. The greater speed of the new media, which permits instant polls, instant referenda, and instant voting, promotes an individualistic, plebiscitary brand of democracy. The new media's heightened potential to target messages to particular audiences strengthens pluralistic tendencies. Greater volume, interactivity, and user control invite a more informed and involved communitarian style of participation.

But the degree to which one or another of these properties dominates is not fixed. Nor is it beyond human control. Just as one can change the color balance on a television set to suit one's taste, so should it now be possible to change the balance of media technologies to suit the national interest.

We have already seen what can happen to politics when this element of choice is lacking. In recent years, our almost exclusive reliance on the mass media, especially broadcast television, has lent the electoral system an excessively plebiscitary cast. Mass media have contributed to a system that is dominated by candidate-centered campaigns, the mobilization of highly personalized followings, and the registering of private opinion by isolated individuals. The media have promoted an atomized and anonymous mass electorate.

The flip side of such individualistic politics is the erosion of those pluralistic forces that are so vital to a vibrant democracy.

Contemporary electoral processes do not foster a rich diversity of group life. Nor do they encourage communitarian values such as dialogue, deliberation, and participation. As political scientist Nelson Polsby has argued, traditional agents of political intermediation—such as the family, the school, primary communal groups, voluntary associations, and especially political parties—have been losing ground to the mass media.[77]

The new media have the potential to magnify this trend, perhaps even leading to electronic voting—push-button democracy. Yet that is not inevitable. Carefully managed, the new media could help foster the democratic ideal the electoral system sorely needs: the form of democracy we have called "pluralism with a communitarian face."

Perhaps the area most ripe for reform is the nomination process. In the "good old days," nominations hinged on conventions and caucuses. But these old-fashioned political gatherings are not very hospitable to the mass media. Television is much better suited to covering the fast-paced and direct primaries that now dominate the nomination process. Again it is no coincidence that the current process has degenerated into a public-relations and personality contest—individualistic democracy at its worst.

One way the new media can promote pluralism with a communitarian face, then, is by making it possible to resurrect caucuses and conventions.[78] These gatherings are settings where both pluralism and communitarianism can flourish. The assembled party activists, elected officials, and candidates must negotiate and testify to their commitments and interests. They must form alliances and deliberate over issues and offices, both in public and behind the scenes. Caucuses and conventions are arenas where groups can compete over the issues that divide them while keeping in mind—and ultimately asserting—the common goals that unite them. Of course, the kinds of caucuses and conventions we have in mind would not be exact copies of their historical antecedents. Those earlier bodies shared with other communitarian gatherings (like local town meetings) the tendency to be elitist, exclusionary, and closed.[79] In order for caucuses and conventions to serve effectively the democratic ideals outlined here, they must be open and representative.

Unlike broadcast television, the new media—with its decentralizing, localizing, and segmenting qualities—should be quite at home at such gatherings. Caucuses and conventions are multi-stage events that begin in neighborhoods and then move to precincts, wards, districts, and eventually to states. These are ideal audiences for local media outlets, including cable systems. Moreover, conventions include a wide variety of demographic, geographic, interest, and issue groups who will be excellent audiences for targeted narrowcasting before an assembly convenes. And interactive technologies such as videoconferencing can promote exchanges among groups, as well as allow more people to participate in the assemblies.

Of course, this is only one example of how the new media can be mobilized to improve the democratic process. The ultimate balance among plebiscitary, pluralist, and communitarian democracy in the future will depend on which properties of the new technologies are exploited and emphasized. Our hope is that, in making such choices, political leaders will have the wisdom to draw the best features from each of the three democratic visions.

CHAPTER 4

COMMUNICATIONS TECHNOLOGY AND GOVERNANCE

POLITICS DOES NOT END when elections have been won and lost. Governance, the normal conduct of political life, the reason for all the campaign balloons and hoopla, begins again—or, more appropriately, continues. To adapt a definition of politics from political scientist David Easton, governance produces an "authoritative allocation of values."[1] Though many citizens do not believe that politics is important to their daily lives, real values are at stake in public policy: scarce resources are distributed to some, denied to others.

Whereas the politics of elections accentuates the formation of majorities, the political processes that decide and implement public policies are susceptible to the mobilization of minorities. Because most political values are collective in nature and because individuals working in concert can usually muster greater resources, interest-group organization determines much of the politics of governance.

Among the more enduring features of governance in America is its pluralist or interest-group character. In *Federalist* No. 10, James Madison observed that

the latent causes of faction are thus sown in the nature of man; and we see them everywhere brought into different degrees of activity, according to the different circumstances of civil society. A zeal for different opinions concerning religion, concerning government, and many other points, as well of speculation as of practice; an attachment to different leaders ambitiously contending for pre-eminence and power; or to persons of other descriptions whose fortunes have been interesting to the human passions, have, in turn, divided mankind into parties, inflamed them with mutual animosity, and rendered them much more disposed to vex and oppress each other than to co-operate for their common good.[2]

As discussed in chapter 1, the genius of Madisonian politics has been to combat faction with faction. A governmental process was bequeathed to us through which tyranny of the majority is checked by effective coalitions of minorities. Visiting the United States in the 1830s, Alexis de Tocqueville commented extensively on the power ordinary citizens could exercise over public policy by joining voluntary associations.[3] Modern political science has built on these Tocquevillian and Madisonian observations by emphasizing the group basis of American politics. In an influential work, *The Process of Government*, the political scientist Arthur Bentley noted the complex and cumbersome process by which the national interests of the United States are articulated:

On any political question which we could study as a matter concerning the United States . . . we should never be justified in treating the interests of the nation as a whole nation as decisive. There are always some parts of the nation to be found arrayed against other parts. . . . When the groups are adequately stated, everything is stated. When I say everything, I mean everything.[4]

In this chapter we consider the impact of the new media on the channels of communication among interest groups in the United States and between these groups and the government. More specifically, we focus on three areas where the nature of democracy seems vulnerable to changes in communication. These areas are new ways in which (1) citizen groups lobby government; (2) government mobilizes citizen support for policies; and (3) officials of government communicate among themselves.

Citizen Pressure on Policy Making

In a democracy we must be concerned with the possibilities for citizen influence in public policy—that is, with the capacity of the political system to deliver on the promise of governance of, by, and for the people. Guided by the pluralist conception of democracy, our attention is directed to the development of interest groups and manifestations of collective citizen presence in policy making. Specifically, we will examine how the new media affect lobbying activity, the formation of interest groups, and organized efforts to mobilize citizen pressure on public officials from the grassroots.

Direct Lobbying Contact

Thus far many who run national interest organizations have concluded that the new media work best in helping them to put pressure on political leaders by arousing the public. Even so, there are some prominent examples in which some of these leaders have attempted to use emerging technologies to influence policy directly. The distribution of a controversial videotaped documentary titled *The Silent Scream* provides a prominent example.

In the fall of 1984, the "right-to-life" organizations in Washington, D.C., were searching for some way of recasting the debate over abortion. Politically, the issue had stalled; recognized players on each side repeated well-known positions with little gain or loss of support to either side. Seeking to break out of the familiar point-counterpoint lines into which the debate had fallen, the "pro-life" forces turned "high-tech," using both sophisticated medical technology and video distribution techniques that were unavailable a few years earlier.[5] *The Silent Scream* contains ultrasound images of a twelve-week-old fetus *in utero* during an abortion. According to the narration provided by Dr. Bernard Nathanson, the pictures provide dramatic evidence that the fetus undergoes pain and suffering during abortions, attempts to escape the suction probe by vigorously lurching away, and opens its mouth in a piercing, silent scream.

In January 1985, after the film was screened at the White House, Ronald Reagan stated during a speech to the Annual March for Life gathered at the Washington Monument, "It has been said that if every member of Congress could see that film, they would move quickly to end the tragedy of abortion . . . and I pray that they will."[6] Three weeks later, responding to the president's cue, the Crusade for Life announced that they were sending every member of Congress and every Supreme Court justice a copy of the videotape.

Although the Washington media gave the film a great deal of attention, contacts with a small number of congressional offices several months later revealed that many members were unaware that their offices had actually received the tape.[7] Though most congressional offices now have videocassette players, the groups pressing the Congress on both sides of this issue discovered that political organization was essential to ensure that members and staff actually watched the film. Both the pro-life community (Crusade for Life, American Life Lobby, and Senator Gordon Humphrey of New Hampshire) and their opponents (Planned Parenthood, the National Organization for Women, the National Abortion Rights Action League, Catholics for a Free Choice, and Congresswoman Barbara Boxer of California) organized screenings of the tape followed by question-and-answer sessions with doctors favorable to their views. These sessions were well publicized and were responsible for a good deal of the media attention the tape received. Even so, while many congressional staffers attended these sessions or viewed the tape in their offices, few congressmen or senators actually did so.

This shortfall in direct viewing does not alone imply, however, that *The Silent Scream* had little effect on Capitol Hill. In fact, the videotape became a media event in its own right. Most major news outlets covered the White House screening as a news story, and, before the discussion died away, parts of the film were shown on each of the three networks. This exposure—more than the videotape's accessibility—accounts for the commotion that resulted. The opponents felt obliged to respond, and congressmen moved quickly to develop a position on the film.

The Silent Scream did not lead to the shift in congressional politics the antiabortion movement had sought. In the final analysis the production itself, rather than the issue it raised, quickly became the focus of attention. Opponents were able to damage the credibility of the film and blunt its effect. The instance underlines, however, how difficult it is to capture congressional attention. Watching the videotape demanded more time than many congressmen and most of their staff were willing to give to one piece of information.

A slightly different variant has been attempted by the Labor Institute of Public Affairs, a new division of the AFL-CIO that is exploring the opportunities created for labor by the new media. It has produced videotapes of working men and women that its lobbyists can carry with them to Capitol Hill to dramatize how federal policy affects ordinary citizens, such as farmers or blue-collar workers. The expense of producing these testimonials, however, has precluded taping constituents of the individual congressmen whom they are trying to reach. As a result, the institute's director, Larry Kirkman, admits that it has been hard to get congressmen to sit down and watch the tapes.[8]

The pro-life movement has been no stranger to other aspects of the changes in communications. For her research on the sociological aspects of the abortion controversy, Kristin Luker interviewed many activists in the movement and found that technology enabled many volunteers to contribute their time to the movement while working at home.[9] Home computers for keeping mailing and phone lists meant that with twenty-four hours' notice, these groups could arrange to have over one thousand letters sent to the relevant representatives in the House and Senate. A "rollover" feature on the organization's telephone line directed incoming calls to the homes of volunteers who signed up to answer calls during given hours, while they went about their normal lives. Finally, by arrangements with their banks, many members set up a regular monthly electronic funds transfer to donate five or ten dollars per month. These contributions provide a stable source of money for the organizations.

Luker concluded, moreover, that technology had a more profound influence; it allowed many members in the pro-life organizations to remain active while attending an average of only four meetings per year. This pattern stands in sharp contrast to the normal finding that interest-group activists are constantly attending meetings. As a result, Luker concluded that in this instance technology was able to break down the dominant socioeconomic pattern of political participation, namely that activists come from the more prosperous levels in society.[10] Many of the women working in pro-life organizations came from socioeconomic backgrounds that normally exhibit much lower rates of activism.

Lobbyists are also using the new communications media to gather political intelligence. On the national level, at least two firms ("Legi-Slate," owned by the *Washington Post*, and "Washington Alert Service," owned by the *Congressional Quarterly*) supply on-line information to their lobbying clients. Through a computer network, subscribing lobbyists can immediately access and search the text of bills before Congress, the committee calendars, the voting records of individual congressmen, and data bases containing political contributions. This proprietary information is offered at rates that generally mean only the most well-heeled organizations and firms can afford it. For example, subscriber fees to the *Washington Post*'s "Legi-Slate" vary from $6,900 to $12,000 per year, depending on the level of service purchased. As a result, most of the subscribers to Legi-Slate are lobbyists, associations, or news media, although several senatorial offices subscribe, as do the Washington offices of a number of states.

Arnie Thomas of Legi-Slate gave an example of how daily access to the *Federal Register* might be useful, by citing an Executive Order that changed the interpretation of legislation on the books:

One day they were changing the definition of teaching institutions to mean not only universities but to mean large corporations also, because they, indeed, have classes. That showed up in the Federal Register for a week. What happened was that when the universities came back for their money, the piece of the pie wasn't as large as it once was. That's because the major corporations came in and also took a piece. So, we also show that you can lobby the federal government as well.[11]

Mobilization of Membership

To influence government, interest groups must be able to mobilize their memberships in support of or opposition to particular policies. Such mobilization has been going on from the days of the outdoor rally and torchlight parade. But many of the generic properties of the new media discussed in chapter 2—their speed, reach, targeting capacity, and two-way channels of communication—are allowing lobbyists to mobilize their reserve troops as never before.

Consider the following example, in which speed played a crucial role in a lobbying campaign. The Local Government Information Network (LOGIN) contains data bases on matters affecting municipal government. Acting on information added to the network by the Washington offices of the National League of Cities and the U.S. Conference of Mayors, approximately three hundred subscribers can follow and participate in Washington politics despite their physical distance from the capital. In March 1985 Congress was considering an antitrust bill when an amendment was attached on the floor that the National League of Cities (NLC) opposed, considering it harmful to urban concerns. A staff member posted an immediate electronic bulletin on LOGIN, asking local municipal officials to call their congressmen to voice their opposition. The amendment was defeated, and the NLC staff remains convinced that the resulting flood of calls from mayors to their congressmen helped decide the issue.[12]

In the past few years labor unions have turned to teleconferencing and videoconferencing as other means of mobilizing their dispersed memberships. In an effort to assess the need for a "Solidarity Satellite Network," the Labor Institute of Public Affairs (LIPA) reviewed the lessons from ten videoconferences that had been staged in a year and a half by seven unions in the AFL-CIO and in which 25,000 union members participated.[13] The purposes served by the events were diverse—bringing more members to a union constitutional convention, arousing support for presidential candidate Walter Mondale, initiating a membership drive or organizing campaign, and orchestrating pressure on Congress. The latter example interests us most directly in this chapter.

When the Reagan administration proposed to include postal workers under the Social Security Act, the American Postal Workers Union staged an extensive teleconference linking ten thousand letter carriers gathered at forty-seven Holiday Inns.[14] To sharpen the exchange of information, questions from twenty-five of the field locations were telephoned into the Washington studio, so that the two-hour teleconference served as something of a national legislative strategy meeting. Three weeks later, when union members flooded into Washington to lobby their cause, they were already well versed in the arguments that the organization wanted to raise against the administration's proposal. That year's Washington visit attracted more activists than ever before. Attributing that response to the videoconference, one union official remarked, "I think we hit a nerve."[15] The proposed revision was defeated in Congress.

Learning from these experiences, the National Education Association (NEA) has operated since early 1983 a studio and transmission facility in its national offices and has encouraged its state teachers' associations to equip their headquarters with satellite receiving antennas. State organizations are linked by a closed-circuit network that features one-way video from Washington and two-way audio among all sites.[16] Regular weekly conferences and special events are serving to bind the association more closely together.

Educating the General Public

Judged by their efforts, those who lead national groups and organizations believe that the new media can be more useful in reaching concerned citizens in the public at large than in direct efforts to affect congressional behavior. In recent years, several new Washington lobbying firms have sprung up, specializing in so-called "grassroots lobbying." These firms are essentially middlemen used by interest groups interested in quickly mobilizing public opinion on a given issue. "Using phone banks, computer-aided targeting strategies and direct mail techniques, these middlemen can quickly manufacture and channel public support that otherwise would not exist."[17]

To cite a prominent example, the firm of Communications Management Inc. arranged to have two thousand Mailgrams sent to one senator's office in one week urging decontrol of natural gas prices. These citizens had been contacted by a phone bank, read a statement, and asked if a Mailgram could be sent in their name (paid for by the Natural Gas Supply Association). Communication Management had used U.S. Census data and polling results to locate neighborhoods in which citizens were likely to distrust government and believe strongly in private enterprise. In some instances the citizens contacted were not told that gas suppliers were behind the campaign; the effort was called the Alliance for Energy Security. In addition to the Mailgrams, Communications Management asked 38,000 volunteers in fifteen targeted congressional districts to distribute pro-decontrol literature and postcards to their neighbors, and they arranged for personal letters to be sent from business leaders on stationery with the sender's name and address printed as a letterhead. The whole orchestrated campaign was designed to find citizens outside the natural gas industry who would agree with the decontrol argument. Commented Communication Management's Mike McAdams, "We know we can find a constituency for almost any issue . . . we make it easy for them to respond."[18]

The effectiveness of these campaigns is, however, open to question. A *National Journal* survey of lobbyists, congressmen, and Capitol Hill staffers found that 87 percent rated computer-generated letters or postcards as ineffective while 91 percent thought handwritten letters were "most" or "very" effective.[19] An earlier survey of congressional staff conducted by the Congressional Management Association[20] found that spontaneous letters from constituents ranked at the very top of ninety-six different kinds of influential information, while orchestrated mail and petitions were ranked much further down the list (ninth and thirty-second respectively). Even so, much of the huge increase in mail arriving on Capitol Hill (see table 4.1) can be accounted for by the organization of citizen pressure by groups and lobbyists.

There are abundant signs that political groups are also using the newer communication vehicles in an attempt to influence the general climate of public opinion. The best example is provided by the U.S. Chamber of Commerce, which, back in 1982, established its own television network in an effort to reach its scattered membership and to present to a broader slice of the American public the business point of view on Washington politics. The network consists of a state-of-the-art studio in Washington, a satellite uplink, and both subscribers and cable companies on the receiving end. Five days each week, the Chamber airs its principal show, *BizNet News TODAY*, which by 1985 was carried by three national cable networks (USA, Financial News Network, and The Learning

TABLE 4.1

Receipt of Mail by the U.S. House of
Representatives by Year, 1973–1986

Year	Number of letters (millions)	Number of "flats"[a] (millions)
1973	20.6	11.3
1974	25.8	14.6
1975	25.1	14.5
1976	24.3	13.1
1977	26.8	12.4
1978	28.0	13.5
1979	27.5	13.6
1980	29.4	13.3
1981	40.1	17.8
1982	32.5	12.3
1983	36.4	13.0
1984	40.4	13.2
1985	42.3	13.5
1986	32.4	13.9

SOURCE: Norman J. Ornstein, Thomas E. Mann, and Michael J. Malbin, *Vital Statistics on Congress, 1987–1988* (Washington, D.C.: Congressional Quarterly Inc., 1987), p. 175.
[a] "Flats" are either large manila envelopes that contain many individual communications or bundles of postcards not counted separately.

Channel), by an additional twelve cable systems directly, and by forty-two commercial broadcast stations.

Given their point of origin, the content of these shows tends to focus on government activity that affects business. Fearing that totally one-sided, pro-business presentations would diminish their credibility and truncate the distribution of its shows, however, BizNet has tried to preserve some balance in its programming. For example, labor leaders are often invited to appear on a BizNet show entitled *It's Your Business*. Each week for half an hour, Richard Lesher, president of the Chamber of Commerce, teams up with an invited guest to debate a topic on which the Chamber has taken a position opposed by two other guests. The show is carried each week by approximately 150 broadcast stations and by the USA cable network and Ted Turner's Atlanta "superstation," WTBS, which can be found on many cable systems.

The Chamber of Commerce supplements the BizNet enterprise by renting its facility to other groups that would like to hold videoconferences or to film shows or other productions in their studio. Before the White House set up its own studio and microwave relay to an earth station, for example, Ronald Reagan crossed Farragut Square on numerous occasions to "attend" videoconferencing meetings or fund raisers. In short, the BizNet studio, with its established access to a satellite uplink, has become an important center of activity for Washington political elites who wish to bypass the television networks and still send video communications out to the American public.

BizNet's changing nature over its short history is quite instructive as to the current uses of these new media. The Chamber of Commerce initially planned BizNet as a private network connecting its member affiliates across the nation. Originally affiliates of the national Chamber, larger corporations, or local branches were supposed to purchase and install a receiving dish and decoder (about $10,000) and pay a yearly fee ($5,000) in order to receive a continuing stream of political programming from the Chamber's headquarters. Offerings would include shows such as *BizNet News Today, It's Your Business*, and *Ask Washington*—the latter another of BizNet's daily offerings on which viewers can use an "800" telephone number to pose questions to Washington insiders. But more important, these subscribers would also receive scrambled communications so that, over BizNet, businesspeople could hold confidential strategy sessions to discuss pending legislation in Congress, litigation underway, and administrative implementation of policy. In other words, the private network was designed to aid the Chamber of Commerce's lobbying efforts in Washington by welding pressure from prominent citizens in local constituencies with national coordination and strategy.

Its planners ultimately wanted BizNet to replace much of the intraorganizational communication of the Chamber of Commerce. With 200,000 members on its mailing list, every legislative alert or bulletin costs more than $40,000 in postage alone.[21] Those costs were, moreover, just for one-way communications, which did not easily permit responses from the field or follow-up messages. The early enthusiasm at the national headquarters was filled with ideas of "a cheaper, faster and more flexible system of talking to its members and letting them talk back."[22]

The vision of a finely tuned effort to orchestrate business lobbying receded during the first few years of BizNet's operations, due to a complicated set of reasons. First, potential subscribers encountered a plethora of unanticipated logistical problems in constructing "downlink" facilities, including microwave interference, local zoning and beautification ordinances, and landlord refusals. These retarded the growth of the private network. But even more important from our perspective were the problems of focus: the national headquarters may have overestimated the interest of affiliates in Washington news. The Chamber of Commerce found it very difficult to produce a full agenda of programming that would speak to the concerns of local affiliates in the problems peculiar to their communities. In other words, the content to be carried by the system was never really attractive enough to provide an incentive to override the logistical problems.

Thus BizNet's intraorganizational communications did not develop successfully; yet the growth of the Chamber of Commerce's general-audience programming has succeeded well beyond any of the original expectations. Three years after its startup, *BizNet News Today* could be seen by approximately 42 million households, and an independent telephone survey estimated that 800,000 watched parts of the show daily and around 2.5 million viewers tuned in for at least six minutes in an average week.[23]

Instead of an effort to focus specific lobbying pressure on Congress, BizNet evolved into a general effort to shape public opinion more broadly in favor of business positions. While this longer-run strategy may prove just as effective as the original plans for a highly focused, coordinated lobbying effort, there is nothing very original in the attempt to create a climate of public opinion favorable to business even when conducted through the new media.

One seemingly immutable law of interest-group politics is that organization stimulates counterorganization.[24] Not to be outdone, the AFL-CIO has begun to move in much the same direction to get labor's side of the story out to the American people. Its vehicle is LIPA. In addition to the videotaped testimony carried up to Capitol Hill, LIPA has been producing spot advertisements intended for broadcast on commercial television stations. Like those produced by the Garment Workers ("Look for the Union Label") and the National Education Association, these ads are intended to create a generally favorable climate of public opinion about organized labor. More focused goals of some LIPA spots include efforts to raise the visibility of issues such as "right to know" legislation pending in many state legislatures or to condition public support for a major strike. For example, LIPA produced several ads that were run on Detroit stations during automobile industry negotiations. These efforts are justified in terms of their impact on union members and the general public:

> Union members are part of the media world too. They are going to be tremendously influenced if they don't see the union side on television . . . These spots helped set the agenda for the members, for the press and for the general public, and created a media context in which the bargaining could take place on an even playing field.[25]

The Labor Institute has also produced a wide variety of other video materials, such as a television series entitled *America Works*. It endeavors to promote these products with individual stations in the Public Broadcasting System after having been turned down by the network as a whole. A measure of the sophistication with which the Labor Institute produced and refined this series can be found in the fact that they used both focus groups and Arbitron rating to observe viewers' reactions to their shows.

In August 1985 LIPA sent out "video news releases" on cassette tapes that local broadcast stations could use to tell the labor story over Labor Day weekend. Institute Director Larry Kirkman argued that providing this footage to local stations would compensate for a lack of resources, such as a regular reporter assigned to cover labor or existing material on that subject.

Additionally, LIPA has been trying to demonstrate that membership organizations can use public access on cable television systems more successfully than individual producers have been able to do in the past two decades. Armed with surveys showing a high concentration of labor homes in Atlanta, Pittsburgh, and Seattle, LIPA established a pilot project in each locality in which some labor programming would appear on the access channel every night for ten weeks. These productions were supported by a network of union organizational and personal contacts. In other words, local labor unions attempted to generate an audience beyond that which might serendipitously turn to the access channel.

Technology has made little headway in facilitating efforts by group leadership to contact and influence a very select target, the policy makers themselves. While some groups have tried to produce more gripping material through the use of video communications, they have found it difficult to use this product effectively. Greater success can be observed when group leadership uses the new media to communicate with a finite group membership in order to enlist their participation in lobbying activity. The key appears to be the interest of participants on both ends of the communication. Where there exists a commonality of purpose, the media can impressively magnify the ability to coordinate action. But without shared interest, the new media cannot easily be used to create concerted lobbying.

Uses of the new media that mobilize political activity from the public at large appear to be more prevalent than these narrower-gauge communications. Here, prominence and seeming success may well be an artifact of the attention lavished by news reporting on such activities or of the fact that they are more easily observed. But it is also likely that those involved in political communications naturally lean toward replicating the mass media, which are, after all, the dominant means of exchanging political information. The experience of the Chamber of Commerce is instructive. It set out to establish an instrument of targeted political communication and failed. So it moved over into efforts to reach the general public.

This observation may well signal a change in the strategy and tactics of political mobilization, a change induced by technology. Organization building becomes analogous to the biblical parable of the sower of seeds. The word is cast out broadly, but only a small amount of it falls on fertile ground. Nevertheless, so long as the return is sufficiently high, this strategy may extract the resources necessary for political influence. Contributions support the group's activity; a large bank account becomes synonymous with perceived political clout. Alternatively, the organization may be able to stimulate a flow of letters and petitions to policy makers that at least demonstrates some minimal public awareness and pressure on office holders.

No clearer example of these forces at work can be seen than in the emergence of televangelism, electronic preachers using television to reach a far-flung congregation. The names of Bakker, Falwell, Roberts, Robertson, Schuller, and Swaggart and their programs and organizations (*The Old Time Gospel Hour*, the Praise the Lord ministry, *The 700 Club*, *The Hour of Power*, the Moral Majority, and so on) have become visible symbols of the developing force of fundamentalist Christians mobilized by technology. The word goes forth by satellite and cable. When it lands on fertile ground, the word begets contributions that engage a sophisticated direct-mail apparatus which thereafter maintains a constant stream of contact with supporters, much of it centered on the force of religious values in contemporary society and politics. The multimillion-dollar organizations that have been built through this process in turn create a demand for a continuing stream of contributions.

As with many other aspects of the relationship between technology and social activity, it is easy to overstate the significance of this development. No doubt vast sums of money have been raised and spent. No doubt a huge number of people are on the receiving end of the electronic word. But considerable doubt can nonetheless be cast on the television ministries' political potency. Given the requirements of maintaining such organizations, the ministries' large bank accounts may be more potent symbolically than in actual political use. Moreover, though fundamentalists certainly number in the tens of millions, they are by no means a cohesive political force. As a candidate for the 1988 Republican presidential nomination, Pat Robertson demonstrated both the potency and the limits of mobilizing these small bands of ardent followers. Since electoral politics generally demands mass appeal, Robertson had limited success with primary electorates but fared best in caucuses, where turnout was small. Then too, by the spring of 1988, several of the more prominent electronic ministers had gotten themselves into well-publicized trouble, so that in some cases their robust empires appeared to be on the verge of financial ruin.

The political influence of televangelism, therefore, rests upon the less visible, less direct impact of opinion influence among smaller segments of the public. Using the new media technology, the electronic preachers and their staffs have been able to promote an agenda of public issues for millions of citizens who otherwise might not participate in politics. The resulting mobilization of evangelicals flows into the representative system as interest-group pressure rather than through a mass impact on the electorate. The power to mobilize group pressure upon sensitive decision points can be considerable nonetheless, for as Jeffrey Hadden and Charles Swann note, televangelists have "more undisputed access to the airwaves than any other social movement in American society."[26]

These general developments are carrying interest-group activity in a different direction than the theories that value pluralist democracy would suggest. Rather than groups of citizens with a common identity and a shared sense of belonging and purpose, the new technology is permitting the collective mobilization of autonomous individuals. Citizen involvement in group activity—that which Tocqueville found so vital 150 years ago—has traditionally meant more than a desired response from 5 percent of those who receive a communication. Face-to-face involvement has allowed reciprocal influence and greater political equality within the group or organization than can ever be achieved when citizens merely write out a check or sign and mail a prepared letter or postcard.

Group activity in American politics is changing. One observer discusses this evolution by differentiating between *interest* groups and *issue* groups. The former had the economic self-interest of their members as the clear goal of collective activity. The latter, a recent phenomenon in American politics, pursues ethical principles that have less to do with self-interest and more to do with perceived benefits for the whole of society. Public-interest groups such as Common Cause and pro-life organizations come immediately to mind as examples of issue groups, although it cannot be said in either of these specific cases that the organization leadership has exclusively opted for mobilization rather than the creation of an involved membership.[27]

There is no inherent reason why the new media cannot serve the internal communication needs of organizations such as the National Education Association. In practice, however, many of those experimenting with using these emerging means have concluded that they can better mobilize individuals from mass audiences than they can reach a definable roster of members. Thus the new technology may work to underwrite a change in American pluralism.

Government-to-Citizen Contacts

Public officials need to reach out to citizens: to understand the impact of their policies, they need to contact those most affected; to carry on disputes and to form coalitions with other leaders and authorities, they need to maintain public support for their actions; to obtain compliance with their policy decisions, they need to communicate to citizens an appreciation of the rules, regulations, laws, and policies.

The public-relations activities of public officials confront us with something of a dilemma. On the one hand, their need to communicate with citizens is both legitimate and desirable. We wish citizens to be well informed about the substance of public issues. Because many citizens remain passive in their acquisition of information about political life, political leaders must actively seek to educate the public. Moreover, the desirability of this communication extends beyond civic education; in a democracy, we value advocacy: citizens must be exposed to the different views of their leaders in order to choose among competing elites and policies.

So far so good. We can evaluate whether the ongoing changes in the media will facilitate the ability of officials to communicate with the public. Unfortunately, however, improving this contact is not universally beneficial, for distinctions between civic education and manipulation are not easily drawn. Putting citizens in direct contact with political leaders will also give those elites expanded opportunities for bypassing intervening institutions and secondary opinion leadership, for appropriating public resources to pay for communication that reinforces their own visibility and power, and for framing in self-serving terms the agenda to be considered, the information provided citizens, the timing of decisions, and the alternatives to be considered.

Numerous laws and codes of ethics attempt to distinguish between civic education and self-serving efforts to build and maintain political support. For example, Congress follows an established set of rules governing the use of franking privileges and office resources. These rules, which are intended to prevent the use of public resources for electioneering, necessarily leave a wide "gray area" between educating the citizenry as to the public's business in Congress and reinforcing the political position of the individual member. But, in practice, we cannot definitively separate public-spirited from manipulative communications. Accordingly, our commentary will consider all the efforts that public officials are making to use the new media to reach citizens.

During the nineteenth century, a rather high percentage of

those elected to serve in Congress were freshmen.[28] Distance, the inconvenience of travel, and the lack of amenities in Washington made congressional incumbency a dubious privilege to many officeholders. Reinforced by shorter legislative sessions, the high turnover in Congress resulted in citizen-legislators who shared much in common with their constituents. As the federal government became more consequential and as transportation and communication improved, the percentage of congressmen staying on for many terms has markedly increased.[29] As a result, a principal problem faced by many incumbents who prize reelection above all else is keeping in touch with constituents back home.[30]

For at least twenty-five years, members of Congress have been using robotype and signature machines to send seemingly personal form letters to constituents. We should not be surprised, therefore, to find incumbent congressmen in the forefront of the use of computers and laser printers to handle an ever-increasing volume of mail. As the figures in table 4.2 reveal, the outflow of mail from Capitol Hill has been keeping pace with the escalating amount of incoming mail. While the general trend is ever upward, these data also exhibit a "sawtooth" pattern in which the outgoing mail surges during election years, which confirms that, in addition to public service, the self-interest of incumbents lies behind these communications.

The more sophisticated congressional offices now employ a correspondence management system that allows them to use computers to track and respond to letters received. Each incoming communication is initially logged into the computer before being passed over to an aide who will prepare the response. In many offices a "thirty-six-hour rule" mandates some immediate action from that staff member. Supervisors are automatically notified if someone falls behind in responding to a letter. In most cases, after the matter at hand has been resolved by return mail and/or other suitable action, the constituent's name and address is added to the office data banks for future mailings on policy areas linked to subjects raised in this initial correspondence.

While congressional offices have been sending out large volume mailings for many years, as a result of record keeping by computer, letters can now be tailored much more closely to the interests of constituents. Every time a major event occurs in the Middle East, to make up an example, a congressional office can

TABLE 4.2

*Volume of Mail Sent and Expenditures
for Mailings by the U.S. House of
Representatives by Year, 1960–1986*

Year	Letters Sent (millions)	Cost of Mailing ($ millions)
1960	108.0	—
1965	120.9	—
1970	201.0	—
1971	238.4	11.2
1972	308.9	32.9
1973	310.6	21.2
1974	321.0	30.5
1975	312.4	38.8
1976	561.3[a]	73.6[a]
1977	293.3	46.9
1978	430.2	48.9
1979	409.9	64.9
1980	511.3	30.7[b]
1981	395.6	52.0
1982	771.8	75.1
1983	556.8	93.1
1984	924.6	117.2
1985	675.0	85.8
1986	758.7	95.7

SOURCE: Norman J. Ornstein, Thomas E. Mann,
and Michael J. Malbin, *Vital Statistics on Congress,
1987–1988* (Washington, D.C.: Congressional
Quarterly Inc., 1987), pp. 153, 174.
[a] Includes change in fiscal year from July 1 to
October 1.
[b] Reflects decrease in bulk mail rates.

mail the congressman's position to those who have written to express their support of Israel. At the same time, another letter might go out to constituents in the same community who support stronger environmental laws or who oppose abortion. In all our interviews on Capitol Hill, we encountered a working assumption that constituents pay more attention to letters discussing issues that concern them specifically. The assumed result is that these constituents will be more likely to support the incumbent politically than will recipients of the Postal Patron Local mailings, which must be written for a more general audience.

Since the mid-1960s, both the House and Senate have maintained recording studios in which incumbents can produce films documenting their activities and policy statements. Many members stage regular shows that they send home for airing over the principal broadcast station in their district. The advent of videotape and satellites has accelerated this process. For example, as mentioned in chapter 3, both senators from New Jersey participate in a regular cable show distributed by a network of cable systems that reaches about 42 percent of the homes in the state.[31] Changes are occurring as well in another old standby of congressional offices: distribution of "radio actualities" over the telephone to stations back home, in the hopes that they will include the incumbent's remarks as part of their news broadcasts. In the last three years, a growing number of senators and congressmen have been using satellites to distribute video clips of their remarks addressing the major issues of the day. In 1982 the Senate Republican Conference took the lead in these communications by instituting "Operation Uplink," which distributes nationally to over two hundred television stations a half-hour videotape of six senators speaking in five-minute segments.[32] Each Senate office involved alerts the stations in his or her state so that they will tape the entire half hour and slice out the remarks of their senator for the local television broadcast. By 1985, the service had become so popular that the conference was feeding the Westar IV satellite twice each day when the Senate was in session.

The conference activity could make a tangible difference in the amount of news coverage received by Republican senators. For example, Paul West of the *Dallas Times Herald* reported that the two Florida senators received vastly different attention for roughly similar actions.[33] When Senator Paula Hawkins arranged hearings on legislation designed to combat so-called designer drugs, her staff taped her comments and sent them via the conference satellite connection to thirty-eight Florida stations that did not have Washington bureaus.[34] About the same time, Senator Lawton Chiles held related hearings on a very similar bill, but his activity received far less attention in Florida since his staff did not use the satellite. If, as Yale political scientist David Mayhew argues, credit claiming is a major part of congressional activity, Hawkins was able to use technology to perform something of a media coup by grabbing center stage away from her senior colleague.[35]

In many states and in the U.S. Congress, legislators have also begun experimenting with videoconferencing as a means of taking committee testimony from citizens in distant locations. For example, in a National Science Foundation–supported experiment in the early 1970s, a congressman held office hours and took testimony from constituents back home via videoconferencing.[36] In 1982 two senators arranged to go to the public television stations in their two states (Vermont and Minnesota) and take telephoned testimony from farmers calling in to the studio. In Alaska, teleconferencing has helped legislative hearings overcome the obstacles that the size of the state presents to taking live testimony from witnesses at the state capitol. We will study this example in greater depth in chapter 5. And, more recently, a subcommittee of the House Foreign Affairs Committee asked the U.S. Information Agency to set up a two-way video link so they could take testimony directly from Latin American educators and government officials who had gathered in Panama City.[37]

Federal legislators have also begun experimenting with cable television as a means for holding electronic office hours, either in one locality or to a broader audience through a hookup of cable companies. In New Jersey these procedures have been established on a regular basis; both senators and the governor have a monthly, statewide show. In Connecticut, to cite another example, Senator Christopher Dodd held four "electronic town meetings" over cable during 1985 and 1986. During one session observed, eleven cable companies serving half the state's population were interconnected by microwave relays. Dodd's staff sent postcard announcements of the event to their entire mailing list in the relevant towns. As soon as the senator opened the hour-long show, the twelve telephone lines of the host cable company filled up with callers. Although Dodd spoke directly to only about ten constituents, many more tried to get through to him.

Of course, the most dramatic advance in the provision to citizens of political information has come about through the creation of C-SPAN. Since the late 1970s, the House of Representatives has allowed coverage of its floor sessions by television cameras operated by the House itself. C-SPAN brings these activities into more than 20 million American homes. The proceedings of the Senate are now covered on a separate channel (C-SPAN II).

C-SPAN is an anomaly: in the competitive world of television, the cable television industry chose to band together to create a public service. The network was the brainchild of a group of cable companies that decided in 1977 to reserve a channel on their systems and to provide funds to underwrite a network to carry the sessions of the House into American homes. With initial donations totaling $400,000, C-SPAN began programming with only four staff members, telecasting only the House sessions—a few hours a day of programming, at most.

C-SPAN remains a not-for-profit cooperative of the cable industry, although its programming has grown to round-the-clock and its budget to $6 million. In off hours, C-SPAN brings its viewers committee hearings; coverage of significant political events such as the national party nominating conventions; call-in shows in which members of the home audience can question government officials or other Washington insiders; editorial board meetings of newspapers and magazines; and meetings of interest groups and political organizations, such as the U.S. Mayors' Conference, the National Governors' Association, or the National Rifle Association.[38]

The fact that this new channel is available to bring government into the homes of those wired for cable raises important questions: Who watches such programming? How many? For what reasons? To be sure, there is a value associated with having information available, whether or not it is consumed. But it must also be recognized that any impact of such a channel on the national forum of public ideas and debate depends, in the end, on whether or not it is watched and by whom.

By the end of 1984, C-SPAN had almost two thousand local cable affiliates, a number that represents approximately 20 million homes or slightly over 23 percent of all American homes with televisions. A careful survey of C-SPAN viewing was conducted that year by the Media Analysis Project (MAP) at George Washington University under the directorship of political scientist Michael Robinson. According to the MAP study, 38 percent of those interviewed watched C-SPAN at least one hour per month.[39] The data documented a "three-tiered" audience: 20 percent of the sample reported watching somewhat less than five hours per month, 13 percent watched between five and twenty hours, and 5 percent watched more than twenty hours per month.

Additionally, the study found that those who watch the channel are an "advertent" audience; they watch C-SPAN because they enjoy or are interested in the programming it brings. This finding contrasts with other studies by Robinson that the general audience for network television news is inadvertent—watching as much because they enjoy television as because they wish to receive news. Not surprisingly, C-SPAN viewers also tend to participate in politics and government more than their counterparts who do not watch the network.[40] C-SPAN President Brian Lamb describes the network's audience as follows:

On an ongoing basis, it's the political infrastructure of the country who watch it. That may be a million people; I don't know the number. It includes everyone from a city councillor, or a university professor, or a reporter who works for a local paper, to elected officials at the local, state, and federal levels, and to corporate executives concerned with issues that affect their businesses.[41]

Several commentators have argued that C-SPAN has changed some of the ways in which Congress operates, ranging from use of floor time, to the nature of leadership, to the ways in which officials communicate. Political scientist Norman Ornstein, for example, argues that the advent of C-SPAN, and other changes wrought by cable, has had significant effects on how leadership on issues is exercised. Through C-SPAN's live coverage of floor proceedings, he argues, the network "has altered the tactics of congressional politics." C-SPAN has revived the importance of floor debates for congressional representatives and "underscored the fact that television, not the political parties or other institutions, has become the major vehicle for political mobilization."[42]

Journalist Sidney Blumenthal points to the change that has occurred in the open hours of time after the regular session on the House floor, a period known as "special orders." A "dead zone" prior to the advent of television, special orders has now become a highly charged partisan spectacle. Members use these hours to reach constituencies outside the House and often outside their own geographical districts.

In one instance, C-SPAN's coverage proved to be a particularly valuable medium for a group of young House conservatives. The Conservative Opportunity Society (COS) found that C-SPAN allowed them to get their message directly to President Reagan. One afternoon the president had retired to private quarters and was watching C-SPAN. When he telephoned one of the COS congressmen to express his approval of his speech, word spread back to the floor that the president was watching. Through televised floor and special-orders speeches, the COS was able to achieve access to Reagan that the senior White House staff had denied them. Blumenthal quoted Congressman Newt Gingrich of Georgia as saying: "The White House staff protects [Reagan] from us by sending him upstairs, and he watches us on television. . . . It saves us the cab fare."[43]

Lamb treads lightly in appraising the changes that C-SPAN has brought to the Capitol. He does concede, however, that the network has some impact—he believes for the better—on federal legislating and governance.

The fact is that the number of hours the House is in session has gone down since TV was introduced. They were in session 1,000 or more hours in the two years before TV; and they have not been in session 1,000 hours since 1978.

It seems to me, though, that members are reluctant to go to the floor now unless they are pretty well prepared. They can't make statements as frivolously as they did before TV. Now they know somebody is watching—often lots of somebodies. It seems to have sharpened their comments.[44]

Regarding the White House's use of the channel, Lamb adds:

The use is tremendous. We have direct evidence that the President watches C-SPAN. All of the departments of government have C-SPAN. The President, we think—they won't actually confirm this for us—can watch it at Camp David and Santa Barbara. [White House staffers] can grab people as they come off the floor in the cloakroom and congratulate them or buttonhole them based on what they've seen and heard them say.[45]

Lamb notes that even the congressional hearings have changed some with the advent of television coverage:

There isn't more attendance, it was always pretty good, but they do seem to try to schedule hearings when the C-SPAN cameras will be available. And they seem to be better organized [than before television] and have more visual aids in their presentations. Some people are offended by that, but I find that ridiculous. You don't have a Congress in order to confuse people, and if the presentations are better and more easily understood I think that's great.[46]

While the network itself eschews partisan politics, it is impossible to cover Congress without covering partisan rhetoric. The best-known example was a series of exchanges between former House Speaker Thomas P. O'Neill, Jr., and Representative Gingrich. As described by Blumenthal, it is only one illustration of the intrusions of partisanship that can now be viewed on C-SPAN:

During one of the C-SPAN shows, in mid-May [1984], Gingrich denounced by name House liberals he claimed were soft on communism. The next week O'Neill retaliated by having the cameras scan the empty galleries, puncturing the illusion that conservative orators had the ears of their colleagues. Then O'Neill charged that Gingrich's assault on members' "Americanism" was the "lowest thing that I have ever seen in my thirty-two years in the House." Because his attack was personally aimed at Gingrich, the Speaker was declared out of order. That night this extraordinary incident elevated the C-SPAN boys from the cable ghetto to the network news.[47]

Ornstein believes that through exchanges like these, the coverage on C-SPAN has been responsible for a reinvigoration of partisan rhetoric and ideology on the floor of the Congress.[48]

Efforts similar to C-SPAN have been started in several states, including Florida, Massachusetts, New York, and North Carolina. Most of these broadcasts or cablecasts consist of conveying directly to the public the activities of legislative assemblies, without a great deal of editorial or programming input by the information carrier. In Boston, for example, gavel-to-gavel legislative sessions are carried by a UHF public television station, WGBX, whereas in Florida the statewide Public Broadcasting System presents one hour of daily coverage plus a thirty-minute satellite broadcast in both Spanish and English. Unlike C-SPAN, the Florida broadcasters can influence the content of their programming through editorial decisions as to which segments of floor debates will be made available to the public.

Eleven state governments have recently begun to distribute public information through electronic means other than television.[49] Alaska and New York provide contrasting examples in their efforts to provide a service much like the commercial computer network Legi-Slate discussed earlier. In about fifteen locations scattered around our largest state, Legislative Information Offices provide citizens the opportunity to examine computer records containing the text of bills under consideration in Juneau; the calendar under which subcommittees, committees, and the chambers will take up legislation; and the voting records of their elected representatives.[50] From these remote locations, citizens can also voice their opinions to legislators over an electronic mail system. Access to the system is provided free of charge to all citizens as a service of the state government.

In New York roughly the same information, minus the messaging system, is available to citizens who are willing to subscribe to the state's service.* The $1,500 yearly fee effectively restricts access to this information to associations and organizations rather than individual citizens. Private citizens can still write to or visit the state capitol to obtain paper copies of pending bills, and a free terminal in the State Legislative Library will give them on-line access to the same information sold on a proprietary basis. But obviously this access is not really equivalent to subscribing to the remote, on-line service. Written copies of bills do not allow one the same speed or quality of information as a capacity to search a data base for key words tailored by individual interest. Public access through one terminal in the state capitol, moreover, is a narrow bottleneck and undoubtedly requires more expertise than most citizens are likely to possess.[51]

In a few cases citizens can also make their policy views known to officials through these same systems. The Alaskan system allows legislators to take testimony from citizens in remote communities via a teleconferencing network permanently in place.[52] As noted, citizens can also voice their opinions in electronic mail messages over the Legislative Information Office's computer network. They can send their views on pending legislation either to specific representatives or to categories such as all Republicans, all members of a committee, all representatives from Anchorage, and so forth. The Alaskan system is discussed further in chapter 5.

In the fall of 1986 the California legislature was beginning to follow the lead of Michigan State Senator William Sederburg, who has used his office accounts to establish two computer bulletin boards for citizen education and comment. The "Political Forum" is available to his constituents, while the "Higher Education Forum" serves the committee he chairs. In 1985 he logged ten thousand calls from over four thousand different people who left over twelve thousand messages on his computer for the senator

---

* In California, an equivalent service is provided by a private corporation, Legi-Tech, which has also been involved in a legal dispute with the New York legislature over access to that state's computer network.

and other legislators, their staffs, and other callers to read.[53] A random-sample telephone poll in his district revealed that 17 percent of his constituents had heard about this novel method of reaching their legislator.

In North Carolina executive branch commissions and legislative committees have established OPEN/net, a regular show on many television systems throughout the state. State officials can present their policy deliberations and hear from citizens who call in to the studio. These mechanisms are on their way to becoming permanent political institutions underwritten by communications technology.[54] For example, in three years of operation, OPEN/net has moved from patchwork funding from a variety of sources to major support in the North Carolina state budget, and from an office that sought to convince legislators to appear on its programs to one that now receives strong political support and numerous suggestions from state officials who would like to appear. The network survived a change from a Democratic to a Republican gubernatorial administration. And it has recently received a major foundation grant to help extend its concept to other state governments. OPEN/net is not supplanting the traditional means of communication by which representative politics takes place, but it is very likely to grow into a permanent feature of North Carolina's political landscape.

Intragovernment Communications

By design, American government has always been highly decentralized and fragmented. The same constitutional architecture that provides political protection against governmental tyranny— the separation of powers into three branches of government and the reservation of residual powers for the states—also ensures that most policy problems will be the responsibility of divided authorities. The fractured nature of American government puts a premium on effective communication among the separate branches and levels of government. Here the new media are already playing a role.

The U.S. House of Representatives again provides a convenient starting point for our discussion. In the decade and a half since the House Information Services (HIS) was established by the House Administration Committee, the Congress as a whole and individual member offices have come a great distance in adapting to the opportunities offered by computers.[55] As discussed earlier, the staff offices of most individual members have seized upon the computer to handle the large volume of mail to and from constituents. In 1979, only two years after the initial authorization to add computers to the approved list of office equipment, roughly one-third of the member offices were using computers.[56] Today the percentage is approaching 100 percent.

Initially, however, the pace of implementation was rather slow due to the decentralized nature of the institution and the reluctance of senior members to alter patterns of activity established over many years.[57] An instructive example can be gleaned from an early attempt to rationalize the scheduling of committee meetings by computer. As the House goes about its business, 22 committees and 140 subcommittees schedule meetings for 435 members. No single authority has control over the available meeting rooms. The resulting scheduling problems looked like a natural for computer solutions.

The HIS staff discovered, however, that behind this seeming anarchy lay an important strategic weapon of committee chairmen: their ability to time meetings so as to influence results or to maximize the impact through timing, or to avoid publicity or even to discourage unwanted members from attending.[58] In effect, the HIS system threatened to withdraw strategic resources from key committee chairs. Naturally they resisted and eventually defeated HIS's plans. As a result, the proposed information system had to be withdrawn, providing us with a reminder that because power and communications are intertwined, rationalizing the latter cannot be undertaken without accommodating the former.

Despite this experience, HIS has continued to grow and expand its services, and now offers the Congress two new packages of information management. The first concerns the budgetary processes. The second is the Member Information Network, which provides information to the individual member offices. We describe these two below.

The last fifteen years have witnessed tremendous growth in the staff support available to the Congress;[59] among the most visible changes have been those associated with the Budgetary Act of 1975. The Congressional Budget Office (CBO) and the House and Senate Budget Committees have established an institutional counterpart to the Office of Management and Budget (OMB) that serves the president. They provide the Congress with alternative proposals for expenditures and revenue raising in broad categories. The tasks that support these endeavors are essentially information collecting and management. Here computer technology has become indispensable to government.

For example, in addition to the publicly available published budget prepared by the executive branch, OMB now provides Congress with access to the master computer tape that contains much greater detail as to the monies requested for different programs. The fact that these detailed data are on computers enables the budget, taxing, and appropriating committees to get to their work without a great deal of information searching. The data can also be easily broken down into the various accounts that fall under the jurisdiction of different authorizing committees and subcommittees, providing them with information they did not have prior to computerization.[60] The computer-based proposals coming from the executive branch can now be quickly compared to alternative plans developed by congressmen. Once general targets have been agreed on for the different agencies, internal changes such as new programs must be balanced by cuts in other categories. This process too is considerably aided by the ready availability of detailed financial data.

Another major area of the CBO's responsibility involves economic forecasting for the Congress of the larger consequences of various expenditure and taxation packages in terms of fiscal policy. In this domain, the existence of computerized information has helped the Congress emerge as an equal to the executive branch. In 1981 CBO projections yielded a much higher estimate of the consequences of Reagan's tax-cutting and spending proposals. This projection was extremely controversial at the time; that ultimately the CBO's numbers proved to be more accurate added enormously to the credibility of the process of an independent review of administration proposals. In a ironical twist, the fact that the CBO must work within a bipartisan structure makes the executive branch estimates appear somewhat tainted by comparison.

The emergence of Congress as an equal in the budgetary planning process has reportedly had another interesting effect on information sharing arrangements. Before the 1974 Budget Act, congressmen were in a decidedly subordinate position vis-à-vis the administration in access to information. They had to request, beg for, and accept whatever the executive branch would release. In the present climate, the congressional committees have something to bargain with; they can exchange their information with the executive branch. Primarily this means allowing the other side to share the assumptions upon which different forecasting models are based, especially in the difficult area of assessing the effect of changes in various aid formulas in entitlement programs.

A second recent development, the Member Information Network (MIN) provides congressional offices with a wealth of information that makes it easier for them to perform their legislative functions. Status reports on pending legislation, brief descriptions of the content and intent of floor amendments, roll-call vote results, morning notices, current floor proceedings, summaries of debates, and so forth are entered into the network as activities take place on the floor.[61] All these services could be performed without a computer network; the technology does, however, make the whole process more instantaneous and efficient.

The MIN also allows the individual congressional offices access to information that helps congressmen better serve their districts. A "Geographic Profiles" data base contains census information and federal grants and contract dollars for various geographical units, including congressional districts. Thus a congressional office can monitor the nature of federal contracts awarded to its districts and compare those figures with other districts or with past circumstances. The network also delivers a current assessment of federal assistance funds in different categories flowing into the district. Yet another service of the MIN provides an inventory of these assistance programs such as grants, loans, direct payments, insurance and cooperative agreements,[62] and information about eligibility, requirements, restrictions, and the applications process. The congressional staff can use this facility to assist local private organizations and government units to find sources of federal support for their activities. Again, while this information may well have been available before the advent of computers, its existence in on-line form greatly facilitates the problem of searching through voluminous material in order to uncover the existing opportunities.

We turn now to uses of the new media within the executive

branch. During the Reagan administration, the White House has established a true computer communications system. The system is called EOPNet and was introduced by John Rogers, assistant to the president for management and administration. Of the state of technology in the White House upon his arrival, Rogers says: "Most people would think this is the leading front office in the free world and would have the latest in everything. It didn't. I wanted to get the White House into the 20th century."[63]

The EOPNet system combines both information transfer among presidential aides and availability of information from outside sources. As a result, executive branch officials now have available a number of services, such as electronic mail, data and report retrieval, word and data processing, and news and data base services. Specifically, EOPNet provides word processing, spreadsheet development, in-house electronic mail, a library of wire service stories, a White House guidance data base system, and access to Nexis/Lexis (a news and data retrieval service).

Another feature of the system is the White House guidance service, which provides an in-house listing of presidential positions on eighty-nine topics. These position statements are updated on a daily (or more frequent) basis. The impetus for this kind of service is to prevent presidential assistants from incorrectly stating White House positions on major issues. While no system can stop them from misstating executive positions intentionally (for example, for the purpose of advancing or hindering a particular cause), EOPNet can help them avoid missteps because their information is out of date.

Other agencies in the executive branch have begun making use of computer communications systems. Rogers's next task, after developing the White House network, for example, was to begin work on a similar system for the Office of Management and Budget. The federal government's use of the new technologies is clearly growing, as can be demonstrated by the sharp increases recorded in government outlays for the purchase of information and communications technology. In fiscal 1983 the outlay was slated to be $10.4 billion; by fiscal 1984 expenditures grew to $13.9 billion, a 33 percent increase.[64]

Even so, the executive branch is probably moving slower than other institutions in our society to install new technologies. A prime reason for this lack of speed is politics, not technology.

Communications Technology and Governance

During the Carter administration sociologist Amitai Etzioni was asked to help create a computer management tracking system in order to monitor the variety of initiatives undertaken by the president. Etzioni encountered some vexing problems:

One major difficulty in providing the president with a proper tracking system was the issue of what constitutes a presidential directive. For instance, if during a speech the president reassures a group of American exporters that he has every intention of helping them increase exports next year, and that he will seek to open 20 new trade offices overseas for that purpose, does this constitute a directive? To whom? Should a management tracking system encompass only those matters the president orders personally—or also the many other instructions issued in his name by the presidentially appointed White House staff?[65]

The political problems with such a system become clear almost immediately. Should all the statements a president makes be recorded and tracked by computer? The omission of a statement from such a tracking system immediately raises doubts regarding the chief executive's sincerity. Moreover, those who are allowed to define what constitutes a directive will certainly gain a greater measure of power.

Etzioni encountered other issues as well:

There was also a highly charged authority and "access" issue: who would be in charge of such a White House tracking system? Note that this person would in effect oversee the performance of all the president's men, women, and agencies. Even what seemed like a minor question—where to place the computer—turned out to be tricky. In the White House? It would smack of 1984. Outside? Where?[66]

Questions like these abound as new communications systems are designed for the government. Virtually each feature—access, data stored or not stored, program choices—seems able to change subtly the balance of power among a variety of government players.

In his book *The Rise of the Computer State*, David Burnham, a *New York Times* reporter, provides another clear example of how a system originally thought to increase efficiency changed lines of authority and power. In July of 1981 the Department of Justice installed seventeen computer terminals in the Newark and Trenton offices of the United States Attorney for New Jersey, and hoped to expand this operation to include similar setups in over two dozen other offices around the country over the next several years. The computers, however, had potential effects other than efficiency:

The computer systems . . . installed in the separate U.S. attorneys' offices almost certainly will improve the management efficiency of the federal prosecutors. But because the tapes from these computers will be sent to the attorney general in Washington, something more subtle but perhaps more important is also happening. Without any discussion in Congress, without any change in law, the power of the attorney general to influence public policy is being enormously enhanced. From the beginning of our government, U.S. attorneys have been somewhat independent from the attorney general. To this day, for example, no one is nominated to be a U.S. attorney without approval of the senators in the state where the federal district is located. . . .

The fact that U.S. attorneys are beholden to senators, as well as to the president and his attorney general, has meant that federal prosecutors could be a little bit independent from the dictates of the Justice Department. Federal law enforcement in Wyoming has not been a carbon copy of federal law enforcement in Massachusetts. . . .

But with the installation of the computers in every office, the attorney general will be able to keep track of every investigation, every prosecution, every conviction and every acquittal. He will be able to do this on an individual basis—the name of the defendant, the name of the prosecutor, the name of a defense lawyer—or by broad categories of law-enforcement actions.[67]

At the state and municipal levels, one can find counterparts to many of these federal examples. In 1983 Governor John Sununu of New Hampshire requested funds to computerize the state's budgeting. Two years later the legislature woke up to the fact that the resulting system had been designed to provide access only to the executive branch.[68] Michael Hutchings, one of the supporters of a bill to give the legislature equal access to the data base, argued that

the conflict will determine the balance between the two branches of our government, relative to the flow of information. We are setting a precedent with this bill, and if we set the precedent caving in to the executive branch, we will be fighting like dogs and cats for the next ten years, trying to change what was done in this session.[69]

The governor wanted the power to veto requests for access to the data base, citing separation of powers and arguing that during the decision-making process managers needed to protect their thoughts and conclusions until they were final. Ultimately the governor's view carried the day. While legislators were given the access to information they would normally have, they could request additional access only in writing, and the executive branch retained the power to consider whether or not to grant that request.[70]

In 1979 the National Science Foundation (NSF) supported an experiment to connect science and technology advisers in state legislatures together in a computer conferencing network.[71] By logging on to the Electronic Information Exchanges System (EIES) at the New Jersey Institute of Technology, science advisers discussed such topics as the standards different states were applying in environmental legislation or information regarding the hazards of different toxic substances that might require state regulation. Moreover, a permanent record of their comments back and forth was available, indexed by subject so that other members of the network could learn from prior discussions if an issue subsequently became relevant to their work.

Overall, representatives from about half the state legislatures participated in the network during the experiment. Despite its success in providing needed information across states, the network collapsed after NSF funding ran out. But the lesson was clear enough so that by the mid-1980s the system was reestablished by a private association, the National Conference of State Legislatures (NCSL). Now in its beginning stages, Legis-Net facilitates the exchange of state legislative research reports through an on-line index. Only a portion of each report is actually entered into the computer, but knowing that a report has been prepared allows legislators in one state to request a full written copy from another state. In addition, NCSL allows private research contractors to add to the network titles and extracts of their work, which state legislative research staff can then arrange to purchase.

Those concerned with facilitating (and improving) policy making and public administration on the municipal level have seized upon the opportunities for information distribution through computer networks. As alluded to earlier, the National League of Cities and the U.S. Conference of Mayors provide information to the LOGIN network. In addition, the NLC cooperates with the International City Managers Association in providing yet another network, LINUS (Local Information Network for Universal Service). Both networks serve to exchange information that concerns public officials working in city government. In addition to announcements from Washington about federal policy that affects cities, subscribers to LOGIN—who pay a sliding-scale fee depending on the size of their city (from $900 to $5,800 per year)—can add and retrieve information on a range of topics such as energy conservation techniques for city governments. In other words, in addition to bridging the federalism gap, LOGIN provides horizontal communication among similarly situated political authorities. Those who organized LOGIN hope that the processes of diffusing innovation will be sharply sped up by this technology.[72]

Discussion and Conclusions

In evaluating the consequences of all this technology on the processes of governing, we should reiterate emphatically that to date there is not all that much technology in politics. The adaptation of political institutions to new possibilities for communicating, moreover, takes place gradually, and this "revolution" has not yet gathered force. If we can learn from the work of political scientist Richard Rubin, the institutional effects of television upon the presidential selection system did not begin until 1968 or 1972, fully fifteen years after the medium had reached near-universal penetration. So, even if the newer media had firmly established themselves (and they have not), we still might expect that political consequences could not be accurately assessed for decades. In cataloging here the uses of emerging communications technology in politics, we have deliberately ignored the preponderant fact that most communications in government take place through means that have existed for a very long time. Nevertheless, we feel that it is still possible at present to advance some defensible statements as to how communications media will affect governing.

The New Media's Effect on Process

In the short run, the emerging communications media will buttress the position of established political organizations and actors within our present system. It is not accidental that when we examine who is leading the way into the newer media, we come up with a list of Washington's most prominent forces, organizations like the Chamber of Commerce, the AFL-CIO, the Republican National Committee, and incumbent members of Congress. In these early stages, the uses of these communications conduits are experimental and the initial investment costs can be quite substantial. Even though the drop in price for computers or in the per-unit cost of communicating has been significant, for many of these media the economies of scale in the human resources needed to utilize them dictate that one must go into them in a big way or not at all. Accordingly, access may initially be limited to well-heeled organizations and individuals.

Because communications and power are so closely intertwined, it would be notable indeed if powerful political forces did not seize upon new opportunities to reinforce their position. The trend toward increasing advantages for incumbent congressmen, for example, has been going on for most of this century. They have consistently displayed an interest in using public resources in ways that might benefit their prospects for reelection.[73] Without knowing anything about the new technology, we would have predicted that incumbents would experiment with using these new technologies if for no other reason than that they fear losing their competitive edge to challengers.

Putting these new media to political use is a function both of having the hardware and knowing how to use it. In establishing BizNet, the U.S. Chamber of Commerce brought in the latest in studio equipment but overestimated the enthusiasm of their local affiliates for Washington-oriented video material. A "Vanguard Network" for progressive public-interest organizations was proposed in 1983 but never materialized.

Several observers of the new media suggest that in the long run established forces will not be able to control the revolutionary potential of the new technologies. Once successful techniques have been mastered, they argue, the lessening costs will generate greater political equality between the status quo and its challengers. Futurists Alvin Toffler and John Naisbitt have both suggested that the new media will allow the currently disenfranchised citizen a substantially greater access to political information.[74] Benjamin Barber has argued that, if appropriately designed and implemented, the communications revolution can greatly ease the problems of political inequality.[75] A few practitioners agree. Asked whether the high fees charged by his company meant that only well-heeled lobbyists could afford access to the on-line data base, Arnie Thomas of Legi-Slate argued that the costs were much less than would be necessary to pay a staff salary to obtain the same information:

They can take this [service], save a great deal of money and be as effective as a large corporation. On the other hand, a large corporation may feel that they don't need it, because they have 20 lobbyists out there on The Hill and they know everything. Some clients you think that we should have, we don't; and some clients you'd think there's no way we would have them, we do.[76]

A second observation is possible: modern communications will exacerbate the problem of factions in American politics. When James Madison worried about this problem two hundred years ago, he found some comfort in the very size of the new nation. Now we have an even larger nation than Madison imagined, but, if our research documents anything, it is that groups today have the means to overcome the obstacles of size and to forge the kind of majority coalition Madison feared.

In the last one hundred years, the mass media gradually replaced party organizations as the principal instrument of political discourse. Politicians were put in the position of either renting the services of media that existed essentially for entertainment or informational purposes (that is, through paid political advertisements) or generating information that would merit news coverage (that is, in extreme form the so-called media event). As a result, editors and producers who decided which news stories deserved coverage and businessmen who made advertising policies came inadvertently to exercise substantial power in the workings of political institutions.[77]

In the contemporary era, we are witness to a reversal of this trend: politicians are seizing for themselves the means of communication. Much of the activity discussed earlier involves efforts by politicians to bypass the gatekeeping that journalists exercise over political discussion. This activity is a further step toward more direct, less mediated forms of politics. National interest groups are now able to reach their membership directly, bypassing the local and state level affiliates that used to filter messages. Citizens no longer need to wait till the dinner hour for network anchors to tell them what happened on Capitol Hill; congressmen now can be seen in 22 million homes on a more or less continuous basis. Senators beam their smiling faces to local news editors, thereby circumventing the more informed and cynical Washington press corps. Direct mail now conveys highly partisan appeals into citizens' mailboxes, absent any independent editorial judgment, honed to the particular interests of the recipients, and designed so as to mask for recipients an appreciation of the information about them upon which the message has been crafted.

The existence of intermediate groups between the individual and the central government has been an essential tenet of pluralist democracy. Tocqueville, for example, saw the strength in American democracy grounded in local diversity and the plethora of groups and organizations that involve Americans in politics.[78] More than one hundred years later, his thoughts were echoed by sociologist William Kornhauser, who recognized that these organizations protected citizens from manipulation by national leaders in a mass democracy.[79] Mass society was said to occur when citizens were directly related as individuals to the few leaders. Through groups, however, citizens are exposed to multiple opinions, more abundant information, and divergent perspectives—all of which afford them a broader basis for deciding what is right or wrong than just the words of national leaders. Strong group leaders are more likely than are individual citizens to be able to deal as equals with political authorities and thus hold them publicly accountable.

The politics of interest groups are not likely to be eliminated by the emerging media, but they could be changed. For one thing, most of the attempts to exploit the potential of the new media are occurring on the national level. In the competition for citizens' attention, voices from Washington are likely to grow even louder, drowning out local leaders who used to mediate much of the opinion formation process. More important, there is a difference between membership groups and organizations, on the one hand,

and those constructed through electronic media. For example, two political scientists, Kenneth Godwin and Robert Mitchell, found that participants recruited into environmental organizations through direct mail tended to be more extreme in their views and less supportive of the association itself than did members recruited at meetings.[80] In other words, the electronic media may lend themselves more readily to issue mobilization, or what Nelson Polsby calls "factional mobilization," than to building a participant membership.[81]

Kristin Luker's interviews among pro-life activists also support this conclusion.[82] Modern communications technology achieved the beneficial result of mitigating the well-known inequalities in rates of participation across social strata. The women mobilized by pro-life organizations were drawn from groups that normally have low rates of participation in voluntary associations. But the basis of their participation was quite different: although they volunteered an average of ten hours per week, they attended only about four face-to-face meetings per year. Instead, they became involved in group activity as isolated and autonomous individuals, more heavily dependent on group leadership and less able to share opinions with similarly situated members.

As a result, the classical pattern of politics shaped by membership-based interest groups described by Cornell political scientist Theodore Lowi[83] may be in the process of giving way to issue groups, a more fluid and agitated politics of mobilized "categories" of citizens. Collective action may no longer demand mutual recognition of collective interest.

Pondering how a politics of mobilized categories might be different from that of interest-group pluralism leads us to consider the differences between electronic communications and face-to-face contact. In the former, citizens are contacted in isolation from one another, they do not receive political information in a social context, they do not have an opportunity to communicate directly with other group members, and they do not enjoy anything approaching parity of power and influence with the organization's leaders.

Moreover, because the newer media are interactive, they may appear to respond to the concerns of individual citizens, while failing to convey equal power to the speaker-initiator versus the audience-responder. In contrast to group meetings, the feedback component of interactive communications is likely to be carefully controlled by political leaders. The techniques of television appeals and direct mail as forms of political communications transform political activists into consumers. Their only power over the organization is their option not to contribute further. In short, the new media allow a much more transitory definition of membership: a reaction by 5 percent of the recipients of a direct-mail piece will allow the sponsoring organization to extract the resources it needs to be "a player" in governance. Moreover, those who support the organization by responding may be changing constantly, but individual members are completely substitutable as long as there is a sufficient quantity of them. Even among interest groups that have a concrete, definable membership—such as the AFL-CIO or the Chamber of Commerce—we found that there were significant efforts toward using such a marketing approach and new technology to reach out and attract support from the general citizenry. The size of a group may come to be the sole measure of "throw weight" in politics. On the surface this may seem democratic, but it is a majoritarian conception of democracy hostile to the liberal tradition, in which the rights and interests of different groups need to be respected and taken into account.

The fact that citizens will hear from (and may belong to) many groups and organizations means that cross-cutting cleavages are likely to weaken social conflict. The organization of interests on one side of a question is likely to produce the counterorganization of opponents, thereby enhancing the prospects for a negotiated compromise. As a result, most policy choices will not seem unambiguously good or bad to many citizens because they belong to groups and interests on both sides of policy disputes. Across the whole gamut of issues faced by a polity, furthermore, few citizens are likely to find themselves permanently on the losing side.[84]

On the other hand, among those who remain interested in politics, increased competition for their attention may bring about the creation of more intense "issue publics," to use a term coined by Philip Converse, a political scientist from Michigan's Survey Research Center.[85] That is, citizens may increasingly specialize in political topics to which they will pay attention, ignoring the discussion of other issues that do not interest them so vigorously and ignoring channels of communication that impart information outside their range of intense concerns.

These issue publics may indeed respond to the efforts of categorical mobilization directed at them by interest groups and other political leaders. The net result could be greater participation by citizens in governance. For example, while precise measurements of political contributions are not available, we can be fairly certain that the number of citizens making such contributions has increased sharply with the advent of direct mail. In addition, much of the increased flow of mail to congressional offices is evidently the result of organized mobilization campaigns. Through contributions and letter writing, much of it mobilized by interest groups, citizens transform their concerns into pressures on political leaders and political institutions. But rather than a general pattern of civic involvement in public matters, the net result is more likely to be a compartmentalized involvement.

Thus the new media promise sharper delineations of political interest. In some cases, these pressures may transcend the geographical boundaries that ground our political system. Such a trend would put increasing strain on our national institutions of government, particularly the Congress. While congressmen and senators have long sought support from groups whose membership stretched beyond their districts and states, these bases of support do create a tension between the representatives' policy-making role in committees and their representation of constituents in a sharply defined geographical area. While the two roles are not necessarily contradictory, they can impose different agendas and time constraints on representatives. If the new media free national political interest groups from geography, these tensions will be heightened.

The American political system already exhibits a degree of fragmentation in the subcommittee structure of the Congress, in the separate agencies of the executive, and in the divided authority of the federalist structure.[86] On the national level, political scientists refer to "iron triangles" of issue networks that exist among congressional staffers, bureaucrats, and interest-group activists to deliberate policy within narrowly defined domains.[87] The effect of these politics is to diminish presidential influence over policy and to make it difficult for the political system to deal with such overarching questions as, for example, the appropriate level of overall expenditures. Unfortunately, the communications revolution promises nothing in the way of alleviating these problems. They may even be exacerbated as the actions of political leaders become more accessible to concerned and attentive citizens, making it more difficult for them to bargain, maneuver, and compromise.

This argument runs directly counter to the predictions of those who trumpet the evolution of a populist, plebiscitarian political system in the United States.[88] While political authorities may become more responsive to citizens, especially to mobilized categories, that does not necessarily mean a more responsible politics in terms of the other tasks of leadership in a democracy, such as forging new coalitions out of colliding interests.[89] Nor can one be assured that a greater volume of political information, a larger number of political speakers, and the existence of feedback mechanisms will reinforce a politics of near-universal involvement necessary to government by plebiscite. In chapter 5, we will study at length the pitfalls of plebiscitarian views of democracy.

Our examination of the emerging communicating behavior of public officials leads to one final conclusion of a beneficial nature for American politics. To the extent that the problems of federalism are born of ignorance or the inability of political authorities to communicate with each other, then the emerging media will ease the problems of coordination across branches of government and across levels of the political system. There is already ample evidence that one of the earliest uses to which emerging means of communicating will be put is to allow political elites the information they need about the actions of other political authorities.

Not all observers will greet this development with enthusiasm. Suspicion of government runs deep in American political thought. A serious worry, to which we return throughout this book, is that better governance means greater ability to penetrate citizens' privacy. In perfecting the communications power of government, we should not forget that there are some things—many of them intimate—that government ought not to know. Moreover, as we noted earlier, the notion that the problems of governance are entirely created by poor communications within complex governmental machinery should be greeted with skepticism. Political interest and power enter to complicate both policy making and implementation. Here we return to the genius of our constitutional architecture, in which abuse of governmental power is limited by counterposing ambition with ambition. Ambition will not be swept away by better means of exchanging information.

CHAPTER 5

THE NEW MEDIA
AND DEMOCRATIC
PARTICIPATION

NO POLITICAL PROPHECY figures more prominently in the popular literature on the communications revolution than the prediction that a new age of direct democracy is dawning in the United
States. "Spectacular advances in communication technology,"
surmises futurologist Alvin Toffler, "open, for the first time, a
mind-boggling array of possibilities for direct citizen participation
in political decision-making." In the face of "computers, advanced
telecommunications and polling methods," Toffler continues, representative democracy is "increasingly obsolete." We are witnessing a fundamental "shift from depending on representatives
to representing ourselves."[1] The same theme is sounded by John
Naisbitt in his best-selling book, *Megatrends*:

We created a representative system two hundred years ago when it was
the practical way to organize a democracy. Direct citizen participation was
simply not feasible, so we elected people to go off to the state capitals, represent us, vote, and then come back and tell us what happened. . . .

The New Media and Democratic Participation

But along came the communication revolution and with it an extremely well-educated electorate. Today, with instantaneously shared information, we know as much about what's going on as our representatives and we know it just as quickly.

The fact is we have outlived the historical usefulness of representative democracy and we all sense intuitively that it is obsolete.[2]

In chapter 1 we stressed the profound disagreement among democratic theorists over what type of citizen participation is desirable in a democracy. The plebiscitary theory of democracy takes its ideal of participation from the initiative and referendum process writ large. Individuals must be empowered to decide issues directly and not just to select those who will do the deciding. The democratic potential of the new technology, the plebiscitarian argues, lies in its unprecedented computing and polling capacity, in the automated and instant feedback it permits between citizen and government. These new technologies for surveying public opinion invite a radical increase in the direct, plebiscitary character of American democracy—in the opportunities for individuals, no matter where they are located, to have a direct say, a vote as it were, in the setting of public policy.

The communitarian vision of democracy assigns far less importance to polling as a form of participation. It is not that polling is entirely suspect. So long as it is but one form among many in which citizens communicate their politics, almost all would concede that polling serves our democracy in many ways. It provides an informal method for making representatives responsive to public opinion, an occasion to mobilize public concern on a given policy issue, and a source of information to candidates about potential voter support. The criticism is that polling, in itself, can be only a partial kind of participation. By culling from citizens their most immediate and raw responses, polling tends to divorce public opinion from public debate—from the richer reflections implicit in the concept of *collective* self-government. Moreover, rampant polling encourages a confusion of democratic process with pure majoritarianism, as if public opinion should rule on every issue, as if representatives should function only as their constituents' barometer. Such a tyranny of the majority is foreign to American political culture, and therefore polling of individuals one by one cannot encompass the whole of democratic participation.

Given the shallowness of polling as a form of democratic participation, the more communal visions of democracy express a hesitancy about the new media. Many features of the new communications environment, especially the speed and volume of information exchanges today, make it likely that in the future we will see more, not less, of electronic plebiscites, voting from the home, and instant polls. If this happens, the new media will impoverish, not enrich, the sustained public debates through which democracy thrives. Only if the technology is used to provide instruments for collective deliberation will the new media prove an ally of citizenship and participation.

This communal vision is the vision of the electronic commonwealth. If the poll symbolizes the plebiscitarian theory of participation, the town meeting symbolizes the communitarian conception. The endeavor is to use the new technologies to overcome the difficulty of practicing town-meeting democracy in an area as large as the nation state. Of course, the revival of the town meeting must be accompanied by respect for the plurality of persons we are and the diversity of values we hold. Only then can the drive for democratic community avoid the pitfalls of exclusivity discussed in chapter 1.

To date, both the plebiscitarian and communitarian conceptions of democracy have sponsored new media experiments designed to improve the quantity and quality of citizen participation. As a case study of the plebiscitarian view, we focus first in this chapter on the Hawaii televote—an electronic plebiscite conducted in conjunction with that state's 1978 Constitutional Convention. As an example of how communitarians use the new media to support the participatory ideals of the electronic commonwealth, we will study the use of two-way cable technology to televise town meetings in Reading, Pennsylvania. The difference between these two uses of the new media goes a long way, we believe, to distinguish what is friend and what is foe of democracy in the new media environment.

Participation by Electronic Plebiscite:

The Case of the Hawaii Televote

As the 1978 Hawaiian Constitutional Convention approached, various civic groups searched for a way to bring public opinion to bear on the work of convention delegates. To this end, the University of Hawaii sponsored an experiment, in conjunction with a course offered for credit, with a novel form of polling known as televoting.[3] Employing a host of old and new media (from the mail to the telephone to the computer), the project surveyed public opinion on two issues scheduled for debate at the convention: adoption of a state initiative or referendum process and appointment versus election of state judges. A survey was conducted according to the following steps:[4]

1. To assure a random, scientific sample, a computer was used to generate a list of random telephone numbers statewide. Because this procedure was not based on listings in the telephone directory, it picked up unlisted and unassigned numbers, as well as telephones out of service.

2. The televote staff (University of Hawaii faculty and students) contacted registered voters from the computer listing, explained the project, and solicited their participation. This was the "call-out" phase of the televote. Approximately 50 percent of those contacted, or 565 persons, agreed to participate.

3. Televote ballots were then mailed to the participants, together with an educational brochure prepared by the staff. The brochure started as follows:

Please read the contents of this TELEVOTE. Take a day or two to think about it and talk about it with your friends. Then fill out the ballot and call us back within 3 days after receiving this TELEVOTE.[5]

The brochure went on to present, in easy-to-read format, arguments pro and con regarding initiatives and referenda and about various methods for selecting state judges.

4. As opposed to the call-out phase, where contact was initiated by the televote staff, televoters were instructed to initiate their own subsequent participation in the "call-in" or voting stage. When calling in their votes, voters were to identify themselves with a preassigned number.*

---

* The 1978 televote relied on back-and-forth communication by telephone and had live persons doing the telephoning. Two high-tech variants of this procedure have been used in subsequent electronic polls or plebiscites. One variant continues to use the telephone but automates at least the call-in stage of the vote by having persons talk directly to a central computer. An example of this is the "900" AT&T instant poll, where by placing a fifty cent toll call, individuals can have their opinions instantly recorded and tabulated by computer. Another variant replaces communication by mail

5. Only 15 percent of the 565 Hawaii televoters called in their votes within the allowed three-day period. The project staff called the remaining participants and solicited their responses. In this way the televote achieved a return vote after two weeks from 400 of the 565 participants.

6. Although the project failed to win official consideration of televote results from the Constitutional Convention, it was granted permission to set up a room at the convention and to disseminate information about televote results.

7. Finally, the project sought to publicize televote results in the mass media. Leading newspapers, major radio stations, and all network television affiliates carried news stories on the televote results.

Rates of Participation in Electronic Plebiscites

As the preceding description indicates, the results of the tele-vote had no binding effect or formal recognition. Perhaps this explains the relatively low rate of participation achieved by the televote. Professor Ted Becker, a chief organizer of the project, credits the televote with achieving an "astounding" 72 percent "return vote," but this statistic is misleading.[6] Becker's own figures show that 50 percent of those asked to participate flat-out refused. Of the remaining 50 percent (565 persons), only 15 percent called

---

and telephone with communication by interactive cable television: here the televote ballot and brochure are published electronically on the screen; the home viewer marks a ballot simply by pushing buttons on a console attached to the set. A central computer scans all participating homes, recording and tabulating all votes. An example of a cable voting system is the defunct QUBE system of Warner-Amex Cable Communications. The speed of the QUBE system was such that a computer would scan home television sets every six seconds, tabulate responses, and display aggregate totals within ten seconds after "voting" closed.

In one important respect—speed—the televote differed from the QUBE or AT&T "900" poll. Giving people time to respond rather than polling for immediate responses was basic to the organizers' sense that the televote could spur reflection and education. We will return to the comparison of instant versus delayed polling later in this chapter. Putting aside the question of speed, the televote shared at least one important political aim with its more instant polling cousins: its goal was to use the channels of communi-cation provided by the electronic media, rather than the more institutionalized and distant channels of communication provided by government or political parties, to amplify the political voice of the individual.

in their vote within the allotted time period. This yielded a timely vote by about 85 persons.[7] Not surprisingly, the televote managers then departed from their own design and, like conventional pollsters, called participants and solicited an on-the-spot response from them. Only with this prodding and time extension did the "return vote" reach 72 percent of *ballots mailed*—which means participation by 36 percent of the sample originally contacted. This compares unfavorably to the 53 percent voter turnout in the 1984 presidential election and is about the same as the 35.7 percent voter turnout in the 1982 off-year House of Representatives elections.[8]

According to one recent survey of experiments throughout the United States with home-centered voting, low voter turnout is the rule rather than the exception. One pioneer project in home voting was the NSF-funded "Feedback Project" at the Massachusetts Institute of Technology in 1971. As a vehicle for soliciting participation in its various plebiscites, the project generally relied on "issue ballots" distributed in newspapers (either as inserts or detachable coupons). In two voting exercises on educational policies in Massachusetts, between 1 and 2 percent of the printed ballots were returned.[9] In a subsequent issue ballot in Troy, New York, 1 percent of the ballots printed as newspaper inserts were returned; and only one-tenth of 1 percent of the coupons were clipped and mailed.[10] While these results were disappointing to the Feedback Project, one researcher dryly notes that they are not "unusual" in plebiscites of this sort.[11]

Those experiments in electronic home voting that have used the more rapid interactive capacities of cable television to conduct their voting have not fared much better. In the state-of-the-art QUBE system, the act of home voting was made about as easy as it can be made: a matter of pushing buttons on a console atop the television set. But on two major occasions where nonbinding electronic plebiscites were conducted over QUBE, participation was low. In 1978 a highly publicized meeting of the city planning commission in the Columbus, Ohio, suburb of Upper Arlington was aired to a potential audience of 32,000 QUBE subscribers. No more than 2,500 residents tuned in to the meeting and voted in the accompanying plebiscite.[12] In Dallas, the Domestic Policy Association used QUBE to broadcast a two-hour television panel discussion on the nuclear arms race. Periodically during and after the discussion, questions were posed on the screen regarding citizen attitudes toward and knowledge of various nuclear issues. Although no official statistics were ever released from the straw poll, there is a general consensus that the invitation to participate in this poll fell mostly on deaf ears.[13]

On the numerical level, then, televoting and its progeny of electronic plebiscites appear to be trivial rather than substantial exercises in citizen participation at this time. In and of themselves, they offer no remedy to the problem of low voter turnout in actual elections. Moreover, there are normative questions about what steps we ought to take to make political participation into a matter of convenience. Democracy thrives on self-initiated participation rooted in civic concern and civic education. Too often, electronic plebiscites substitute entertainment for education in their hurry to provide a quick fix to low voter turnout. For instance, Professor Becker betrays no irony when he treats participation in the televote as analogous to participation in home video games: "Electronic games that plug into TV sets will recondition people to interact with their sets rather than sit passively in front of the tube."[14] This new interactivity will inevitably spill over into politics. The QUBE system shows that "millions of people are already willing to 'play and pay' for electronic town meetings, just as they are already paying to shoot down space invaders."[15] These predictions made in 1978 about the then-current home video game rage seem just as wrong today as the predictions made about the willingness of citizens to pay to play politics over QUBE. (In January 1984 Warner-Amex terminated interactive programming for QUBE, citing its failure to attract a sufficient audience.)[16] But more disturbing is the underlying notion that politics is a game like any other, that anything that makes that game more entertaining— more like shooting down space invaders—is to the benefit of democracy.

Quality of Participation in Electronic Plebiscites

The Issue of Empowerment. To the problem of low voter turnout, televote organizers could rightly respond that it was their purpose to improve the quality of citizen participation, not necessarily the quantity. Specifically, the televote sought to use modern polling and communication methods to accomplish two goals. First, organizers hoped to educate and inform public opinion better than conventional polling does. Second, they sought to empower public opinion and give it influence at the Constitutional Convention. Did the televote accomplish these educating and empowering goals? Does it give us reason to believe that modern communications technology can emerge as media for civic education and citizen power?

Regarding the question of empowerment, it is not at all clear how a nonbinding plebiscite or straw poll serves to empower public opinion. The televote project took its normative understanding of democratic participation from the initiative and referendum process. But the democratic merit of initiatives and referenda—the reason that adoption of a national referendum process has been a rallying cry for democratic reform movements from the Progressive party of the 1920s to citizen movements of today—is that their results are binding. With referenda, the people are actually, not symbolically, enfranchised to decide issues. Participation in the televote, while it resembled voting in a referendum, generated no actual legislation. The hope was for something lesser and looser, variously called feedback, input, or influence. Alas, in the case of the 1978 Hawaii votes, there was only the show, not the reality, of input into the Constitutional Convention. A whopping 86 percent of televoters favored the adoption of some sort of referendum process in Hawaii, but the convention made no proposal for one.[17] The convention also rejected the alternative for selecting state judges favored by 50 percent of the televoters and recommended a system resembling a choice made by only 15 percent of the televoters.[18]

Would democracy in Hawaii have been better served had the convention been swayed by the televote results? If delegates are not to deliberate but only to record majority opinion, then there is no need to convene political assemblies or constitutional conventions at all; we could, as Alvin Toffler advocates, simply "represent" ourselves via the taking of a representative sample of opinion. But, especially in regard to constitution making, American democracy is an attempt to limit the reach of popular sovereignty, to map out a sphere of individual rights over which majorities have no control. The mere fact that delegates to the Hawaii Constitutional Convention did not decide in accord with the majority of televoters does not mean their deliberations were undemocratic. Televote organizers never systematically considered what kind of impact polls ought to have on deliberative bodies such as constitutional conventions.

At times, the organizers eschewed the view that their poll should have had direct impact on the convention. Instead, they justified their project in terms of psychological rather than political benefits. Using new technology to reach citizens customarily left out of the political process, these nonbinding polls and referenda can serve democracy, we are told, by reducing the average citizen's sense of alienation and powerlessness. But it is doubtful that the new technology can perform even this psychological fix. As classically understood, democratic participation has a transformative effect on the individual because participation is coupled with the potential for action. By contrast, straw polls and televotes trivialize participation into feedback—elites promising to "consider" the mass of citizen views pouring in.[19] By divorcing participation from action, one critic balks, the host of new automated feedback or polling devices only underline the posture of citizen as supplicant to those with real power. Such uses of the new media thus "stand out as additional symbols of the lowly state to which the citizen is reduced."[20]

The Issue of Civic Education. If the televote did not serve to empower citizens, did it educate them? Designers of the televote stressed the civic education achieved by their "new polling technology":

All modern issue polling, no matter how scientific the sample and how careful the design of questions, still fails to provide the respondent questioned with much (if any) information. Moreover, the response sought is immediate, with very little opportunity to think about a response. And isn't information and time to think the essence of coming to a good judgment on policy? . . . [Televoting] differs from conventional polling in that it provides respondents with undisputed information, balanced arguments, and a wide range of issue-relevant alternatives. It also yields sufficient time to think about or discuss the policy matters with friends, relatives, experts and other people.[21]

Explicit in the televote project from its inception, therefore, was the argument that traditional courses of civic education were failing the public and that if polling were to serve democracy well, pollsters themselves would have to educate as well as survey public opinion. Or, as Becker put it, the televote project required "acceptance of responsibility by pollsters to serve as the research staff of the public."[22]

But the civic education accomplished by the televote experience must be judged meager. The televote did stimulate media attention to its results, thereby possibly focusing a wider audience's attention on the otherwise insulated work of the Constitutional Convention. But this wider media audience did not actually participate in the televote—they received no ballots or background literature. As originally structured, therefore, the televote had little or no educational impact on a general audience. To correct this problem, subsequent televotes—for instance, a New Zealand version—have included an official and unofficial component. The official component remains just as before, to ensure a scientific sample. The unofficial component does not try to reach a random sample. Instead, the televote ballot and brochures are widely printed and distributed as newspaper advertisements or inserts; a self-selected sample of newspaper readers can then participate alongside the official televoters.[23]

But in either version, the televote's claim to serve as a means of civic education rests on two of its distinguishing features mentioned earlier: (1) the distribution of information to those whose opinions are to be polled and (2) the slowing down of the poll to allow participants three days to ponder their response. We consider each of these features in turn.

The brochure mailed to Hawaii televoters commendably focused on the substantive issues up for vote—unlike media coverage of elections, which is often criticized for concentrating more on style than substance, more on who is winning or losing than on argument over issues. Still, the televote text provided more the caricature than the curriculum of a civic education. It must be judged inferior in fact to current press coverage of issue politics. By way of example, the following quotation cites the entire argument, pro and con, regarding election of state judges:

ELECTION:

FOR	AGAINST
The election system makes sure that the judges are directly responsible to, and representative of, the people.	The election method encourages judges to become politicians. The judge's main interest is to stay in office—which may affect his fairness.
The election of judges makes sure that the court system is an independent branch of government, separate from the governor and the Legislature.	Poorly qualified persons could run for office and win.[24]

173

This information is no doubt accurate, impartial, and objective. But it trivializes the nature of democratic deliberation. The argument is devoid of specifics about the role of political parties in judicial elections or the term of office elected judges would serve. And although the *Federalist Papers* offers perhaps the classic arguments in American politics against elected judges and in favor of life tenure, the televote course of civic education was far too short and quick for such study.

The same formulaic approach to civic education is evident in the subsequent use of televoting in New Zealand, as part of long-range planning for that nation's future. New Zealand voters were asked to choose one of four alternative futures for their nation. One view of the future was that New Zealand should be "a free enterprise system in which major economic growth provides great economic benefits for all." This viewpoint in turn was composed of four concepts, or "building blocks." By way of illustration, block number one of this point of view was "the people of any country benefit more where there is equal opportunity for each person to seek their own best interests. Government must not tell them what to do or not to do."[25]

It is difficult to see how anyone could dissent from such a future, worded as it is, though of course in real life the politics of free enterprise are a source of intense controversy. The text for education here is so short, conclusory, and leading in tone that it could educate New Zealanders only in the crudest of ways. Once again, it was no advance over the education delivered by the organized press.

Even more damning is that televoters played no role in deciding which issues ought to be the subject of the plebiscite, which issues ought to be placed on the public's agenda for constitutional action. Agenda setting—in this case the decision to highlight the issues of initiatives and referenda and of methods for selecting state judges—was the work of students and faculty at the University of Hawaii, as "inspected" and "judged" by a major polling firm in Hawaii. Nor did televoters have the opportunity to participate in framing the "pro" and "con" arguments about the issues under discussion; once more this was the exclusive province of the televote staff. Participation in the televote was limited to picking among prepackaged choices—a political act not much different from that afforded by conventional polling.

The New Media and Democratic Participation

Subsequent experiments with electronic voting are marred by the same thin understanding of participatory democracy. Particularly troubling are the push-button voting experiments over QUBE. In conjunction with the televised city planning commission meeting in Upper Arlington, Ohio, previously described, QUBE subscribers could respond to questions flashed on their screen. But, just as in the televote, Upper Arlington voters had no input into the selection or design of the questions. As one group studying the plebiscite concluded, the responses of home viewers were all but scripted for them, and many complained that the script did not include the choice they would have made under conditions of free choice.[26] As a critic in *The Nation* put it, the act of responding to questions and multiple choices framed by others reduces participation into a "shell game [that] cons us into believing we are participating when we are simply performing as the responding end of a prefabricated system of external stimuli."[27]

We turn now to the second of the two distinguishing features of the televote: its attempt to slow down the pace of citizen feedback. To its credit, the televote architects labored to avoid the pitfalls of instant polling and to provide respondents with the time necessary for informed decision making. Still, the three-day time schedule of the televote offered only token resistance to automated politics. And beyond televoting, the enticement of truly instant polls continues. Perhaps the most noteworthy case in which the speed of the new technology was used to impoverish communication took place during the 1980 presidential election.[28] Immediately following the first Carter-Reagan debate, ABC News solicited viewer opinions as to who had won the debate. The technology involved was the AT&T "900" network previously discussed. Telephone calls were answered in automated fashion, and a central computer kept a running, televised tabulation of the vote (which Reagan won by a two-to-one margin). Nothing prevented individuals from voting more than once, although a fifty cent charge per call kept the poll from surveying a random sample. But the most ominous aspect of the ABC poll was its rapidity —the swallowing up of the substance of the debate by the horse-race question of who won. Televised debates can be an important course in civic education. They can center public attention on the issues and call upon us to continue the debate among ourselves. But the ABC poll divorced public opinion from public deliberation, distracted citizens from the content of the debate, and obsessed the public with "participation" in declaring a winner.

The unscientific nature of the ABC poll has kept major news organizations from using the "900" number for direct political polling in subsequent elections. But the technology continues to be used in a variety of nonpolitical polling (for instance, during the 1984 All-Star Game, baseball viewers became voters on the question of the American League's "designated hitter" rule). And on QUBE the instant poll was a fixture. To take one example, home viewers were asked to respond to the question, "What effect do you think Reaganomics will have on the economy? Do you think it will (1) greatly help; (2) somewhat help; (3) make no difference; (4) somewhat hurt; (5) greatly hurt."[29] Results of the push-button voting were tabulated and displayed on the screen almost instantly. Superficially, this process

may seem democratic: one gets to make one's opinion known. But the "one" in this formulation is the privatized viewer rather than the public citizen, and he or she gives an instant "opinion" rather than concurring or dissenting from a position hammered out through debate and democratic discourse. A compilation of opinions does not make a civic culture; such a culture demands a deliberative process in which people engage one another as citizens.[30]

Here we spy the irony in those uses of telecommunications that choose the plebiscite and home-centered voting as vehicles for democratic participation. In their novel interactive capacity, in the technology for videoconferencing and other forms of electronic congregation, the new media have an unsurpassed capacity to bring persons together and to sustain the fullness of conversation against obstacles of distance and time. But instant polls are a way of avoiding conversation and congregation altogether. Home-centered voting uses the new technology to isolate persons and to privatize their deliberations, communicating only final opinions and not the ongoing process of debate. This makes a mockery of the ideal of an electronic commonwealth.

*Conclusion: Polls, Plebiscites, and the Ideal
of Participatory Democracy*

Designed to avoid the empty participation afforded by conventional polls, the televote did not succeed in its good intentions. Instead, it continued the political drift toward plebiscitarian uses of the new media that shortchange the democratic process. Two points are worth emphasizing by way of summary.

First, the allure of speed is so great that we can expect computers, telephones, interactive cable television, and other new technologies to be harnessed in the future to ever more instant methods of voting. If this pattern continues unchecked, the new media will do more to undermine than to support democratic participation. The very speed of electronic voting will shrink the time for deliberation and debate, persuasion and argument.

Second, there is equal allure in the ability of the new technology to bring politics to the person rather than the person to politics. We can therefore expect continued use of the new media in home-centered voting scenarios. Indeed, across the board, the new technologies may effect an intense privatization of our culture as we move toward home banking, home shopping, home work—and now home voting. Home voting may be no more than a convenience, and the ability of persons to talk with those they cannot meet face to face may yet be a boon for democracy. But in the instant variety of plebiscites, the passivity of communication grows to the point where persons are not engaging one another in mutual conversation at all. Seriatim, they respond on demand to the stimuli of a computer or television set. The computer compiles the aggregate opinion—and this is what we have somehow "decided" together.

Participation in the Electronic Commonwealth:

The Case of Reading, Pennsylvania

Plebiscites and polls are not the only uses for the new technology. In this section we turn to a fundamentally different use of the new media, inspired by classical and communitarian understandings of democratic participation.

Television and the Deliberative Ideal of Citizenship

In 1976 a pathbreaking experiment in the political use of interactive, multichannel cable television was launched in Reading, Pennsylvania.[31] Designed by researchers at New York University's Alternative Media Center and funded by the National Science Foundation, the pilot program put the new interactive capacity of television to use in overcoming the social isolation of the elderly. Three neighborhood senior citizens' centers were equipped with television cameras and videorecording equipment that allowed senior citizens to write and produce their own programs. The three centers were then linked together by cable into a two-way communications network. Special converters were also installed in the private homes of about 125 selected elderly citizens, allowing them to receive the cable programming over their television sets and to respond by telephone.

As originally designed, the program aimed at improving the social welfare of the elderly and did not call for political programming. Early programs included advice on sexual activity, insomnia, when to stop driving a car, and the cost of funerals.[32] But it quickly became evident that senior citizens were interested in talking politics with city officials. Soon the daily programming included videoconferences with elected officials in what one commentator described as "regular town-meeting style."[33] The initiative for these town meetings, it should be emphasized, came from the elderly themselves and was not anticipated by the NYU designers. There is impressionistic evidence that these televised town meetings led "to the political mobilization of the entire [senior] community"—to the entrance of many formerly shut-in senior citizens into the political process and their consolidation into an articulate voting constituency and interest group.[34]

The video experiment with senior citizens ended after thirty months, but the political use of interactive television has spread to the general Reading population. Berks Cable Television Company, the local cable operator, provides a public access channel, known as Berks Community Television (BCTV), over which an extraordinarily rich menu of political programming is broadcast. Most important for our purposes is that BCTV has continued the town-meeting model by using cable to televise city council, city budget, and community development hearings.[35] Indeed, one group visiting Reading in June of 1983 found that most public hearings on city business were conducted over BCTV. At these hearings "the comments of citizens who telephoned in are counted as testimony in the same way as those who participate in person."[36] In 1979 City Councilor Karen Miller was elected mayor, beating the candidate backed by a long-entrenched Reading political machine. Many credit her victory to the exposure she received through cable coverage of the City Council.[37]

The Reading experiment with interactive television differed markedly from QUBE's version of two-way television. As we saw earlier, QUBE programmers became fascinated early on with the novelty of push-button voting and home plebiscites. In the beginning, what QUBE did was to transplant political behavior into the nonpolitical realm. The run-of-the-mill game show became an election, as viewers at home pushed buttons to vote for this answer or that contestant or what was behind which curtain. QUBE went on to use the same technology to permit viewers to be voters on political issues proper, and in this way to achieve a kind of political participation analogous to game show participation.

Implicit in the Reading experiment was a classical understanding of participatory democracy. In the writings of Rousseau or Jefferson or Tocqueville, participation is valued only partly as a way for individuals to express their own views, values, and interests. In fact, in the classical view individuals are quite competent to know their own interests apart from active political participation; electing representatives provides a sufficient opportunity to express these interests and to hold representatives accountable to serving them. But without direct participation in politics, individuals cannot know or express the interests they share as citizens—the choices they themselves might make when judging their own good in a public context rather than a private one. The primary value of participation over representation, therefore, is that, by allowing citizens to act like citizens, participation acquaints each with the interest of all. Participation gives the citizen education in, and responsibility for, the common good. But—and this is crucial —participation can deliver civic education and civic virtue only when it takes the form of deliberation and dialogue, persuasion and debate—and not just the periodic act of voting preconceived interests. Participation, that is to say, has to take communal forms;

it is a collective act to be given the widest publicity, not an individual act to be shrouded in the secrecy of the voting booth. Public participation breeds in turn a public, civic culture, whose symbols are town meetings and town halls, soap boxes, torchlight parades, neighborhood rallies, party caucuses, conventions, even parent-teacher associations and the like.

The Reading experiment and its progeny seek to bring this town-meeting ideal of democracy into the television age. The mission of an electronic commonwealth is to pioneer civic uses of two-way television in transforming citizens from passive spectators of politics into active participants:

From the ancient world to the American founding, the great enemy of democracy has been scale: the repressive effects of mass society on the communication and participation necessary to self-government. Television in its second age *can* be to the problem of scale what drugs were to disease: a miracle remedy. People can be brought together across time and space and be permitted to confront one another in a continuing process of mutual exploration, deliberation, debate, and decision-making.[38]

Assessing the Reading Experiment in Electronic Town Meetings

How successful has the Reading model been in breathing new life into the more classical and communal forms of democratic participation? Is the "electronic commonwealth" a mere catchphrase or a serious ideal capable of sponsoring real politics?

Quantity of Participation. As far as increasing the television audience for political programming, the track record of the electronic commonwealth remains unimpressive. In Reading itself, a 1982 survey of 393 respondents showed that 27 percent described themselves as watching political programs on BCTV "regularly."[39] But this result has not been approached, much less duplicated, anywhere else in the United States. In Dallas, a town meeting regarding rapid transit was held in which citizens could participate by going to one of four videoconferencing studios throughout the city. On average, the four sites attracted twenty to thirty-five persons each, in a city of 984,000 persons.[40] It is estimated that all public-access channels together across the whole nation account for seven-tenths of 1 percent of all viewing time; "at any one time, the number of viewers of access channels is so small as to be trivial."[41] Thus, although the technology supports an increase in public-affairs programming on television, the audience is simply not there yet. As one dissenter from the blue-sky predictions for cable puts it, access to a television station that no one watches is a "benefit not connected to anything of significance.... [It is] the stuff of 1984, not the tool . . . of revitalizing tired democracies."[42]

All of this is not to say that cable television has proved politically bankrupt. Available on cable is a wide and diverse set of political offerings, including C-SPAN's gavel-to-gavel coverage of the House of Representatives and other government sessions, CNN's twenty-four–hour news programming, and a host of televised local government meetings and even some criminal trials. There are also networks to serve the particular political interests of particular religious, ethnic, racial, and linguistic groups. Still, the major fact about cable programming is that mass-audience programming predominates. For the last decade, the prime movers in the cable industry have been the satellite movie networks such as Home Box Office and Showtime. HBO, the largest of these services, has 14.5 million subscribers and is carried on over 5,400 cable systems. Showtime, the second largest pay cable service, attracts 5.4 million subscribers.[43] After movies, the prime fare of cable is certainly not politics but sports, music, concert, music videos, pornography, network reruns, and even the weather. And as pay-per-channel movie services begin to show signs of slowed growth, the cable industry is currently turning to the concept of pay-per-view programming, with predictable emphasis on conventional entertainment fare such as live coverage of boxing matches and concerts.

A 1986 study of politics and the mass media pessimistically concludes that cable is unlikely to change the "deeply ingrained media habits" of the average citizen. The problem is that, "although channels devoted exclusively to the coverage of news and public affairs may become available through cable, all but a small politically inclined elite will opt most of the time for sports, reruns, and movies."[44]

Of special concern here is the emergence of advertising on cable, which was once destined to be a subscriber-supported service. Today most cable systems derive less than 5 percent of their gross revenues from advertising. But a recent study predicts that revenue from cable advertising will reach $2.1 billion by the end of this decade.[45] Were advertising to become substantially embedded in the financial structure of the industry, we could expect the broadcast model of uniform, mass-audience entertainment programming to tighten its already considerable hold on cable offerings.

Quality of Participation. Assessment of the Reading model turns ultimately on a judgment about the quality of discussion in the electronic commonwealth. How well has town-meeting democracy in fact translated to the tube? One preliminary issue has to do with issues of equality and financing. To carry town meetings on cable is to extract a participation tax: one attends the meeting only by paying the costs of cable service. The political use of cable and other new media—especially high-cost computer data services—has the clear potential to widen the information and participation gap between educational and economic classes in the United States. This potential for inequality forms a strong argument for legislation that would provide government subsidies for the new media, much as the government currently subsidizes public television through the Corporation for Public Broadcasting.

If obstacles to equality in the electronic commonwealth can be overcome, then the question becomes how best to use the new two-way nature of television illustrated in the Reading experiment. A persistent criticism of broadcast television has lamented the passivity it demands of the viewer. A modern-day Pericles can use television to reach an audience far larger than the one that gathered in Athens to hear the famous funeral oration, but conventional television does little to allow more people to talk back than could have done so in the fifth century B.C.[46] The result is that televised politics resembles a spectator sport. After all, "you cannot talk back to your TV set, you can only turn it off."[47] And any gesture of response you do make in the privacy of your own home is likely to be politically impotent, unless "you are something of a crank and immediately telephone your friends to inform them that you have tuned out an obnoxious politician and urge them also to turn off their TV sets."[48] In this way, conventional television, no matter how much information it brings to people, "infinitely inhibit[s] the capacity of people to convert that knowledge into action."[49]

The New Media and Democratic Participation

With the advent of new technology, silence and passivity are no longer the iron logic of television. Participants in the Reading experiment reported to field observers that the ability to question city councilors led them to take a more active interest in the doings of the council and gave them a sense that their participation could make a difference.[50] The participants also reported that conversation with other elderly participants enabled them to fashion a common point of view and an agenda of interests for which to lobby. In short, there is at least impressionistic evidence that the interactive capacity of the Reading network enabled the elderly to engage in the kind of deliberations we associate with face-to-face meetings.

Another central feature of the Reading experiment was the involvement of senior citizens in all stages of the planning for their town meetings. They decided on the agenda, selected the officials and experts they wished to hear from, asked their own questions, and rendered their own comments. It is a cause for alarm that in many subsequent experiments with electronic town meetings, this across-the-board participation has dropped out, replaced by something much more scripted. In Dallas, as noted earlier, a television meeting was set up ostensibly to permit citizens to debate certain rapid-transit proposals. Home viewers could call in questions to a panel of transit authority representatives or they could go to one of four videoconferencing studios to appear on television themselves. Either way, their participation was limited strictly to asking questions of the transit authority representatives; comments were out of order, as were follow-up questions. Most striking was the fact that the panel was chosen by the transit authority without any citizen input. Not surprisingly, the panel was packed with transit authority officials in favor of their own proposals. Many who watched this "town meeting" concluded that it offered citizens only a kind of pseudoparticipation. Television was really being used to conduct a sales conference for the transit authority's proposals.[51]

As this example indicates, elite control is as much a danger in electronic town meetings as it is in conventional meetings. And the manipulation is easier to hide. In the traditional New England town meeting, there is a visible moderator. That moderator is held accountable through public challenges, through the informal constraints of having to go on living in the town, and by the formal

183

constraints of recognized rules of procedure. In a televised town meeting, studio personnel become invisible moderators, making behind-the-scenes decisions about whom to recognize and in what order. Insufficient attention has been given to how to translate *Robert's Rules of Order* into an electronic manual.

Certain uses of telecommunications in Alaska provide a striking example of the danger of elite control. There the size of the territory sharply limits the number of citizens who have the time or resources to journey to the state capitol to testify before the legislature. To alleviate such problems, the legislature takes testimony from witnesses at various state-owned teleconferencing sites. The state network employs so-called field managers, who are charged with making crucial decisions about what segment of the population might be interested to know that a legislative hearing on trucking deregulation or park land or gun control is about to take place. These field managers then advertise the hearing to the target groups and invite their testimony via the teleconferencing system. Such decisions, which are passed off as merely administrative or managerial, go to the heart of the political process and place in the hands of these field managers the power to control the results of citizen participation by deciding who is to participate at all.[52]

This teleconferencing system is patently open to manipulation by lobbyists and special-interest groups. Testimony at the various studio sites is taken by the legislature on a first-come, first-served basis. Lobbying groups can always "pack" the studio and monopolize the testimony. Special-interest packing of legislative hearings or town meetings takes place, of course, without the aid of electronics. But there is a tendency to think that political uses of the new technology will result in automatic victory for equality of access and ordinary citizen participation. This is a naive view. Due care needs to be taken to design the electronic commonwealth so as to minimize elite control and lobbyist manipulation.

Interest Groups, Factions, and New-Media Narrowcasting

So far, we have treated the Reading experiment as illustrative of the ways in which the new media can be used to support the more communal aspects of democratic life. But this may be an exaggeration. It might be more accurate to stress the garden-variety interest-group politicking that the elderly were able to accomplish with the help of two-way television hook-ups.[53] As one of the project's organizers put it, "the two-way cable system in Reading demonstrates the potential for broadband communications to reinforce community consciousness *and to reflect the distinct preferences or priorities of an age-based sub-group of the population.*"[54]

As noted in chapter 4, other interest groups have been quick to recognize the lobbying uses to which the interactive capacity of the new media can be put. Groups such as the National Education Association or the Chamber of Commerce, for instance, have used satellite technology to link geographically dispersed chapters into a single network. "BizNet," the Chamber of Commerce network, briefly tried televising business news and lobbyists' messages to satellite dishes at corporate headquarters throughout the nation.[55] The national committees of the Republican and Democratic parties and independent political action committees are likewise making use of videoconferencing by satellite, automated telephone banks, and computerized direct mailing lists to raise money and votes for candidates and issues.

On cable television, narrowcast programming aimed at special-interest audiences is also a standard feature. In part, cable narrowcasting is a boon for democratic pluralism. As opposed to the uniform political culture served by commercial television, cable programming has the potential to serve the different kinds of citizens we are. Ithiel de Sola Pool succinctly summarized the democratic case for cable:

From the social point of view the promise of cable lies in the pluralism made possible by the unlimited number of channels. From the programmer-cablecaster's point of view this may be its horror. A program producer gains from limitations on competititon that compel vast audiences. . . . But for society, the advantage of cable is that it can create for video the kind of diversity of choice that exists in print.[56]

Narrowcast programming is also a potential boon to democracy because it guards against what we isolated in chapter 1 as the characteristic danger of classical or communitarian visions of democracy: the tendency for the commonwealth ideal to be invoked on behalf of closed and monolithic visions of public life. Far from any such dangers of collectivism or exclusion, the public-access television pioneered in Reading and elsewhere fits well with the open community norms of a pluralist society.

But there is always the danger that narrowcasting will foster faction in the body politic. Special-interest programming on cable ignores the public culture at large and focuses "on discrete, specialized, one-issue or one-interest audiences."[57] The new religious, racial, and ethnic cable networks reach separate "audiences who [may] never again be required to share a common channel or talk to each other."[58]

Use of new technology to fragment and narrow communications is illustrated by computerized direct-mail campaigns. The computer routes letters opposing abortion to members of right-to-life groups, letters opposing arms sales to Jordan to people with presumably Jewish surnames, letters opposing gun control to members of rifle clubs, and so on. Each group receives mail about the politics it already favors and is spared news about opposing views. It is not difficult to imagine narrowcasting on cable being put to similar use in mobilizing single-issue constituencies. It is also not difficult to imagine uses of cable designed to escape politics and news entirely: to air only sports programming to the sports fan, movies to the movie buff, or home shopping to the consumer.

If the political strategy of the direct-mail campaign—targeting supporters of an issue for mobilization and forgoing communication aimed at convincing opponents—becomes the model for narrowcast television, then democratic pluralism will be degraded into mere factionalism. Democratic pluralism acknowledges that, absent state coercion, people's patterns of association and communication are likely to be rooted in ethnic, racial, religious, and economic distinctions. But if the nation is to be a community in any sense—a *res publica* or public thing—then democratic pluralism must regain its communitarian face. There must be an identity that unites us as Americans as well as divides us into hyphenated subgroups. There must be a civic education provided in the schools, forged in the army, or taught by candidates, elected officials, and the press. This education must give us a sense of being participants in a joint venture, sharing a *common* wealth and a common vision for the nation. For all its failures, national network television contributes to national unity. It has made us all participants, if only as spectators, in the extraordinary happenings of the age—the assassination and resignation of presidents, the conduct of wars, the landings on the moon.[59] Of course, most often the common television culture is of a different order entirely—a matter of sharing references to Lucy and Dallas, Gunsmoke and Kojak. It is a common culture that remains bland, uniform, and homogenized; it is also the culture of the consumer and not the citizen.

Cable's excess of channel capacity means those who want to watch political programs can now do so. But there is also more of the same old stuff—reruns of situation comedies and detective stories, movies galore, music and sports. More than ever politics is dwarfed on television by comparison to mass-audience entertainment programming. And those not interested in politics can push buttons to avoid it entirely. Before there was UHF and before there was cable, news programs tended to monopolize television's early evening hour. The lack of choice permitted television news to capture an inadvertent audience that watched the news simply because it was on. In the same way, an audience tuning in to watch their favorite situation comedy might have come inadvertently to see some of the preempting presidential news conference being carried live on all three network affiliates. But with cable and UHF, there is no longer a "wall of news" at any one time; the presidential news conference may compete with a dozen other offerings. In these ways, it is quite possible that the new media, so full of civic promise, may in fact reduce the number of persons who receive basic political news via television.

Cable's narrowcast networks also can risk political partisanship in ways that broadcasters seeking to attract a mass audience cannot risk. Partisanship in the presentation of news is not necessarily bad. As previously discussed, alliance with a political party was the democratic norm for the press in the early nineteenth century (see chapter 3). But when partisans watch only their own partisan channel, communication shrivels to positive reinforcement. The historic ills of faction in a democracy return.

Whether the new video age will enrich or impoverish politics along the lines suggested by the Reading experiment thus remains to be seen. The aim must be to harness the power of telecommunications to the cause of civic education. Above all else, civic education requires us to sustain communication with viewpoints not our own, always in search of common ground. This common ground is the commonwealth electronics can help to found.

Beyond Reading: The Convergence of Video and Computer Technology

The Reading experiment tapped only a small part of the new technology. Its progeny have gone on to suggest ways of marrying the videoconferencing used there with computer information and retrieval services commonly known as videotex. From the technological point of view, phrases such as videotex and electronic publishing alert us to the new media's distinct tendency to blur the boundary between print and electronic communications. In videotex, the television set is no longer just a receiver of over-the-air broadcast signals; it is a terminal hooked by a special box, telephone modem, cable, or optic fiber to a remote computerized data service. Any data stored in that service can be retrieved instantly and "published" as text on the television screen. This convergence of video, telecommunications, and computer technology into a single communications network is largely responsible for the new abundance and speed with which information flows in this society. With little more than a television set and one of the connecting devices to computer data, the home becomes the complete library. As of the time of this writing, such corporate giants as Time, Bank of America, Sears, and IBM have all announced plans to enter the electronic publishing field in major ways.[60] The Justice Department has also proposed lifting the restrictions that prevent the local Bell Telephone operating companies from offering electronic information services of their own. In 1989 the original seven-year ban on electronic publishing by AT&T will expire. With commercial backers such as these on the horizon, videotex is a technology here to stay.

One apostle of electronic publishing argues that the computer serves democracy by bringing any and all information to anyone living anywhere.[61] But before the computer can democratize access to information, the cost of subscribing to videotex services must be low enough to attract subscribers across economic classes. This is not the case now. For example, today almost all major private law firms in the United States use computer information services for legal research projects. One such service, provided by Mead Data Central, Inc. ("Lexis"), costs a law firm a flat fee of $125 per month, no matter how many professionals use the service; time charges run about $32 per hour, and there is also a per-search fee, running from $3 to $30, depending on the number of sources searched. None of these expenses include the cost of purchasing or leasing a computer terminal and printer.[62] The cost of subscribing to *Viewtron*, Knight-Ridder's electronic newspaper, was also steep. Viewers had to buy a $600 AT&T terminal, in addition to paying $12 a month in fees and $1 an hour to the telephone company.[63]

Given these costs, videotex's contribution to democracy hinges on lowering price obstacles to equal access to electronic publishing. Market forces have driven the cost of personal computers and accessories down dramatically in recent years. Still, computer information services remain in the hands of the few; it would be rare indeed for an ordinary citizen to have access in a public library to the kind of computerized legal research services that are the expensive commonplace of major law firm practice in the United States. Indeed, across the board, civic uses of videotex and computer services are practically nil.

Here we come to an essential irony about the impact of the computer age on our democracy. In theory, the computer is a vast force for equalizing access to information: no information is so remote or closely held as to be unobtainable by the average citizen. In practice, the computer tends to widen the information gap between economic classes. The most telling sign of the growing gap is the public library's slow entrance into the computer age. Whole carloads of information are no longer bound between covers but are available only by subscribing to some computer service. The result is that the public library, long a forum for democratic and civic education, has fallen behind. It is imperative that Congress and local legislatures search for ways to subsidize civic uses of videotex and computer information services so as to make the power of the new media generally available to the citizenry. Only then will the new media be a common wealth of the people.

CHAPTER 6

POLICY IN A
COMPARATIVE
PERSPECTIVE

WE have come a great distance in discussing how changing technology, driven by invention, discovery, and investment, is affecting political activity and the course it might follow in the near
future. We must also discuss how politics and public policy might
alter the media available for the practice of democracy in the
United States. Our next logical step, therefore, will be to consider
how different media might best underwrite democracy and how
public policy can contribute to an electronic commonwealth.

In this chapter we examine very different models under
which the media exist in democratic countries. The comparative
study of communications media reveals that different nations
have chosen quite distinctive approaches for regulating electronic
media. To some degree, these different patterns parallel the values
emphasized in different models of democracy.

As we shall see, the fractured American policy-making machinery—the Federal Communications Commission, the Congress, and the courts—does not lend itself to dealing easily with the broader questions we raise here, such as the benefits to democracy of different communications policies. Rather, the very nature of the way in which we achieve policy tends to focus our attention on narrow and specific issues, as, for example, whether cable systems must carry local broadcast signals. In the American political system, policy decisions have largely been shaped by the interplay of private interests rather than by calculations of the public benefit.[1] This is, of course, a consequence of the private media system we have accepted in this country. Nevertheless, there have been occasions in the history of American media when policy makers have given more explicit attention to the public stake in alternative structures of media. Examples include the creation of a regulated monopoly in the telegraph and telephone industries, the decisions to grant broadcasting licenses to private radio stations combined with a reservation of spectrum space for educational broadcasting, and the continuing deliberations over public access on cable systems.

When we turn to the available literature on communications policy in the United States, we confront an analogous situation. The writings on the details of narrow policy issues are abundant; much has been produced for public edification by attorneys who work in this area of regulatory law. Many fewer studies treat communications policy with the broad brush that the topic merits. (A notable exception is the volume *Technologies of Freedom*, in which Ithiel de Sola Pool discusses the applicability of different bodies of regulatory law to the new media.)[2] We believe that a discussion more appropriate to our consideration of democratic values will evolve out of a comparative examination of how different nations regulate communications media.

National Patterns of Regulating Broadcasting

At the broadest level, nations have chosen at least three different patterns for making broadcast media available to their citizens: commercial licensing, public ownership, and what we will call subsidized access. The first should be well known to Americans from their daily experience. Many readers will comprehend the basic ingredients of public ownership, as applied by Canada and most European nations. To our knowledge, a full-blown system of subsidized access has been attempted in radio and television broadcasting only in the Netherlands.

The ensuing discussion will not satisfy specialists in communications policy. We need to describe these three models only briefly in order to get to a topic more central to our present purposes: the political problematics that plague the interface between media and democracy. We also frankly acknowledge that our discussion is of ideal types, drawn for heuristic purposes. As it turns out, none of the three models exists in pure form in any country. For example, while the dominant pattern in the United States is commercial media, the Public Broadcasting System has been in existence for almost two decades.[3] Nevertheless, by describing the broadcasting systems in the United States, Great Britain, and the Netherlands, we can present the basic contours of different policies.

After describing these different media systems, we turn our attention to what we will call "political problematics," systematic problems in the interface between media and politics. Our argument is that sooner or later every democracy will have to cope with these problems, such as government censorship or access desired by political candidates.

Commercial Ownership—The United States[4]

The law regulating communications in the United States begins with a strong injunction against any government involvement whatever. "Congress shall make no law . . ." asserts the First Amendment, "abridging the freedom of speech, or of the press." By the time the Founders sought to incorporate unrestricted use of a technology—the printing press—into the Constitution, the tradition of journalistic independence and pamphleteering was already well established. Newspapers had claimed and won the right to criticize colonial administration and to expose its frailty. In fact, it is hard to imagine the American revoluion at all without emphasizing the struggle for men's minds that Paine, Franklin, Hamilton, and others conducted through pamphlets and the journals of the day. So it was natural that, in envisioning the freedoms necessary for the prevention of tyranny, the Founders wanted to guarantee a press unrestricted by government intervention.

The centrality of a free press to democracy is further emphasized by the construction of the First Amendment. Its three clauses deal with the exercise of religion, free speech and press, and rights of assembly and petition. Even in the days when a soapbox could provide a meaningful means of reaching one's fellow citizens, it was recognized that the printing press provided the only practical means of accentuating one's voice over the crowd and beyond it to citizens in other locations. Two hundred years ago effective free speech required a medium of transmission; the same is true today.

If a free press meant anything, it meant emphatically no government ownership of the press, particularly monopoly ownership. Therefore, it seems natural to assume that when different technologies for communication came along, the government would stay well clear of direct involvement in providing services. However, since another clause in Article I (section 8, paragraph 7) empowered the Congress to establish a post office, the United States was deeply involved in communications on another front. In fact, the precedent of the mails reached back equally as far as that of independent journalism; mail had been under government ownership in England since 1656 and in the American colonies since 1711.[5] When the telegraph, the first of the electronic media, arrived in the 1840s, it was therefore not at all clear what the government's role should be in promoting the public welfare by making the service available to citizens.

In 1845, rejecting the recommendation of the House Ways and Means Committee and Postmaster General Cave Johnson, the U.S. Congress refused to purchase Samuel Morse's patent rights for the telegraph, even though it had subsidized Morse in stringing the first "lightning lines" between Washington and Baltimore.[6] In effect, Congress decided to leave telecommunications to the private sector, despite Johnson's warning: "The evils which the community may suffer or the benefits which individuals may derive from the possession of such an instrument, under the control of private associations or unincorporated companies, not controlled by law, cannot be overestimated."[7] At approximately the same time, for example, many European nations concluded that electronic delivery of messages should be structured much like the service most akin to it, the government-run mail service.

We need not probe why the Americans made a different decision[8] so much as understand its consequences. During the 1840s and 1850s numerous companies competed to connect the major eastern cities and to tie them to the expanding West. Out of this initial chaos came Western Union. Formed in 1856, it experienced geometrical growth by acquiring its smaller competitors wherever possible, and within a decade it emerged as the nation's largest corporation.[9]

Efforts to revoke the private ownership of the only existing telecommunications medium continued throughout the nineteenth century. In 1866, the same year that Western Union achieved supremacy by swallowing up its two remaining large competitors, Congress enacted legislation that allowed telegraph companies to build lines along military and post roads, subject to the provision that after five years the government could buy out the companies. Between 1866 and 1900 over seventy bills to reform the telegraph system were introduced in Congress,[10] many of them based on the 1866 act. But the die was already cast: through its alliance with the news monopoly Associated Press, Western Union had gained enough political power to hold off these efforts to bring more government involvement in telecommunications.

The telegraph's dominance faded with the invention of the telephone, but the precedent of private ownership had been firmly established. Western Union became the model upon which future media systems would build. Telephone fell easily into this pattern; in fact, Pool reports that Alexander Graham Bell originally set out to invent a "multiple telegraph," which would allow several messages to be sent simultaneously over the same line at different tones.[11] From the very beginning the two media were viewed as similar services, though natural competitors. Similar treatment in public policy was a logical extension.

The invention first known as "wireless telegraph" evolved into radio. Several characteristics distinguished this medium from the telephone and the telegraph. For one thing, the investment costs in transmitters were not nearly so major as wire-based systems, so the arguments for a natural monopoly were not as strong. Yet the limitations imposed by space on the electromagnetic spectrum implied sharp constraints upon the number of broadcasters, so that some sort of licensing arrangement proved essential. In addition, the interests of government as a communicator in its own right were immediately voiced by the Department of the Navy, which saw the possibility of reaching ships at sea just as land armies relied on the telegraph. These interests were satisfied by the Wireless Ship Act of 1910 and the Radio Act of 1912, which reserved spectrum space for military communications. Within the broadcasting frequencies allotted for public purposes, however, private ownership again became the norm.

The Radio Act of 1927 established firmly the federal government's ability to regulate the radio industry; private ownership was to be circumscribed by government regulation. This prospect worried many, including Senator Clarence Dill of Washington, who sounded an alarm about establishing a "traffic cop of the air":

The exercise of this power is fraught with such possibilities that it should not be entrusted to any one man nor to any administrative department of the Government.

This regulatory power should be as free from political influence or arbitrary control as possible.[12]

Nevertheless, after playing with the problem for seven years through annual renewals of the 1927 act, Congress consolidated the government's regulatory powers in the Communications Act of 1934, establishing the Federal Communications Commission.

The 1934 law specifically directed the FCC to "study new uses for radio, provide for experimental uses of frequencies, and generally encourage the larger and more effective use of radio in the public interest."[13] Over the years, the commission has used the public-interest criterion for a variety of purposes, including some never contemplated in 1934. One important example has been to prevent the entrance of Western Union or AT&T into the broadcasting field. Thirty years later political theorist Ayn Rand would direct a caustic accusation at this weak attempt to derive some collective benefit out of uses of the airwaves:

Since there is no such thing as the "public interest" (other than the sum of the individual interests of individual citizens), since that collectivist catch-phrase has never been and can never be defined, it amounted to a blank check on totalitarian power over the broadcasting industry, granted to whatever bureaucrats happened to be appointed to the Commission.[14]

As Pool has ably described, ownership of commercial media in the United States has been regulated through three models or bodies of law, directed toward either their economic basis or the content of the information they carry.[15] The least restrictive application falls upon the newspaper industry, which enjoys the strongest judicial interpretations of the First Amendment injunction against laws abridging the right of a free press. Common carriers exist under a second pattern of regulation: economic restrictions as to ownership and government regulation of their tariffs, but no government intervention regarding the content of the communications they carry. Common carriers are also prevented from censoring or interfering with the messages exchanged by those using their services, and, in most cases, they are prohibited from being the producer of the content they carry. Finally, the broadcast industry exists under the most severe restrictions on both content and economic factors. As part of the licensing process, broadcasters must show that they have acted in conformity with the public interest as defined by communications law and FCC decisions. For example, they must grant candidates for federal office "reasonable access" and equal time for their commercial advertisements.

We take up the details of U.S. policy in the next chapter. Suffice it to note at this point that in the case of broadcasting, the rules have been justified as a *quid pro quo* under which private interests are permitted to operate using limited spectrum space in the public airwaves. Valuable licenses are given "with strings attached."[16] While dissension has been vocal and the political disputes continuous, the courts have upheld as constitutional the main thrust of broadcast law. In granting radio and television licenses, the FCC and the Congress have imposed some strong obligations, many of which directly affect the content of messages disseminated. This has occurred despite the general injunction of section 326 of the Communications Act:

Nothing in this Act shall be understood or construed to give the Commission the power of censorship . . . and no regulation or condition shall be promulgated or fixed by the Commission which shall interfere with the right of free speech by means of radio communications.[17]

Even within this regulatory framework, radio and television might not have evolved into the advertiser-supported industry that now predominates. A host of different types of broadcasters leapt into the field in the early days, including churches, colleges, labor unions, and sundry other organizations. According to Pool, much of the early broadcasting resembled the current use of citizen band radios: chatter between broadcasters about whether their signals could be heard clearly and discussions of technical improvement possible in jerryrigged transmitters.[18] Unlike telegraph and telephone, however, the operation of one transmitter can directly interfere with others, so that it soon became clear that some sort of government licensing would be necessary. During the early years, some leaders called for government ownership, especially after the period during World War I when the government shut down amateur broadcasting and took over all radio transmissions.[19] According to Pool, however, the alternative of a government monopoly was never considered very seriously.

Licensing sharply limited the number of broadcasters who had access to this form of speech. More important, once CBS founder William Paley had demonstrated the success of selling advertisements, the licenses became so valuable a commodity that alternative uses of the radio airwaves were gradually squeezed out of existence, except for broadcasting in a small part of the available spectrum specifically reserved by the FCC for educational purposes.

The results of this history should be well known to most readers. In the United States, communications media are held in private hands under varying conditions of government influence. Comparatively, the resulting structure is the most *laissez-faire* broadcasting in the world, although those in the industry inevitably compare themselves not to their colleagues in other nations but to those in the newspaper field in this country. As a result, we have set up an enduring and inevitable tension: broadcasters consider their status "second-class citizenship" and continually press for elimination of the content restrictions placed on them as conditions upon which their licenses are granted.

We believe that these conditions imposed on common carriers and broadcasters are efforts to achieve other values in democracy besides those found in the strict adherence to the *laissez-faire* model. The tension between these conflicting values creates unique political problems to which we will turn after considering the alternatives to commercial ownership.

Public Ownership—Media in the United Kingdom

Despite the fact that many Western democracies share with the United States a tradition of a free and independent press,[20] most of them took a different route from telegraph, through telephone and radio, to television. While we shall discuss their approach as a single model, if one probes the precise details of policy there are as many different media systems as there are countries. As a partial remedy, we shall concentrate our attention on the British broadcasting system.

When the telegraph first became a possibility, policy makers perceived the medium as akin to an electronic mail system and thus the natural province of a postal system. The enormous investment costs that were necessary to put such a system in place only reinforced the belief that government had a legitimate role as provider of telegraph services. Finally, it would be difficult to overstate the importance that the closely packed European nations place on communications for defense and preservation of a cultural identity. Accordingly, telecommunications were brought under the aegis of government control, and laws were enacted that sought to ensure a government monopoly. The details of government policy differ considerably from country to country, but in the main, telegraph, and subsequently telephone developed as a service of a separate ministry or department of government, usually dubbed the "PTT," for posts, telegraph, and telephone. There they have tended to remain. In the British case, telephone service remained part of the Post Office until 1980 when a separate government-owned company, British Telecom, was established.*

When radio emerged early in this century, the natural inclination of these European democracies was to expand incrementally the concept of government ownership so as to incorporate

---

* Great Britain has also recently allowed a private telephone company to begin offering services, principally long-distance phone service, to businesses.

the new medium. Moreover, to European eyes, the chaotic American experience provided a sharp counterexample, which many saw as inevitably linked to private ownership. According to R. N. Vyvyan, one of Britain's early developers of radio, "Newspapers and big retail stores soon saw that broadcasting offered a wonderful opportunity for advertising their wares. . . . There were no regulations which forbade this. . . . It did not matter whether one station were interfering with another."[21]

European governments moved into broadcasting not only as an extension of what they had already been doing, not only to preserve and foster a national identity, not only to prevent the disruptions created by rampant growth, but also to limit what they viewed as crass, commercial exploitation of the unlimited potentials of broadcasting. With evident pride, Vyvyan continued:

> Great Britain was slow to start on general broadcasting. The restrictions imposed on private activities in England, while frequently annoying, are generally for the public good, and in wireless matters the British Post Office invariably investigated a new proposal thoroughly before sanctioning it . . . Conflicting interests eventually brought about an agreement to form the British Broadcasting Company, financed by these various interests, but under severe restrictions, wisely imposed by the Post Office.[22]

Most European democracies quickly recognized some important problems in applying the telegraph model of public ownership to broadcasting. These crop up primarily because in radio and television the service provider is also the principal generator of program content. Because elected politicians in a parliamentary system manage the various departments of government, direct involvement of a government ministry in radio could produce unwarranted distortion in the information reaching citizens. Accordingly, in many countries radio, and subsequently television, has been at least partially insulated from politics through some kind of publicly owned corporation specifically chartered to provide broadcasting services.[23]

Of course the difference most noticeable to citizens and consumers is the method of financing publicly owned systems. Instead of product and service advertising, the most frequent means of paying for broadcasting is to have users pay an annual tax on the sets in their homes. In Great Britain, for example, the fee now amounts to about $25 for a black-and-white set and $80 for color.

However, it turns out that only four countries (Britain, Japan, Sweden, and Denmark) "have a public service broadcasting system paid for directly and entirely by license fees."[24] In Canada, France, Italy, West Germany, Ireland, and Switzerland, to cite some prominent examples, the publicly owned systems are at least partially funded by advertising of commercial products, usually under very restricted conditions.[25] In other cases, monies are allocated from general tax revenues. However the broadcasting system is funded, the important principle is the effort to provide the broadcasting authority with the financial independence necessary to make independent judgments about allocations for the costs of program development and signal maintenance. This strategy can be only partially successful: while governments can write laws guaranteeing this independence, the political reality is that yearly requests for funding from general tax revenues or occasional proposals to raise the tax on sets make the broadcaster susceptible to informal influence.

The argument most frequently raised in favor of this method of financing radio and television is that it allows broadcasting to be unlinked somewhat from popular consumerism; though this is not totally true, public broadcasting does allow other societal values to be factored into broadcasting decisions. In the case of the British Broadcasting Corporation (BBC), the Board of Governors—which holds legal title to BBC property, is responsible for policy, and exercises oversight of management—is charged with directing broadcasting "in the public interest."[26] As described by the Crawford Committee, which recommended the creation of the board in 1926, the governors are "trustees of the national interest in broadcasting."[27] Whether or not the board is able to put its stamp on broadcasting, however, has in fact varied markedly over the years, depending primarily upon the board's relationship with the director-general it appoints to be operationally in control of the BBC staff.

A germane example of values outside the marketplace that might be pursued under public ownership might help clarify the point. The larger European countries emphasize the civic importance of equality in the receipt of broadcasting signals. The BBC in Great Britain (and Radiodiffusion Television Française [RTF] in France) made sure that every area of the countryside was reached by a transmitter before starting a second network. In the process the national networks nearly exhaust the spectrum available to television. Larger audiences could be obtained if transmitters were concentrated in London and Paris (much as there are seven VHF channels in New York City), but then viewing options in some areas of the country would be sharply reduced.

Equality of reception is but one example. Educational goals and cultural enrichment can be given weight as values that should be promoted in programming in addition to popularity. And, what is important for this study, rather than complaining about public-service commitments forced upon them by government regulations,[28] European broadcasters spend a great deal of time debating how well they are performing their role of informing and educating citizens and whether or not their programs conform to the national interest. Defending his organization against attacks in the British press, Alastair Milne, the current director-general of the BBC, recently drew an example from radio of the subtle interplay between the values of cultural enrichment and popular demand that must be considered in programming within a publicly owned system:

As far as Radio 1 is concerned, it was the government of the day in the sixties that urged a pop channel on the BBC because pirate radio has squatted on other nations' wavelengths. . . . Now 30 percent of all BBC listeners tune in to Radio 1, and Radio 1's audience has an age profile some 10–15 years below that of the other radio services. Anyone who asks that the BBC should give up this service has not thought deeply enough about the *real* nature of public service broadcasting; its vitality depends upon offering the widest cultural choice *and* on addressing itself to the whole community, not to a part singled out by education or class.[29]

Just as the United States Congress established public broadcasting in 1967, so many European systems have been slowly loosening their publicly funded monopolies. Many now permit limited advertising to supplement tax revenue or receiver fees.[30] The British now have four networks, while the French, Germans, Italians, and Swiss have three.[31] In many instances this loosening has entailed the elimination of the absolute government monopoly. In 1955 Britain allowed the creation of the Independent Television Authority (ITV), which functions as a commercial network, drawing large audiences away from the two BBC channels. Competition definitely forced the BBC to change its programs to maintain its audience share and thereby diminished the degree to which the cultural values of education or class could permeate broadcasting. Even so, the present-day Independent Broadcasting Authority (IBA) is controlled by a board of governors appointed in the same manner as the BBC's governors, operates under very strong government regulations, and is very far from the model entrepreneurial ownership we experience in the United States. In fact, George Wedell has argued in *Broadcasting and Public Policy* that British broadcasting is in reality a single system with two variants rather than a dual system.[32]

Subsidized Access—The Netherlands

Historically, the Dutch have lived in a society "characterized by an extraordinary degree of social cleavage" and governed by an abundantly pluralist political system.[33] The polity has remained remarkably stable, effective, and legitimate, despite deep religious and class divisions that separate the population into "distinct, isolated, and self-contained" groups.[34] The Dutch refer to their style of politics as "pluriformity"; their political system emphasizes the values of pluralist democracy. The Dutch broadcast media both reflects and magnifies this social diversity: "The main principle as it is now stated is that pluriformity in society must be reflected and strengthened by pluriformity in the media: in broadcasting, airtime should be available to independent organizations in relation to proven support given to each of them."[35]

Specifically, in Holland the government provides the transmitters for two television and five radio networks, but most of the actual programming is produced by independent groups and organizations that meet certain qualifications as codified in the law. An independent broadcasting authority, Nederlandse Omroep Stichting (NOS), oversees the allocation of time and generates programming that compensates for gaps in that produced by the various broadcasting organizations. But the NOS has no authority to intervene in the content of those programs produced by the independent broadcasting groups.

In the briefest of terms, groups are allocated a given amount of broadcast time by demonstrating a certain level of viewership or listenership for their programs. Once awarded air time, these groups all experience a natural tension between responding to and emphasizing their group interests and boosting their own membership through programs that appeal to the widest possible audience. At present, nine organizations have met the following qualifications for substantial access to the airwaves: (1) they must be legal, nonprofit entities; (2) broadcasting must be their principal activity; (3) they must aim to satisfy the cultural, religious, or ideological needs of the population in such a way that their broadcasts can be considered as being of general benefit to the community; (4) they must not threaten public order, morals, or national security; (5) their programming must be varied and must include information, education, and cultural material as well as entertainment; and (6) they must have at least 150,000 contributing members.[36]

The distinguishing feature of Dutch broadcasting is the way access is subsidized based on audience numbers. Each would-be broadcasting group must be able to demonstrate the number of dues-paying contributors to the satisfaction of the broadcast commissioner. The 1965 broadcast law specifies the minimum dues that broadcasting organizations must collect from individual citizens, and grants them the exclusive right to publish guides that list and describe their programming. That is, subscriptions to these guides may be the basis for documenting membership. For some of the broadcast organizations the guides also provide an important source of income.

Membership is not based solely upon tastes in radio or television programming but is rooted in the social and political cleavages of Dutch society. Of the nine broadcasting organizations, four have religious affiliations (Roman Catholic, orthodox Protestant, liberal Protestant, and evangelical), one is linked to socialist labor organizations, and four are neutral in that they have no strong ideological or religious connections. Moreover, most of the broadcasting organizations have alliances, formal or informal, with political parties in the Dutch Parliament (see table 6.1). They may be either associations with a definite membership or foundations with supporters or contributors. Operationally, for some broadcasters these affiliations with other institutions may be tangential; others clearly draw their strength from their ability to use organizational ties outside broadcasting to reinforce their membership. For example, political scientist Aaron Lijphart cites several examples in which edicts within the Catholic church have served to buttress support for church related media.[37]

TABLE 6.1

*Principal Broadcasting Organizations in the Netherlands,
with Affiliations and Time Allotments, 1987*

Organization	Religious or Ideological Affiliation	Party Affiliation	Number of Members (thousands)	TV Time (hr/wk)	Radio Time (hr/wk)
NCRV	Orthodox Protestant	Anti- Revolutionary	532	11.5	64.0
AVRO	neutral	Liberal	807	11.5	64.0
VARA	socialist	Labor	580	11.5	64.0
KRO	Catholic	Catholic	641	11.5	64.0
VPRO	Liberal Protestant	Radical and Pacifist	330	7.0	38.5
TROS	neutral	Liberal	701	11.5	64.0
VOO	neutral	None	877	11.5	64.0
EO	Evangelical	Conservative Protestant	329	7.0	38.5
NOS	Government-Operated Network		N/A	85.5	37.5

SOURCES: Herman Wigbold, "The Shaky Pillars of Hilversum," in *Television and Political Life: Studies in Six European Countries*, ed. Anthony Smith (New York: St. Martin's Press, 1976), pp. 199–215; *Broadcasting News from the Netherlands*, No. 1 (Hilversum, Netherlands: Nederlandse Omroep Stichting, Communications Department, January 1985); and telephone interview with Margaret Ottink, International Affairs Department, NOS, March 15, 1988.

Among these groups, allocations for air time are apportioned in plateaus according to membership. Category A organizations have over 500,000 members and receive the most time (10 hours per week on TV and 65 on radio); B-level broadcasters, which must have over 300,000 contributors, receive about half the maximum air time (5 hours and 35 hours, respectively); while the lowest category, C, must qualify with 150,000 members (for which they receive 2.5 television hours and 13.5 on the radio).[38]

In addition to these regular broadcasters, the act permits the NOS to allocate time (usually one hour per week) to "candidate organizations" of 40,000 or more members for a trial period of two years, by which time they must cross the 150,000 threshold and become full members of the broadcasting club. In the years since 1965, several organizations awarded candidate status have been dropped when they failed to garner viewership, but at least four others have won a viewership and gained acceptance.

The first five organizations in table 6.1 were established between 1924 and 1926, a reminder that, from its very beginnings in radio, Dutch broadcasting has been characterized by alliances between programmers and interested listeners. In fact, the diversity of programmers and their organizational basis was not too dissimilar from the range of interests that leapt into radio broadcasting in the United States during the 1920s. But in Holland the diversity became cemented, probably because it was a manifestation of the sharp cleavages in Dutch society.

Lijphart describes four *zuilen* (literally, "pillars") or vertical social blocs that cleave Dutch society and politics: Catholic, orthodox Calvinist, and secular groups that divide into liberal and socialist blocs.[39] These divisions began around the turn of the century when religious groupings demanded equal subsidies for their schools, and in succeeding years established hospitals, sports leagues, social clubs, banks, travel organizations, and numerous other institutions. Socialists followed suit, each bloc hoping that its institutions would form a base from which it could become a majority of the Dutch population.[40] In time, social divisions became mirrored in politics and the mass media. Each bloc has its own political party, geographical stronghold, interest groups, and newspapers.

The divisions among these groups are very sharp; for example, 87 percent of "regular" Catholics report reading a Catholic newspaper, while 66 percent of the Reformed church membership read a Protestant paper. The solidity of readership among the Catholic bloc was undoubtedly heightened by a 1954 church edict concerning Catholic newspapers, which urged all Catholics "to support these and these alone." In broadcasting, these divisions continue in somewhat muted form today. For example, KRO argues that it "deserves its right to exist from the 600,000 Dutch people who support the KRO through a special type of membership. It will not be a surprise that 95 percent of them are Roman Catholic."[41]

Collectively, the original broadcasters are known as the "pillars of Hilversum" after the town in which the transmitters, offices, and studios of the broadcasting industry are located. The 1965 Broadcasting Act, however, opened access for new groups that could carve out an identity among Dutch listeners. Since that time, four organizations have risen to the status of major broadcasters, three of which are neutral (that is, nonpolitical) in their orientation. EO, the evangelical organization, was founded in 1967; it attained "candidate" status ("as if by Divine miracle," as

EO described it);[42] passed the C threshold in 1972; and moved into the B ranks in 1982. TROS and VOO were originally pirate stations that decided to come in from the North Sea under the new policies. As TROS, the first and largest of the newcomers, describes its *raison d'être*:

In the sixties . . . many Dutch people could no longer identify with the traditional organizations. These organizations were using the new television medium as they had used the traditional radio medium, for informative and expressive purposes without sufficiently wondering whether the public wanted this. The TROS on the other hand adopted the adage: We are there for you.[43]

But the open system allows even more diversity of access: a provision of the 1967 law permits the NOS to grant time to minor broadcasters ("kleine zendgemachtigden") in order to satisfy cultural, religious, or spiritual needs not adequately addressed by the other programming. These groups are not primarily interested in broadcasting but are, nonetheless, "sufficiently representative of a current group or opinion to justify the use of radio and television and to arouse a reasonable interest in their broadcasts."[44] Thus charitable societies, emerging political movements, and political parties are given small amounts of time. For example, at 10 P.M. every Monday night, right after the major NOS news broadcast, the parties with members in Parliament are given ten minutes on a rotating basis to state their views on current issues. By agreement, the prime minister appears every Friday evening in an interview program conducted by the organization to which that time has been allotted.

The Media Act passed by the Dutch parliament in April 1987 significantly revised many details of broadcasting policy, strengthening in many respects the position of the various broadcasting organizations *vis-à-vis* the NOS. For example, the act split NOS's duties as the provider of broadcasting facilities from its role as a programmer supplementing the offerings of the membership broadcasting organizations. The transmitter functions were assigned to a new, independent corporation, the Netherlands Broadcasting Production Company (NOB).

At the same time, the act changed the allocation of air time to various programming entities, expanding the percentage reserved to qualified broadcasting organizations from about 55 percent up

TABLE 6.2

*Minimum Percentages of Programming
Categories Required of Broadcasting
Organizations in the Netherlands, 1987*

Entertainment	25
Informational	25
Cultural	20
Educational	5

Source: Compiled from data in *HilverSummary*, November 1987 (Hilversum, Netherlands: NOS, 1987), pp. 2–3.

to 70 percent. The act allocated 20 percent of the available air time to NOS (for news, national events, culture, and sports) and set aside the final 10 percent of the available air time on the existing two transmitters for a wide range of minority broadcasters.

Furthermore, the 1987 act established "minimum levels" of different categories of programming which broadcasting organizations must produce and left the allocation of 25 percent of total air time to their discretion. For example, under these levels, which appear in table 6.2, broadcasters must insure that at least a quarter of their broadcasts constitute informational programming. Entertainment programming, meanwhile, must constitute a similar 25 percent, but can be expanded upward to 50 percent of the allocated air time, if broadcasters decide to use all their undesignated time for entertainment. The new law also required that at least 50 percent of the programming of these broadcasters be produced domestically.

Perhaps most significantly, the act provided for a third television channel to begin transmitting in April 1988, enabling each channel to take on a distinctive "color" depending on the type of broadcasters it carries: Nederland 1 contains programming by religious or political broadcasters; Nederland 2 offers programming targeted at more general audiences by the "non-ideological" or neutral broadcasters; and Nederland 3 is reserved for NOS and approximately ten other small nonmember broadcasters, including churches and political parties.

Because Dutch broadcasting is less likely to be familiar to the reader than either the U.S. or BBC model, we will briefly discuss two additional topics: its organizational structure and its financing.

Finally, the 1987 act rearranged the governing structures of broadcasting, providing a new layer of insulation between the broadcasters and the government of the day. Formerly, the Minister of Culture was responsible for such administrative arrangements as allocating air time, distributing funds, checking membership rosters, and monitoring compliance with broad program content guidelines. Now a new National Media Board will be responsible for these duties. Since the government appoints the members of this board, we cannot be certain whether this new buffer will make a real difference, although we should emphasize that the "heavy hand of government" on broadcasting in the Netherlands has been very light indeed.[45]

Approximately three-quarters of the funds for broadcasting in the Netherlands are paid by citizens through their license fees for reception sets. Individual citizens may also choose to support one or more broadcasting organizations through membership contributions or subscriptions to their program guides. The remainder of funds for the NOS system come from commercial advertisements, which have been permitted since 1965 on a limited basis through time allotted to the Television and Radio Advertising Association (STER). Ads occur, both on radio and TV, in blocks just before and after the NOS news broadcasts. Interestingly, from 1965 to 1970 newspapers were compensated for the presumed loss of revenue out of a "press fund" surcharge collected from advertisers.

Media Problematics in Democratic Systems

In modern democratic societies, the issues surrounding free speech through communications media yield to no easy solution. Basically, the attendant problems are a consequence of the fact that the electronic media inevitably create vast inequalities in political speech. The existence of telecommunications media thus injects into the policy arena the highly contentious questions of whose voice will be amplified and what accountability will constrain one's use of mediated speech. Behind these issues lies the matter of content, the exercise of editorial judgment by whomever controls the conduits of electronic speech. The higher the exclusivity of the media, the more intense these questions. By providing more channels, therefore, the new media may serve to lessen conflict over access both as a matter of rights and of practice.

Effective political speech, however, not only requires a transmitter, it requires an audience as well. An audience results from social investment that produces habitual behavior, whether it is the compulsion to answer a ringing telephone or to turn on the television each night. Both elements—technological possibility and the creation of social habit—are essential to any medium. This realization is necessary in defining communications policy. While we can conceptually distinguish the transmitter function from the editorial role, as the Dutch have done most formally, in practice the two cannot be so neatly separated. An audience is not, in short, a product of happenstance; it results from the editorial decisions (that is, content) of those who communicate through a medium. This proposition applies quite clearly in the case of broadcast media, but it holds equally well for the telephone: if, for example, the proportion of obscene or telemarketing calls becomes too high, for many subscribers the utility of answering the telephone will collapse.

In broadcasting, we should not minimize the definite stake that those who provide the conveyance have in the messages that are communicated. That is essentially the dilemma confronting the Catholics and socialists in Hilversum: should they dilute their content in order to reach out more broadly? But this problem faces policy makers and broadcasters in England and the United States as well: if the mass media are used too extensively for advocacy or civic affairs, they will become less massive. Much as we might like to use the mass media as a broadly encompassing and involving instrument of civic democracy, we cannot. They must be used sparingly and tangentially to be preserved.

Before we begin to chant a litany of the problems created by electronic media, we should recognize and appreciate the contribution they make to the essential tasks of a responsive and responsible political system. The mass media bring with them some rather spectacular benefits to democracy. In fact, unless some form of mediated communications are available to a society, democracy may not be possible beyond a finite and compact *populus*. The larger and more complex a society, the more significant grows its need for extensive communications to conduct democratic politics. Without mass-communications media, democratic politics in each of the arenas discussed above—in elections, in governance, in civic participation—would simply not be possible on a national scale in a country the size of the United States.

The discussion of problematics to which we now turn needs to be introduced with three caveats. First, none of the comments that follow is intended as criticisms of those individuals who operate mass media under any of the three models we consider here. We seek rather to analyze the implications of the structure in which communications media function. Given that we are dealing with contradictory values, each system will demonstrate weaknesses that are the concomitants of its strengths. A second limitation results from the fact that our attention will be primarily directed toward the broadcast media. We might equally well analyze the impact of the printed press or the telephone and telegraph. Third, while the list of problems generated by media in a democracy is intended to transcend national differences, we should be cognizant that we view these issues through an American lens. An observer grounded in a European tradition might invoke a very different inventory. Our task is, however, to understand the evolving changes in American politics, so we will concentrate on that perspective, using the other two models as the means to expand our awareness of what is possible to achieve in broadcast policy.

With these caveats in mind, let us turn to the problems that occur in any democracy regarding whose voice will be amplified by the electronic media, and what accountability will circumscribe one's words. We will discuss seven interrelated problems. We start with one that is primarily a matter of accountability, then discuss three that fall mainly into the access domain, and finish with three more that are essentially accountability problems.

The Creation of an Informed Citizenry

The great contribution of electronic media to democracy should occur in the widespread distribution of public-affairs information to citizens. In a sense, most of the provisions under which media operate in democratic societies are intended to achieve this fundamental goal, so we shall be discussing this matter throughout this section. We can, however, point to some specific measures designed to ensure that radio and television promote public political education.

In the United States, the government imposes regulations on privately owned broadcast companies as a condition of their licenses to operate. These regulations will be studied in detail in the next chapter, but we will summarize them briefly here because they constitute efforts in the U.S. context to deal with media problematics.

The Communications Act of 1934 and its subsequent amendments contain numerous specific provisions that affect the content of material broadcast; they also provide a more general directive to uphold the "public interest, convenience and necessity."[46] While the concept of the public interest is extremely vague and controversial, the FCC has used this authority to order radio and television stations to devote a certain amount of their programming to the public's business. Until recently stations applying for license renewals have been required to document the hours they have devoted to news and public affairs in years past. In addition, within their news programs, television stations have been required to give "reasonable coverage" to controversial questions or issues within their communities. The commission has wisely been loath to formulate a general definition of what is reasonable; instead, any disputes under this provision are settled on a case-by-case basis, in which the decisions of the broadcasters are usually given the benefit of the doubt. A further requirement upon broadcasters is for "fairness" (section 315) in news reporting. Under this provision, treatment of controversial issues is supposed to be free from editorial bias imposed by the broadcaster. Quite recent court rulings, however, have thrown this requirement into question, and it remains uncertain as to whether the Congress will provide a firm legislative basis for the Fairness Doctrine. Finally, licensees have been required to give a certain amount of their commercial time over to public-service announcements. In the American case, the mechanisms of compliance work retroactively, during considerations of relicensing or through the FCC complaint process or, finally, through court action. In each case, the burden is placed upon those who would alter the amount and quality of public-affairs information.

Recently the FCC has been moving to mitigate some of these

requirements. In early 1981, noting that competition among the eight thousand commercial radio stations had led to the development of "all news" formats, the FCC relieved radio licensees from their news and public-affairs requirements. The FCC argued that the public interest was satisfied by the balance of programming among radio stations and did not require enforcement within each station's offerings. In another move, the commission has told television stations that they no longer have to submit with their license renewal applications the voluminous logs that document their efforts to meet this obligation. A recent FCC ruling led to the elimination of the Fairness Doctrine as unconstitutional on its face. However, as of early 1988, the matter had not been resolved and the issue was pending both in the courts and before Congress.

In the Netherlands, each broadcasting organization is required to offer comprehensive programs embracing information, arts, entertainment, and so on. Recently, however, the popular TROS organization in effect challenged the seriousness of this commitment by offering wildlife films as informational programs. After much contentious debate, a new minister of culture finally forced TROS to produce and transmit a current-affairs program. In any case, the NOS is charged with presenting a major news show every night between 7 and 8 P.M. so that, on the whole, this goal is well achieved within the structure of Dutch TV.

In Great Britain, the Board of Governors holds the requirement for education in current affairs very high on its agenda of the type of programs it expects the staff to produce. Current affairs constitutes a major division within the BBC; its mandate includes both one-time documentaries and regular program slots such as *Panorama*, a popular show that has run for thirty years. In fact, over the years the current affairs division has led the BBC staff into some nasty confrontations with the Board of Governors and the government of the day on precisely this issue. Several times documentaries have been withheld from broadcast or revised to satisfy complaints from officialdom. On the other hand, more latitude has been given to the news division, which has been world-famous for accuracy and detail in reporting. Again, the strength of this organization is a direct result of the values instituted in the Board of Governors, charged with acting in the public interest.

The American experience yields a complicated assessment. First of all, one finds an important distinction between network corporations and local broadcasters. To be done well, public-affairs programming and news can be costly. Broadcast executives are hard-pressed to invest substantial money in an area that they do not see as profitable. However, this basic tendency is not absolute: over the years the national television networks have viewed their news operations as items of corporate prestige and have been willing, within limits, to support them beyond the "bottom line."[47] In addition, the importance of documentaries, the Sunday interview shows, and other public-affairs specials have waxed and waned, but in general they have been maintained at least partially out of a commitment to the goal of civic education and partially because, if they are not shown too frequently, programs of this sort will draw an audience (as the popularity of CBS's *60 Minutes* reveals).[48]

Writing in the early 1970s, however, one observer from overseas came to a rather dismal conclusion:

It is almost impossible to compare the amount of regular current affairs and documentary output of public service organizations like the BBC in Britain, ARD in Germany, and NHK in Japan with the American commercial network's serious programming in prime time; the ratio is more than 20 to 1.[49]

With the growth of news programming and magazine shows, the imbalance has become somewhat less, but the basic conclusion remains true.

Among local broadcasters, moreover, the commitment to public-affairs programming has been honored only begrudgingly. The budgets for news and current-affairs shows have generally been small and the shows usually deliberately placed at times of low viewership. Similarly, because they bring in no revenue, public-service ads appear much more frequently in the late-night slots than in prime time.

The American system necessarily entails an antagonism between the goals of broadcasters and the interests of a democracy. Regulation becomes odious, minimally observed, and not very successful in accomplishing its purposes. Congress could certainly enact more precise requirements that would move public-affairs information into the prime-time hours. But to do so would only exacerbate the situation and invite constitutional challenges.

Beyond quantity, moreover, there are abundant critiques of the quality of news programming in the American system, where popularity produces profits. Several content analyses of the network evening news shows are available that second-guess the editorial decisions of television executives, finding them overly reliant on values of drama or suspense, focused on personalities and conflict, superficial in detail, and so forth.[50] In general, these are not so much criticisms of the impact of government regulation as they are complaints that in a privately owned system, news presentations will be responsive to the tastes of viewers but less responsible in terms of the information that citizens need to participate actively and effectively in public life.

In this domain, the public corporation model clearly performs in a fashion superior to the other systems, probably because the objective of creating an informed citizenry lies closer to the central goal of the broadcasting organization. While private broadcasters do have a commitment to public affairs, to some degree this objective is antagonistic to the basic purpose of profit-making broadcasters. All the efforts of government regulation will not erase that fact.

The Dutch experience led them to create NOS to fill the program gaps of the broadcasting organizations. Private interests would not spontaneously solve this problem. In some cases, organizations direct their programs toward their narrow groups; in others they downplay public affairs in reaching for the broadest possible audience. Herman Wigbold cites only one broadcaster (VPRO) out of the nine that continues to produce high-quality programs and does not shun controversy. That organization has made an explicit decision to remain in the smallest category of broadcasters.[51] In other words, it has eschewed the value of expansive popularity in preference for its own view of the public interest.

The Conduct of Elections

Democratic elections necessitate communication between candidates and voters. Because elections are the basic means for providing democratic influence, the weeks immediately before an election constitute a special period in which the legitimate requirements of contending politicians for access to the airwaves are greater than at other times. We examined the constraints under which the media operate in several other democracies in addition to the three nations used as model cases and, in every instance, we found that media laws or practices make some special allowance for election communications.

In the Dutch system, each party that puts forward a full slate of candidates receives the same amount of transmission time. These broadcasts are scheduled at the end of the day's programs so that they are available to those who wish to see them but do not intrude upon regular viewing habits.[52] In addition, the broadcasting organizations frequently stage interviews and debates among the major candidates. Such programs do not have to give equal time to all candidates.

"Party political broadcasts" are the primary vehicles through which British politicians can address the nation during election campaigns. The basis for arranging these broadcasts is found not in laws but in precedents established through agreements reaching back into the 1930s. Representatives from all parties with members in Parliament meet with officials from the BBC and the IBA to negotiate an agreement as to how much time will be made available to each party.[53] The governing party and its leading opposition have been given equal time; smaller national parties, such as the Liberals, have received about half their allocation. Other minor parties qualify for some time if they run candidates for at least fifty seats. The parties are entirely free to determine the content of these broadcasts, which normally run five to fifteen minutes. The BBC exercises no editorial control, even though it might be liable for libelous statements. Party broadcasts are also transmitted simultaneously through the IBA system, which is prohibited by law from producing them on its own or from allowing parties or candidates to purchase advertising time.

It is a matter of some importance that the procedure for allotting time is largely informal, occurring as a matter of BBC policy rather than of law or regulation. As a result, one cannot be sure whether minor parties have been given time based on their representation in Parliament or the votes they received in the last election. This question can be critical to the practical results. For example, during the 1983 election, the alliance between Liberals and Social Democrats garnered almost as many votes as Labour, but received far fewer seats in Parliament. Because of its performance, the Social Democratic/Liberal alliance was awarded five party broadcasts of ten minutes each during the 1987 general elections, the same as the Conservative and Labour parties.

Neither Great Britain nor the Netherlands allows political commercials. This policy is more generally the rule than the exception: political scientists Howard Penniman and Austin Ranney report that of sixteen publicly owned systems, most of which are in Western European countries, twelve do not accept commercial advertising of any type.[54] They examined intensively six democracies and discovered that France, West Germany, and the United Kingdom prohibit political ads, while Italy, Canada, and Venezuela do not. Only Venezuela has the completely unrestrained system we enjoy in the United States; Canada allows parties, not candidates, to purchase time and places a limit on the total time available to them.

In the United States, several provisions of the 1934 Communications Act influence the access to the electronic mass media that political candidates and parties enjoy during election times. Most important, broadcast licensees are mandated to make "reasonable time" available to candidates for federal office, on either a paid or free basis at the broadcaster's discretion. Section 315 provides, moreover, that candidates must be given "equal opportunities" to use the station during election times. If broadcasters sell ad time to one candidate, they must make equal time available to the opponents.[55] They must, furthermore, sell a reasonable amount of time to all federal candidates at the same rate, equivalent to the lowest rate they charge their best customers (section 312).

While on its face the equal time rule (section 315) appears justifiable and innocuous, its operation means, among other things, that until very recently broadcasters could not sponsor debates between major party candidates that excluded minor candidates. As of 1983, the FCC had granted and the courts had affirmed an exemption to the equal time rule for candidate debates. Regularly scheduled news broadcasts are also exempt from the equal time rule, but many local broadcasters are not aware of this.[56] In general, broadcasters find it easier to balance news coverage by having a report from one campaign matched by a report from the other.

Critics of these regulations argue that their practical effect is to decrease the total amount of public affairs and news devoted to election campaigns. Broadcasters, for example, cannot put together a preelection special in which journalists report upon the credentials and proposals of the major candidates. Nor can they provide free time to the candidates with reasonable prospects of winning so that they could present their ideas in more detail than a sixty-second spot ad allows. In other words, the uses of radio and television that are comparatively common during election campaigns in Europe are virtually prohibited in the American system.

Many of the most vocal critics of these regulations are broadcasters themselves who rail against what they see as an unjustified abridgement of the First Amendment precept of a free press.[57] By directly shaping the amount and content of public-affairs programming on the airwaves, these regulations turn them into second-class journalists. Their concerns are complemented by many who criticize the current practices of political broadcasting in the United States as inadequate, even though they might not trace the causes back to government regulation. Attacks on political ads as misleading, superficial, image-building, and emotional are fairly common.[58] Politicians are frequently criticized for staging media events on the assumption that entertaining visuals will be more likely to appear in nightly news broadcasts directed to mass-audience tastes.[59] All of these complaints essentially derive from a privately owned broadcast system together with the attempts of policy makers to ensure that the broadcasters' influence over election outcomes cannot be exercised unduly.

Interest-group Access

While those involved might not think it so, media coverage of government officials and election candidates is an easy problem compared to the difficulties of providing access to political activists. Essentially, the problems arise in establishing who merits entry to the media. The legitimacy of threshold tests is clearer when public office or candidacy is involved than when one is confronted by a vast array of groups and secondary leadership attempting to raise a plethora of issues.

Without a detailed content analysis to prove the contrary, we assume that the news reporting process is fairly standard across the three different systems. Individuals and groups make it into the news to the extent that their actions are deemed newsworthy by the editors and producers.[60] While the canons of journalism may differ slightly, and allowances for depth of coverage may permit more detail in one system than the others, group activities will be covered as television news to the extent their actions are exceptional, dramatic, conflictual, visual, and influential.[61]

Surmounting this problem is, in fact, the *raison d'être* for the Dutch broadcasting system. Group access becomes routinely handled through quantification of the threshold requirements: a group that has more than 40,000 supporters becomes a candidate organization, one of 150,000 members qualifies for so much time, and so on. Although this process takes effect only after these groups become somewhat established in terms of membership and organization, the broadcasting law directs the NOS to grant small amounts of transmission time to emerging political and social forces. Given that most of the broadcasting organizations connect tangentially to political parties and social groups, they are likely to be on the lookout for causes, issues, and social forces that they can espouse. Access for these groups is secured as a normal part of the system's current affairs programming. As a result, the media system functions like a vacuum cleaner, sucking political issues into media coverage.

Of the three systems, public ownership places the highest burden on the editorial judgments of the broadcasters. The provision of civic information at BBC, for example, has historically been divided into separate news and current affairs sections. The latter, which concerns us here, is rooted in the immediate postwar period, when Director-General William Haley decided that the news operation should return to its rather timid style before the war, not gathering the news independently but merely reporting information generated by others. In contrast, the current affairs group drew upon a long tradition of documentary films and feature journalism. In the early 1950s Grace Wyndham Goldie, Britain's first television critic, joined the BBC and assembled in the current affairs division a team of journalists dedicated simultaneously to controversy and public education.[62] "Above all, they value flair, imagination, and the ability to tell a good story. They are skeptical of official sources, and often adopt a man-in-the-street view of society." As a result, the civic education provided by the BBC originates in "two tribes, each with its own traditions,

values, and heroes."[63] As we shall see later, its current-affairs programming has led the BBC into a number of crises with the political authorities. The efforts of this division have been independent,
innovative, and creative—especially in comparison to the news
division.[64]

Inevitably the BBC structure depends heavily on the judgment of its broadcasters as to the social forces that merit coverage
and the content of their programs. Groups that feel aggrieved by
the content of their reports or by the absence of coverage can
appeal to the BBC Board of Directors, but that agency acts primarily as a restraint on the BBC staff rather than as a positive goad
pushing it in specified directions.

Meanwhile, in the United States this issue has become the
subject of the most bitter and protracted struggle in broadcasting.
Essentially, the debate revolves around the question of how far
broadcasting should lean toward the common carrier model of a
communications medium versus the newspaper model. Obviously, broadcasters strongly prefer newspaper status, with its
extensive protections under the First Amendment. Critics and
groups that desire access to the airwaves believe that such a policy
would concede unwarranted power to a very few voices. They
prefer that broadcasters be forced to open their transmissions to
content (for example, programming and advertisements) that
these groups would provide.

The Fairness Doctrine, a compromise advanced by the FCC
under its mandate to provide for the public interest, required
broadcasters "to spend a reasonable amount of time discussing
controversial issues of public importance and, when they do so,
provide a reasonable opportunity for opposing views to be
heard."[65] But, in broad terms, the Fairness Doctrine merely defined a battleground on which groups seeking direct access could
launch their crusade. In the late 1960s media reform groups such
as the Office of Communication of the United Church of Christ and
the National Citizens Committee for Broadcasting (NCCB) filed numerous court cases and complaints to the FCC arguing specific
instances of poor performance under the Fairness Doctrine. In
one pivotal case in which these groups were active (*Red Lion
Broadcasting Co. v. F.C.C.*), the Supreme Court upheld the constitutionality of the Fairness Doctrine, advancing the argument that
"It is the right of the viewers and listeners, not the right of broad-

casters, which is paramount."[66] In 1974 Congresswoman Patsy Mink of Hawaii provided another example by filing a complaint with the FCC against a radio station in West Virginia that refused to broadcast a program supporting her legislation directed at strip-mining. The commission's decision was the first that affirmatively directed a station to cover a specific controversial issue because of its importance to the local community.[67]

Organized groups pressing for access to the airwaves have not been content merely to rely on the broadcasters to address adequately all sides of controversial issues. These groups have also pressed for the right to create their own messages and have broadcasters transmit them as paid advertisements. For a short time, the American Cancer Society was able to force broadcasters to accept antismoking spots to provide balance to cigarette commercials, based on an FCC interpretation of the Fairness Doctrine that was later withdrawn.[68] The broadest possible interpretation of the doctrine was narrowed significantly, however, when the Supreme Court ruled, in CBS v. Democratic National Committee, that broadcasters should be able to choose how to comply with the Fairness Doctrine rather than being forced to accept paid advertisements promoting an opinion.[69]

The CBS ruling meant that broadcasters did not have to sell away their editorial judgment, but it still left them bound by the Fairness Doctrine. Virtually nobody was satisfied with this balance. Broadcasters were restive under regulations that cannot be constitutionally imposed on newspapers,[70] while citizen groups seeking access argued that they were locked out of the major avenue of effective political speech. Then, in 1987, the U.S. Court of Appeals threw the whole area open to question by ruling that the FCC could determine whether the Fairness Doctrine was constitutional. When the FCC subsequently decided that the doctrine was unconstitutional, groups demanding access to the airwaves immediately began to exert pressure upon Congress to provide a firm legislative basis for fairness in broadcasting and went to the courts for redress.[71]

But throughout the 1980s, many citizen groups had directed their energies toward securing entree to television through the public-access channels of cable systems.[72] Initially, many cable operators offered these access channels as part of their franchise applications. But frequently citizen groups found that promises went unfulfilled or so underfunded that programming on access channels suffered from poor quality and infinitesimal audiences. By the 1980s, the rise in program providers for cable meant that many operators preferred to use the existing channel capacity for such paying services as premium all-movie networks or home shopping channels. Again, the tension between the interests of service providers and those of groups demanding access ran high. Then, passing the Cable Act of 1984, Congress stipulated that municipalities could require public-access channels as a condition of the franchise.[73] Even so, it is clear that the dispute over access will continue, probably in the courts, where much of it has taken place in the past two decades.

The Dutch case demonstrates that television can provide a voice to many groups. Access can be structured in a noncontentious system and can facilitate the electronic discussion of public issues. Yet the recent evolution in the Netherlands toward more broadly appealing and bland programming should remind us that the message delivered affects the size of the audience reached. In the United States, the television networks have built huge audiences that would likely be driven away by a large dose of advocacy from different social groups. That is, if these groups gained the access they would like, in the process they probably would diminish the utility of the medium and the very reason they so ardently desire the airwaves. Moreover, as unsatisfactory as it is to social groups of all stripes, the present construction of policy is a direct outcome of the American emphasis on individual freedom and the importance of private property in guaranteeing political liberty. It is likely to remain that way.

In addition to the provisions determining access, whether by government spokesmen and their opponents, by competing candidates, or by groups raising controversial issues, other aspects of media policy in the United States have attempted to promote diversity in the policy and political views presented over the media through restrictions on ownership of broadcast stations. No single corporation is permitted to own more than one station in a single media market and no more than six nationally. Efforts have also been made to prohibit the owner of the newspaper in a community from also owning a television station. The operating assumption behind these policies is that diversity in ownership will promote diversity in content. That premise remains unproved and subject to some skeptical comment. Some critics charge that television news and entertainment programming remain all too similar despite these policies; others maintain that the Fairness Doctrine rather than ownership restrictions has been responsible for what diversity in sources can be found on American television.

This problem simply does not exist in the European system. In England the BBC and the IBA own all the transmitters and licenses; in the Netherlands it is the NOS. The American regulations are a direct consequence of our system of private ownership combined with our reluctance to accept the consequences of that monopoly structure. Nevertheless, while the Europeans may have created acceptable procedures for containing these problems, Western Union's early history of intrusion into the structure—and quite possibly the content—of news reporting through cooperation with the Associated Press should provide a clear illustration that the dangers are not mere myth.[74]

Responsiveness to Social Groups

In another sense, media organizations in any democratic society must respond to the general climate of opinion within which they broadcast. Here the problems involve a general responsiveness to citizen pressure and complaints rather than efforts to deal with requests for access. Given the extensive reach of broadcasters into modern society, it is entirely understandable that political leaders of various persuasions and secondary opinion leaders continue to raise a stream of criticism about the appropriateness of values embedded in broadcast programming. In each of the three media systems studied, for example, critics have complained about the level of sex and violence on entertainment shows. To cite another example, Dean George Gerbner and his associates at the Annenburg School have shown that entertainment programming can project systematic stereotypes about different social groupings.[75] Naturally, complaints that derive from systematic continuities in the programming offered by broadcasters can become matters with considerable political strength.

The mechanisms for coping with these disputes are much the same as those already discussed. While individual shows broadcast on the Dutch system may trigger protests, over the long term, any group differing with the overall content of programming feels a natural pressure to join the system and produce shows it deems more suitable. For example, in railing against drugs, abortion, homosexuality, strikes, and left-wing critics of South Africa, the newest organization (the evangelical EO) has returned to an older style of broadcasting: it never gives its opponents an opportunity for rebuttal.

The BBC's Board of Governors provides a ready-made lightning rod for pressures of this sort. Criticism is certain to be brought into their discussions on "the perennial problems of taste, language and sex in our programs."[76] Observers of the BBC find that the board's control over the "creative people" in the programming departments is extremely delicate and difficult.[77] The board can act as a general barometer and nudge programming in desired directions, but basically it cannot provide direct control over the staff.[78]

In the American case, these problems are handled in two ways, one of them informal, the other of untested legality. When they have overall complaints about programming standards, pressure groups have urged the FCC to exercise its rule-making authority and pressured both networks and stations to adopt codes of standards. One of the most notable examples was provided in 1974 by the efforts of Action for Children's Television (ACT), which pushed for requirements that each station carry fourteen hours of children's programming each week and to ban ads during those hours.[79] In a related effort, responding to pressure from Capitol Hill, FCC Chairman Richard Wiley was instrumental in getting the National Association of Broadcasters to add to its Television Code a "family viewing period" from 7 to 9 P.M. each night.[80]

Citizen groups have also used the licensing process to develop leverage over programming. In 1966 the U.S. Court of Appeals for the District of Columbia directed the FCC to permit the United Church of Christ to file a "petition to deny" challenge to the license renewal of a Mississippi broadcaster for discriminating against its black viewers.[81] The decision opened the door to numerous efforts to rectify complaints about programming tastes and employment practices through renewal decisions. The threat of these lengthy battles, moreover, led many broadcasters to enter into agreements directly with citizen groups.[82]

Finally, from both the political right and left, citizens have used economic pressure on broadcasters. In 1976 the NCCB published an analysis of violence in prime-time shows and ranked advertisers according to their sponsorship of violent programs.[83] Four years later the Coalition for Better TV announced that it would monitor prime-time shows for "sex scenes, gratuitous violence intended to injure, and abundant profanity" and urge a boycott of sponsors of the offensive programs.[84] According to *Advertising Age*, the networks responded by asking Hollywood producers to tone down the shows.[85]

Systematic Media Problems of Governing

During nonelection periods, problems infest relations between public officials and the broadcast media. These entanglements have two aspects: negative restraints such as censorship and control of the content of information broadcast, on the one hand, and proactive efforts to transmit the government's position to the people, on the other. Most Americans find it difficult to see that anything positive or legitimate could be at stake here; to our way of thinking, the first aspect involves direct government abridgment of First Amendment rights and the second constitutes propaganda and manipulation.

We will discuss the protections against government censorship later. Here, we consider the legitimate needs of public officials to communicate their policies and proposals to citizens both in times of national emergencies and under less extreme conditions. Basically, the problem is one of establishing an appropriate balance between communicating information required in representative processes and restraining government dominance. The latter can come in two forms: (1) government officials can have so much access that their voices drown out opposing views, and (2) government access can be a convenient cover for undue influence over content.

The great bulk of communication between government authorities and citizens takes place through news reporting. In all three media systems studied, broadcast journalists function comparatively unfettered by laws or regulations that influence the content of their reports. Rather, the actions of public officials have a certain news value that producers appraise in deciding which stories to cover. To be sure, politicians work hard to boost their own visibility by anticipating these news judgments and accommodate to them in an effort to reap coverage.[86] In the American system, moreover, local television coverage overwhelmingly emphasizes the activities of incumbent congressmen over those of competing elites.[87] But neither of these relationships necessarily means that the editorial judgments are unduly swayed by political influence. In this area, broadcasters are able to lay claim to the traditions of independent journalism developed in the printed press.[88]

Government involvement in both the public ownership and the subsidized access systems raises the possibility of government misuse of the airwaves. As a result, these systems generally go to great lengths to protect against abuse. As in most aspects of democracy, however, legalities provide only so much protection; the system works because of the norms and behavior of the people who staff the machinery.[89] For example, until quite recently the French government viewed the broadcast system primarily as a means for countering the antigovernment press. For much of its history and through repeated restructurings, French broadcasting has been under the control of the minister for information[90] and has implemented the general philosophy enunciated by President Georges Pompidou:

Being a journalist working for the ORTF is not like being a journalist elsewhere. Whether you like it or not, ORTF is the voice of France. You who write the news must always keep in mind that you are not talking for yourself, you are the voice of your country and your government.[91]

In England and the Netherlands, such a statement would produce an immediate political crisis. In the United States, broadcasters would view the Pompidou approach as a glaring example of exactly what the First Amendment was designed to prevent.

Even disregarding the impact of the First Amendment, the system of private ownership appears to be the model best suited to prevent undue domination of the news process by government officials.

There have been, however, instances in each system in which public officials have, in effect, commandeered the media and used them for direct contact with citizens unencumbered by editorial control or broadcasters' influence. The Dutch system of dealing with these problems is the most elaborately specified. As mentioned, every Friday evening after the regular cabinet meeting, the prime minister is interviewed by whichever organization happens to have been allocated that night's programming. The procedure falls well short of simply turning the airwaves over to the politicians. While the official can say whatever he or she wants, editorial processes are at work in the questions journalists pose. In addition, regular party broadcasts occur every Monday night at 10 P.M. on one of the two television channels, and there are six radio broadcasts per week on two of the five channels. These are assigned on an equal, rotating basis to all parties having representation in Parliament. The parties control this time totally, without editorial intrusion from the NOS or any other broadcast organization. They are, therefore, like the party political broadcasts that occur in England only during election campaigns.

Under the Dutch media law, the prime minister can also request time to address the nation, so-called ministerials. These are rarely used; only two such broadcasts were aired during the 1970s, and in both instances there were strong complaints that the situation did not merit the request.[92] Under even more extreme circumstances (for example, in times of war), the minister of culture can direct the NOS to turn over the transmitters to a designated government spokesman. This authority has not been invoked since World War II, but it remains "on the books."

In the United Kingdom, the prime minister can also claim a ministerial broadcast that the BBC and the IBA must grant. Initially, by informal agreement among the political parties, these broadcasts "were 'meant' to be confined to non-controversial measures: they were to be used to make factual pronouncements, to explain legislation approved by Parliament, or to appeal to the public to co-operate in national policies."[93] During the war years they acquired a distinctly national policy, national interest flavor.[94] However, if the opposition believes that the ministerial has transgressed into matters of party controversy, it can claim a right of reply. The procedures followed in these instances are revealing. The opposition chief whip contacts his counterpart in the governing party, claiming reply time. The government then has three days to yield a reply, after which the opposition can appeal to the BBC Board of Governors to arbitrate the matter.[95] Notice that the first recourse is to the politicians, then to the broadcasting agency.

In the American system, the procedures for handling these circumstances are even less formal. The president requests time to address the nation on a matter of national urgency, and the networks have complete discretion whether or not to honor the request. The situation is inevitably political. On the one hand, the networks wish to be responsive if the subject merits the address, but, in order to preserve the surprise, presidential advisors are often reluctant to reveal the content of the message. For their part, the network executives are cautious: the procedures have been abused in the past by presidents wishing to bolster their popular performance ratings, and there will inevitably be requests from the party out of power for equal time. On occasion, one or more of the networks have refused presidential requests. While the private ownership of media provides a clearer capacity for broadcast authorities to resist the inappropriate demands for access by government officials, the consequence can be a good deal of unfortunate behind-the-scenes politics.

The very openness of the Dutch system works to finesse these problems, perhaps because political leaders have abundant access built into the regular broadcasting. Moreover, their policies, pronouncements, and opinions are offset in the normal course of broadcasting by those of the diverse broadcasting agencies, expressed in their current affairs programs.

Government Censorship

The American Constitution was drafted after a prolonged period of perceived injustices, in which government was viewed as intervening illegally in private affairs. The resulting sharp limitations on the authority of government clearly reflect those concerns. Two hundred years later, fear of government censorship still constitutes one of the strongest complaints voiced about proposed policies or political maneuvering. The absence of government control is, in fact, the *raison d'être* for the American media, much as access is the prime value in the Netherlands and national interest in the United Kingdom.

Even so, the United States is not entirely free from instances in which political officials have tried to use their power and authority to determine the content of broadcast transmissions. In fact, among the countries studied, the honors in this regard probably should go to the Netherlands. The Dutch government has only retroactive powers, which it has exercised only once: in 1933 it punished the socialist broadcasting organization by withdrawing an hour of transmission time. The action was roundly condemned at the time; the other broadcasters refused to fill in the blank air time. These tactics have never been repeated, although on a few occasions the government has issued official reprimands for "deplorable" programs, such as VPRO showing a naked girl impersonating the queen and a scene in which VARA placed the pope in juxtaposition with some attractive young women.[96] Recently, the Parliament has seriously debated eliminating this power, on the principle that the government should have no more power over broadcasters than it has over newspapers.[97]

In large measure, the system in which different broadcasting interests are interlaced with political forces produces respect for one another's freedom of action and expression, if only to retain those benefits for oneself. In many ways, therefore, the Dutch have been able to replicate in their broadcasting the condition of the American press during the early days of the Republic, when the press was partisan and free speech was therefore synonymous with a free press.

In the United States, the privately owned media take a very different posture. Privately owned, limited in number, and reaching mass audiences, they have assumed an Olympian posture toward politics and government. They are objective, uninvolved observers. Frequently they pose as the watchdog of the people whose task is to bring to light the failings and hypocrisy of politicians.[98] In the process, they become natural targets for political activists who resent their power and independence and would steal their audiences. Not surprisingly, there have been instances in which political authorities have exerted tremendous pressure upon broadcasters to alter the content of their messages.

The lowest days in the relationship between broadcasters and public officials came during the Nixon administration. The much-publicized attack by Vice-President Spiro Agnew on the networks as a "tiny enclosed fraternity of privileged men" was only the tip of the iceberg. Meanwhile, in private conversations with executives at all three networks, Nixon aide Charles Colson maneuvered to kill the CBS series entitled *The Loyal Opposition,* in which Democratic party leaders in Congress were given an opportunity to reply to presidential broadcasts. Colson argued that when the president speaks as president (rather than as a party politician) the Fairness Doctrine did not apply and that giving the Democrats equal time would restrain "the President's right of access to TV."[99] In an internal White House memorandum to H. R. Haldeman that came to light in the Watergate investigations, however, he candidly noted that the FCC had "always ruled that the Fairness Doctrine always applies."[100] Nonetheless, he concluded his memo with the promise to pursue "the possibility of an interpretative ruling by the FCC . . . as soon as we have a majority on the FCC."

On a more public front, Clay T. Whitehead, head of the White House Office of Telecommunications Policy (OTP), argued that the networks exhibited an intolerable absence of accountability. In the months after Nixon's landslide reelection, he insinuated that the administration might use the Fairness Doctrine to challenge the license renewal of local broadcasters who failed to provide political balance to what he saw as a strong liberal bias in network programming.[101] He also made administration support for extending the license period to five years conditional on increased affiliate pressure on the networks.[102]

Four years later, when the Carter administration took office, they "regarded the White House-based OTP as politically dangerous because there might be an irresistible urge for White House staff members to use it to prod the FCC to advance the president's political interests."[103] Accordingly, in order to give this agency some political distance, they pulled this operation out of the White House and established the National Telecommunications and Information Administration within the Department of Commerce.

On the broadest level, the BBC is intended to be responsive to the British regime, as political scientists use that term to describe the set of values and principles that undergird a political system. On an operational level, while the BBC is very far from the circumstances of French broadcasting, in a variety of instances the BBC has yielded to pressure from the government of the day. Equally numerous have been situations in which the corporation has resisted political pressure.

During the General Strike of 1926, when the BBC was just

being formed, Winston Churchill, then Home Secretary, tried to take over broadcasting in order to disseminate the government's position.[104] He was quickly rebuffed by Lord Reith, the first director general. A more serious case, which established several precedents for later disputes, occurred in 1932, when the BBC proposed to interview a German submarine commander.[105] The Cabinet felt strongly that the interview should not be transmitted but was reluctant to use its formal statutory powers to prohibit it. Instead they dispatched the postmaster general, under whose jurisdiction the BBC fell. He put fierce pressure on the chairman of the board, J. H. Whitley, even threatening to have the king cancel a planned visit to Broadcasting House. Although Reith resisted, Whitley decided to cancel but sent a strong letter to the Cabinet:

In the early stages of its existence one of the greatest obstacles to overcome was the impression that the Broadcasting Company had become a Government Department. This unfortunate idea is by no means eradicated today. There have been occasions on which, without justification, Government suggestion or Government domination has been alleged by critics. The Corporation is a new and important experiment in the management and control of a public utility service. Its progress is watched with closest attention, not only in this country but in most foreign countries. Its detachment from the Government of the day has been a cardinal element in its international prestige.[106]

Having won, the postmaster general wrote back, arguing that he knew of no stipulation that his power could be exercised only in time of national emergency, but adding: "It is certainly not my desire to invoke, nor have I invoked, this power of prohibition which if generally exercised would make me a Censor of the programs of the Corporation. The matter was, I understand, regarded by the Cabinet as quite exceptional . . ."[107]

In *Governing the BBC*, media historian Asa Briggs reports on four instances in which the government took strong exception to the BBC's programming.[108] Three involved broadcasts the BBC planned to transmit. In 1936 the BBC yielded to government pressure and cancelled interviews with a communist and a fascist. During the Suez Crisis in 1956, the BBC failed to rally behind the policies of the Eden government by editing the foreign broadcasts so as to deemphasize the growing criticism within Britain by the Labour party leader. Finally, in 1972 the BBC again refused to cancel a show on the Ulster question that featured eight different viewpoints by prominent spokesmen.

The most recent, and possibly most severe, confrontation occurred in 1985 over another proposed show on Ulster political extremism, featuring an interview with an elected politician from Sinn Fein, the political wing of the Irish Republican Army. The crisis was initiated by remarks of Prime Minister Margaret Thatcher; visiting in Washington shortly after the hijacking of an American plane, she joined President Reagan in condemning manipulation of the media by terrorists.[109] When asked by a reporter, she stated that she would "utterly condemn" a program that featured an IRA spokesman, although she was not at the time aware that such a show was being readied for transmission. Home Secretary Leon Brittan, learning of the BBC plans in press reports, wrote to Stuart Young, the BBC chairman, to ask that the show be cancelled, although he was quick to point out that "he fully recognized the editorial freedom of the BBC" and "did not wish to exercise powers of censorship."[110] The board met, viewed a tape of the show, and, against the urgings of the Director General Alastair Milne, voted to postpone its transmission until the offensive parts could be replaced. The BBC staff reacted with a one-day strike and employees in the IBA joined them, blacking out all radio and television news and live programming in Britain.

To admit that government censorship had occurred, however, is very far from saying that the independence of the BBC has been totally compromised. Despite a huge outcry in the British press, the incident was not unprecedented; one can reach back right to the initiating years of the BBC, to the 1930s, to find two cases that were rather strikingly similar. Inevitably, this struggle is a direct consequence of public ownership of the electronic media.

All three media systems—the American, the British, and the Dutch—have mechanisms and procedures for coping with the problems that inevitably plague the use of media in a political democracy. In general, because of the marked separation of media and state in the United States, the processes of responding to these situations are less formal and more conflictual. In Europe, many of these problems have been thought through carefully, resulting in specified and established procedures. The level of formalism is greatest in the Dutch case, where the rules of the game are debated in Parliament and have been the subject of bitter political disputes. Despite the trauma of the recent censorship fiasco in Britain, the government acted within its legal rights and according to precedent.

Each of these structures for broadcast media accentuates the values rooted in a particular notion of democracy. Each conception, moreover, brings forth a different perception of the goals of broadcasting and the political problems to be avoided.

The American system emphasizes the values of independence from government interference. Antipathy toward government's coercive potential naturally led to privately owned media. The system works: comparing media systems, political officials in the United States have the least authority over the structure and content of the media. Our system works to protect individual rights, in this case the private rights of those who would speak. But, in so doing, we create such massive inequalities in political speech that we are not willing to live with the consequences. To compensate, we have propounded regulations intended to mitigate these political problems; that is, strings have been attached to the electronic media (common carrier provisions, broadcast regulations). These are designed to mitigate political abuse by service providers, but in the process they create an enduring conflict of values and a constant political tension. We will study this tension in depth in the next chapter.

In England, broadcasting is undertaken in the national interest, and the machinery that produces programs for broadcast is geared to continual self-scrutiny on this point. As a result, British broadcasting performs better on such dimensions as creating an informed citizenry. Moreover, while complaints are prevalent, less conflict occurs over access questions than in the United States. Nevertheless, the very relationship to the state and to the public that permits the BBC to fulfill, however adequately or inadequately, its role as trustee of the national interest necessarily embroils the corporation with the government of the day. A strong commitment to the independence of broadcast journalism shared by politicians and broadcasters alike serves to lessen this conflict below the level encountered in other nations with a publicly owned system. Even so, the tension is still there, mostly beneath the surface but at times glaringly evident.

Broadcasting in the Netherlands is ideally suited to the creation and maintenance of pluralist democracy: "Dutch broadcasting is theoretically open to every pressure group, whether social, political, or religious, within the country. They proudly point out to visitors that their television system is the most democratic anywhere."[111] Access questions disappear. Censorship is minimal. Perhaps in the process of so much open discussion, the citizenry as a whole benefits as well. But whether it is the most democratic depends, of course, on one's definition of democracy.

Media Policy and Democratic Values

The preceding discussion of media problematics in a democracy reveals that differing global approaches to communications media accentuate different aspects of the media-politics interface. A given design will maximize certain values. In the process, however, the particular construction of media will intensify other problems. There is no ideal solution, except that embedded in the conception of democratic processes held most dear by a given polity.

Beyond this overarching conclusion, the comparative examination of communications policy yields three additional findings. First, the most recent developments in broadcast media may well indicate some convergence of the three systems. Second, the European systems of structuring media appear to exhibit a different patterns of adaptation to the new media. Third, exploring different ways in which the public policies of these other nations make existing media available to their societies can serve to expand the range of alternatives that the United States might apply to the new media.

Technological Determinism?

This comparative, and comparatively brief, examination of media policy in three different nations reveals hints of a technological imperative. Despite the best efforts of national policy makers to mold broadcast media into patterns that conform to

233

political values, there is considerable evidence that these systems are drifting toward similarity. That evidence can be found in the increasing competitiveness of television broadcasting and in the policy tentatively adopted toward the newer forms of communication.

In Great Britain, four broadcast channels—two of them offered by the BBC—now compete for viewer attention. As a result, the capacity to plan the whole agenda of programming offered the public has been somewhat diminished. The result underscores the argument voiced by Director-General Milne that the real nature of public service means offering the cultural choices of the whole community and not just those dictated by an educated or class elite. In a nutshell, here is the essence of competition: competition between channels, competition that transcends the effects of ownership, competition not based on commercial profit but on an effort to achieve organizational goals such as promoting the public interest.

In Holland, critics of broadcasting point out that competition among programmers on the two channels has generated pressures toward similar programming designed for the most popular tastes. The fact that three of the new entrants have been "neutral" with respect to religious or class divisions is also evidence of the impetus to reach more broadly across the demarcations of Dutch society. As one of these newcomers described its contribution:

The arrival and growing popularity of TROS was not only a matter of the Dutch population abandoning the traditional "pillars," but also of the development of the television medium. In addition to its informative and expressive function, Dutch television has increasingly acquired an entertaining function.[112]

Critics of this development point out that this statement of philosophy ignores its consequences: no politics, no controversy, no stimulation of civic involvement.

TROS's success has, however, spilled over into the programming of the other broadcasters. Most current affairs programs were moved out of their flagship positions at 8 P.M., quiz shows began to pop up, the program guides became cheap and slick, and holiday trip prizes were used to attract membership.

So while public policies have produced distinctly different systems, the combination of media and competition may well be reducing those differences. This finding, however, does not constitute a major refutation of the central point of this chapter. Television in England and Holland will maintain its distinctive character. Despite the drift toward mass audiences, we will not witness the emergence of television similar in structure or content to that of the United States. This is a matter of nuance; the values inherent in public policy will maintain their dominant grip.

How are the Different Systems Adapting to the New Media?

Each system is coping with the strains posed by the communications revolution in characteristic ways. If Great Britain, France, and Canada are examples, nations with publicly owned systems appear to be better able to decide what systems bear promise and to invest heavily in those ideas. Consider videotex: in several nations, implementation is further along than in the United States. In France, the telephone system has been moving rapidly to place terminals in homes, to provide directory assistance and classified ads. Meanwhile in England, the Prestel videotex is far ahead of any comparable system in the United States, and the BBC has an operating teletext system, CEEFAX.

A closer look, however, reveals some important qualifications in this picture of progress, especially in instances in which the emerging media threaten the existing media systems. In the case of cable television, for example, most European nations are far behind the United States, in large part due to the vested interests and resistance that comes with government agencies protecting their "turf." In Great Britain, the 1982 report by the Hunt Commission—the latest in a long succession of government-sponsored evaluations of broadcasting—proposed minimal restrictions on the operators of cable systems, a suggestion that was roundly criticized by both the BBC and the IBA.[113] By the mid-1980s the Dutch government had sanctioned only very limited experiments with cable, in order to judge the impacts on broadcasting interests.[114]

Meanwhile, in the United States private corporations are investing large sums in a whole range of possibilities. Many of these efforts are failing: witness the demise of many programming services for cable television. Videotex provides a more explicit illustration. Despite substantial investment, many commercial attempts to establish a viable videotex system have collapsed. By and large, the industry has abandoned the European approach in which the operator functions as a "information utility" much as a newspaper provides information on a broad array of topics to individuals clustered in small geographical units. Rather, the successful developments have come in two very different strategies for using the technology: providing highly specialized information to small groups of subscribers who may reside in very dispersed communities; and using videotex as a means of communication among subscribers rather than each individual interacting only with the service provider.

A critic of the American system of private entrepreneurship might correctly complain that yielding the new media to private interests wastes substantial amounts of investment capital. But in the long run, such a strategy is more likely to create structures and media that satisfy real consumer demands. If that is the ultimate goal of providing communications media, then the American system appears to be better positioned to capitalize on developments in this field across the broad range of possibilities.

Finally, while the direction of policy in the European systems regarding the new media is by no means clear, there are some tentative signs that the national systems may have to yield on questions of ownership and control. Great Britain has recently allowed competition to develop in the telephone industry and appears to be moving in that direction in cable. In Holland, whether the tidy system of centralized control will have to give way to local autonomy in cable production is a lively political topic.

Models for American Policy?

Do the European systems of public ownership and subsidized access offer useful models for the United States? Evidently a corporation like the BBC will not flourish here; witness the low audiences for our Public Broadcasting System and a general lack of commitment to the financial integrity and political independence of the Corporation for Public Broadcasting.

At the same time, the European systems do demonstrate that the abiding American fear of government domination of political discourse may be a bit overstated. An organizational structure can be devised in which media systems enjoy ample protection from intrusion by the government of the day. Despite all the furor created by the British government's request to eliminate a portion of the BBC program on Northern Ireland, the heavy hand of government is applied only in very exceptional cases and then only lightly. Lawyers and constitutional scholars love to speak of "the slippery slope," intimating that one small abridgment will lead directly and inevitably to government tyranny. But the European examples indicate that it is perfectly possible for a political system to delineate the outer limits of state action without inevitably descending to the worst, most indefensible, undemocratic policies imaginable.

These arguments—which are the essence of the debate over media policy in European nations—are, however, difficult to raise in the American context. In fact, to the degree that monopoly or near-monopoly conditions are essential to accomplishing the values inherent in the public ownership model, the whole thrust of the communications evolution in the United States points in the opposite direction. An expanding number of conduits will inevitably undercut the ideal of a medium that effectively promotes the national interest.

On the other hand, to the extent that more channels become available, the ongoing evolution in communications creates the possibility of subsidized access for political groups along the principles of the Dutch system. To establish media such as the civic videotex system that Benjamin Barber recommends[115] is certainly feasible and defensible, even given our own strong emphasis on freedom from government domination of political discourse. The Dutch have demonstrated the possibility of engineering a system free from government intrusion that still offers access to the airwaves for those who wish to exercise their right of free speech electronically. In so doing, such a structure would mitigate the inequalities that currently characterize the discussion of politics and policy through the existing media.

Broadcasting in the Netherlands demonstrates that it is possible to establish a media system that serves other purposes than the protection of private property and a definition of the public good as the sum of individual interests. If Americans so wished, we could do better on equalizing access, nurturing the civic discourse, or addressing the common good. What is more, organizations could be designed to protect these functions against government tyranny. Even though one would not expect that such conduits would be utilized by anything approaching a majority of the citizenry, it would nonetheless be better to have them available for those who were concerned about public life.

In the next chapter we continue our study of communications policy in the United States, especially as it applies to the new media. Once again our focus will be on the recurring conflict between *laissez-faire* conceptions of press independence and a more interventionist strategy of promoting civic uses of the media.

CHAPTER 7

FREEDOM OF THE PRESS
AND THE NEW MEDIA

AT THE CENTER of communications policy in the United States lies an unresolved, and perhaps irresolvable, tension between two competing aspects of our free press tradition. On the one hand, we commonly understand a free press to be an independent and autonomous press—a press that decides what to publish or not to publish without interference from government. For only a press insulated from government is free to criticize it. But prior to World War I, legal protection for an adversarial press was still precarious in the United States; newspapers were successfully prosecuted for editorializing against our entrance into that war and pamphleteers received long prison sentences for leafleting in opposition to the military draft.[1] Much that is heroic in our tradition of civil liberties has to do with the struggle it took to undo the legacy of such prosecutions and to enshrine the principle of press autonomy at the center of First Amendment law.[2]

On the other hand, according to a more recent part of our free press tradition, the crucial democratic value is not an unregulated press but an accessible one. If it takes legal regulation to keep channels of mass communication open to the public and to diverse points of view, then so be it. Such regulation frees speech even as it restricts press prerogatives. For freedom of the press is not just the right of individual reporters and editors; it is the people's "collective right . . . to receive suitable access to social, political, esthetic, moral and other ideas and experiences."[3] Thus we license broadcasters as public trustees,[4] and we refer to all of the press as the eyes and ears of the public, the people's proxy, and so on. The point here is that we rely on the press as an instrument, almost an institution of democracy.[5] Publishers and broadcasters are not just private individuals entitled to the ordinary privileges of property owners but public servants entitled to special protection precisely because their freedom is indispensable to our freedom.

At law we distinguish defamation of a public figure from defamation of a private person, giving the press more room to err in its stories about the former so as to encourage press coverage of government and other powerful social institutions.[6] This distinction in libel law is not understandable if all we care about is preserving press autonomy pure and simple—for autonomy is equally at stake whether the press covers private persons or public figures. What is *not* equally at stake is the needs of democracy itself. Freedom to comment on public issues is not just one freedom among many; it is the very antecedent of democracy—a precondition for any effective exercise of the freedom to vote, run for office, or petition government for redress of grievances. ("Speech concerning public affairs is more than self-expression; it is the essence of self-government.")[7] Democracy presupposes a collective debate on the public issues that is "uninhibited, robust, and wide-open."[8]

When we talk this second language, we value freedom of the press not so much as an end in itself—a matter of individual self-expression needing no further justification—but as a means toward the final end of an informed and alert citizenry. As the philosopher Alexander Meiklejohn described the more collective or public view of free speech, "The point of ultimate interest is not the words of the speakers, but the minds of the hearers."[9] In similar language the Supreme Court has upheld legal restrictions on broadcasters by noting that "it is the right of the viewers and listeners, not the right of the broadcasters, which is paramount."[10]

The two ideals—press autonomy and public access to the press—are never wholly at odds with each other. To the contrary, the classical liberal view, expressed in the metaphor of a marketplace of ideas, is that one produces the other. The liberal argument is that free competition among ideas permits truth ultimately to prevail.[11] But the notion of political debate producing truth is quizzical. Free inquiry on *scientific* issues serves the truth, but what is the truth on whether to have a NATO alliance or a food-stamp program? Political debate on such issues aims not at the truth but at the people's consent (whereas the notion of consent is superfluous in the scientific community—it is irrelevant whether the majority consents to Newton's laws of motion).[12] Thus it would seem better to rephrase the liberal theory of a free market in political ideas as follows: Given that there is no one truth by which to govern a people, we stake our all on the people's consent—on the virtue of living by policies to which we have at least agreed. But if popular consent is to have moral import, then it must not only be freely given; it must be an informed or knowing consent, preceded by and premised on a public debate in which we all have the opportunity to hear and be heard in turn. This freedom of opportunity will be maximized if government keeps hands off the spoken or published word.

It is revealing to review the line of cases that gave rise to the First Amendment principle that government has limited power to interfere with the content of speech. The paradigm was very much the radical demagogue,[13] the fringe press,[14] or the religious dissident[15] being censored by a government bent on policing the entrance to the marketplace.[16] Policing speech in these ways inevitably impoverished debate by closing the market to novel or unpopular views. To defend the autonomy of the press from self-serving governmental oversight was clearly to defend the public's First Amendment right of access to a full range of views.

But does ensuring the press's autonomy from government always secure its service to open debate? Or, in an age of media giants of the ilk of CBS or Time, does the end value of a rich and robust public debate require government today to play an active role in legislating public access to the media? The answer to these questions depends on how persuasive the metaphor of a free marketplace of ideas continues to be. And here, as is well known, American law gives not one but three answers. The applicable answer depends on whether the medium of communication is print, broadcast, or common carrier. A review of these three separate legal traditions is necessary before we turn to the issue of new media regulation.

Print Media: The Tradition of Press Independence

In regard to print media—newspapers, magazines, books, pamphlets, periodicals, leaflets, and so on—the emphasis at law is almost entirely on the value of autonomy. Apart from some narrow areas involving national security,[17] libel,[18] obscenity,[19] or incitement to illegality or violence,[20] government is wholly without power to object to the content of the printed page. Government cannot censor the press on the basis of some perceived harm in press coverage. Indeed, in the leading case involving a government attempt to restrain newspapers from printing a story—the Justice Department's suits against the *New York Times* and the *Washington Post* for printing the classified study of U.S. involvement in Vietnam known as the "Pentagon Papers"—the Supreme Court held that, notwithstanding the national security overtones of the case, the government lacked power to stop the presses.[21] As Justice Brennan argued in his concurring opinion, a direct causal relationship between the publication of the story and immediate harm to our troops would be necessary before the traditional autonomy of the press gave way to national security.[22]

Just as government can hardly ever require the press to drop a story, neither can it force the press to add one. In 1974, in *Miami Herald Publishing Co. v. Tornillo*,[23] the Supreme Court struck down a Florida law requiring newspapers that print an editorial attack on a political candidate's personal character or official record to offer him or her an opportunity to publish a reply free of charge. The Court specifically rejected arguments that right-of-reply laws were a necessary remedy to the alleged skewing of the marketplace of ideas wrought by economic concentration among newspaper publishers.[24] Instead, the Court found that right-of-reply laws would likely have a chilling effect on the editorial decision to criticize a candidate in the first place. Insulating the print press from government regulation, the Court concluded, was still the best way to encourage investigation and criticism of government.

Broadcast Media: The Tradition of Access to the Press

Public access to the media, not editorial independence, has been the driving value behind American regulation of broadcasting. Beginning with the Radio Act of 1927 and then again in the Communications Act of 1934, Congress took the position that the broadcast medium itself—the electromagnetic spectrum over which radio waves travel—was an inherently scarce resource owned by the public.[25] However, Congress seems never to have seriously considered the possibility that the government itself should run the medium. Instead, it settled on a system of public trustee licensing, in which private parties were assigned exclusive use of a broadcast frequency on condition that they use it in the public's best interest.[26] Thus, from the beginning, two things were true about broadcast regulation that were not true about print. First, government was in the business of licensing the electronic press and renewing their licenses. Second, at least in theory, government was in the business of monitoring the content of a broadcaster's programming to ascertain whether the broadcaster was indeed fulfilling the obligations of a public trustee.

The Communications Act of 1934 also empowered the Federal Communications Commission (FCC) to make further rules necessary to carry out the Act's provisions.[27] Historically, the FCC has sought to enforce three different kinds of access rights to broadcast stations: a guaranteed minimal right of access to radio and television for candidates in federal elections; a contingent right of equal access to radio and television for all political candidates; and the listening public's right to hear opposing points of view on issues of public importance. These three variations on the theme of access to broadcast stations are discussed below.

243

Access of Federal Candidates to the Broadcast Media

Congress has legislated an unconditional right of access for only one group of speakers: candidates for federal office. The Federal Elections Campaign Act of 1971 amended the Communications Act to require broadcast stations to give candidates for federal office "reasonable access" to their stations.[28] This has come to mean that, once the campaign has commenced, broadcasters must permit federal candidates to buy a reasonable amount of air time during prime time for their candidacy. Moreover, as is true whenever a broadcaster sells any candidate air time within forty-five days of a primary election or sixty days of a general election, the charge must not exceed "the lowest unit charge of the station for the same class and amount of time for the same period."[29]

Access of All Candidates to the Broadcast Media

The second meaning access has in broadcasting regulations is akin to balanced treatment or equity. For instance, the Equal Opportunities Rule[30] guarantees candidates for public office only a contingent equal right of access: if a broadcaster permits one candidate to use the station, then all other candidates for the same office must be provided an equal opportunity to use the station. What is at stake here is impartial treatment, or nondiscrimination. The fear is that broadcast stations, through a policy of discriminatory favoritism, could skew the outcome of elections, much the same way discrimination by railroads once skewed farmers' access to the market.

From the beginning, controversy has attached to FCC and congressional attempts to foster balance in broadcasting. Throughout American history, much of the press has been partisan rather than neutral, an adversary or advocate of specific political and editorial points of view.[31] The Communications Act and FCC doctrine have prohibited broadcasters from following this older, partisan press model. That model might have served democracy well in an era of small press powers competing with one another. But it ill fits the contemporary media environment, where even major cities are served by few television stations. If these stations have no obligation to provide time to candidates they oppose, then those candidates might be shut out of the local broadcast market entirely.

Access of Listeners to Diversity

The final and most important access right belongs to the listening public. This is their right to have broadcast stations used in ways that enrich debate on issues of public importance. Prior to its repeal by the FCC in 1987,[32] the great symbol of the listener's First Amendment claims upon broadcasters was the Fairness Doctrine. The doctrine, dating back to Federal Radio Commission policy in the 1920s,[33] required broadcasters "both to cover controversial issues of public importance and to broadcast opposing points of view on them."[34] The latter requirement is again a matter of balanced presentations; the former is a more radical mandate to broadcasters to air certain kinds of programs in the first place. The FCC justified the policy by stressing the inherent scarcity of broadcast frequencies, the public ownership of these frequencies, and the need to prevent domination of scarce public resources by the few to whom licenses could be granted. In a major decision upholding the constitutionality of the Fairness Doctrine, the Supreme Court specifically cited the scarcity of broadcast stations as legitimizing greater legal regulation of radio and television than of newspapers and magazines.[35]

In 1959 Congress amended the Communications Act in a way that strongly suggested congressional ratification of the Fairness Doctrine. The amendment exempted certain appearances of candidates on news programs from the standard equal time requirements.[36] But Congress further provided that the amendment "shall [not] be construed as relieving broadcasters ... from the obligation imposed upon them under [the Communications Act] to operate in the public interest and to afford reasonable opportunity for the discussion of conflicting views on issues of public importance."[37] The Supreme Court has characterized this language as expressing congressional acceptance of the FCC's view that the Fairness Doctrine inhered in the public-interest standard erected by the Communications Act.[38]

By 1982 a more conservative FCC began to express doubts about the Fairness Doctrine. In a 1985 report, the commission laid the ground for an eventual repeal of the doctrine by rejecting the view that Congress had ever statutorily authorized it.[39] The report also criticized the Fairness Doctrine for making broadcasters "more timid than they otherwise would be" in airing controversial programs.[40] The timidity was the result of the bureaucratic regulations triggered whenever a controversial program was broadcast. The 1985 report concluded with a call for comments on the FCC's proposal to repeal the doctrine.

Congress responded by passing legislation early in 1987 that expressly codified the Fairness Doctrine but President Reagan vetoed the bill. On August 4, 1987, the FCC formally announced repeal of the doctrine.[41] The commission argued that the "explosive growth" in new media technologies invalidated the original scarcity rationale for the fairness requirements. Even without legal intervention, technology was poised to provide a "multiplicity of broadcast voices."[42] Not only was the Fairness Doctrine therefore no longer necessary; the FCC faulted it for being counterproductive (chilling broadcasters from covering controversy for fear of triggering legal regulation) and unconstitutional (violating the editorial independence of broadcast journalists).

The repeal of the Fairness Doctrine is illustrative of the FCC's wider policy of deregulating the broadcasting industry. Already there are signs that the commission intends to abandon two important spinoffs of the Fairness Doctrine. These are the personal attack rule, which requires that any person or group attacked in a discussion of a controversial issue be given notice and a reasonable opportunity to reply,[43] and the political editorial rule, which gives any candidate disfavored by an editorial the right of reply.[44] The general counsel to the FCC has characterized the "legal standing of these rules [as] questionable, . . . because they may be deemed to derive from the fairness doctrine itself."[45]

In justifying its deregulatory policy, the FCC has stated:

What we have come to realize is that the First Amendment was, to quote Justice Stewart, founded on a belief that " 'fairness' was far too fragile to be left for a Government bureaucracy to accomplish. . . . If we must choose whether the editorial decisions are to be made in the free judgment of individual broadcasters, or imposed by bureaucratic fiat, the choice must be for freedom."[46]

If Congress and the courts side with the FCC in shelving the Fairness Doctrine, then the key legal distinction between print and electronic journalism will be a curiosity of the past. But the Supreme Court has yet to be heard from on this issue. It is worth recalling that the Court's landmark decision approving of the Fairness Doctrine contains language that suggests that the doctrine is rooted in statutory and constitutional law. The statutory argument is that there is no way for broadcasters to satisfy the public interest standard of the Communications Act,[47] except by obeying the essential mandates of fairness.[48] The constitutional argument, hinted at but not endorsed in the Supreme Court's decision, is that the public has a First Amendment right of access to the public airwaves. Broadcasters take their government license subject to this "paramount" First Amendment access right of their viewers.[49] Therefore, they not only can but must be required by government to "share [their] frequency with others and to conduct [themselves] as a proxy or fiduciary with obligations to present those views and voices which are representative of [their] community and which would otherwise, by necessity, be barred from the airwaves."[50]

Now that the FCC has repealed the Fairness Doctrine, it falls to Congress and the courts to settle the long festering issue of whether the sources of the doctrine go deeper than administrative policy.

Common Carriers: The Tradition of Separating the Medium from the Message

In the United States a third paradigm for regulation of communications is the common carrier model, applicable to the private and public postal systems, to the telegraph and telephone, and arguably to cable television and many of the other emerging new technologies.[51] The notion of a common carrier first grew up in regard to the post office and was then applied to the railroad. It soon became evident that if railroads were left wholly unregulated under a private property theory, economic incentives might lead them to prefer one customer to another, give lower rates or kickbacks to large farm customers in preference to smaller ones, or serve some routes and not others. The potential skewing of the market was enormous, and American law responded by imposing on private carriers certain duties of public or common carriage. These principles, which apply to communications as well as transportation carriers, are three:

First, common carriers have their rates regulated by government.[52] The justification is that these are private concerns peculiarly bearing on the public interest and usually enjoying a monopoly advantage made possible through state action.

Second is the principle of nondiscriminatory access: common carriers are legally obligated to accept all comers on a first-come, first-served basis and to charge equal rates for equal service.[53] Thus, for telephone and telegraph companies and mail carriers, there has never been a tradition of pure autonomy that would have allowed, say, Bell Telephone to monopolize its own lines for its own messages.

Instead, the third principle is that common carriers are precluded from publishing messages over their own medium. This is the principle of separating content and conduit; the carrier provides the pipeline and others supply the words. What purpose does such an enforced separation serve? A carrier that published over its own wire would always be in potential competition with its customers, always facing a possible conflict of interest between carrying its own messages and those of others. To avoid such discrimination, American law has historically insisted on a rigorous separation of the medium from the message in the case of the telegraph, the telephone, and the mail.

One recent example of the content/conduit distinction occurred in the 1982 consent decree severing the local Bell Telephone companies from AT&T.[54] Dating back to a 1956 consent decree, AT&T was restricted to providing regulated common carrier services.[55] These line-of-business restraints would have been eliminated in the antitrust settlement negotiated between AT&T and the Department of Justice in 1982. But in approving the settlement, a United States District Court modified it to bar AT&T from providing "electronic publishing" over its own facilities for seven years.[56] Without such a restriction, the court feared that AT&T "could discriminate against competing electronic publishers. It could, for example, use its control over the [telephone] network to give priority to traffic from its own publishing operations over that of competitors."[57] A similar common carrier restriction in the consent decree prohibited the divested Bell telephone companies from providing information services.[58] (Interestingly, however, the Justice Department has recently proposed lifting this restriction on the local Bells and allowing them to compete full force in the business of electronic publishing.)[59]

Common carrier law is generally studied in courses on commercial rather than constitutional law. This is unfortunate, because the principles of common carriage form an important free speech tradition—a tradition that brings to the fore the value of equal access to the media. In a democracy it is crucial that the people have the wherewithal to speak meaningfully, to reach others with their ideas. Private economic powers cannot be allowed to monopolize an entire medium of communication. Short of a monopoly, they cannot be permitted to use their ownership rights in a capricious or discriminatory manner.

Current Regulation of the New Media

The FCC, Congress, and the courts are currently struggling with how the new media fit with our inherited free speech traditions. A hodgepodge of regulations has resulted.

Cable Television

Cable regulations are currently an amalgam of print, broadcasting, and common carrier regulations. In line with the print tradition, the FCC has never required cable operators to obtain a license before commencing operations. Indeed, prior to 1965 the commission took the position that it lacked authority to regulate cable at all, because cable signals did not make use of the electromagnetic spectrum. But pressure to regulate mounted as cable came into its own as a competitor to broadcasting; by 1965 the FCC concluded that it could not adequately discharge its statutory duty to regulate broadcasting unless it regulated the competition emanating from cable. This theory that FCC jurisdiction over cable was "reasonably ancillary to the effective performance of the Commission's various responsibilities for the regulation of television broadcasting" was subsequently upheld in 1968 by the Supreme Court.[60]

The 1965 cable rules applied only to cable systems receiving their signal by microwave; in 1966 the rules were extended to all cable systems.[61] These rules fell into three main categories. First, "must-carry rules" obligated cable operators to carry the signals of any broadcasting station into whose market area the cable brought competing signals.[62] Second, "nonduplication rules" prohibited cable systems from transmitting programs shown on a local broadcasting station for fifteen days before and after the local broadcast.[63] Third, "distant import rules" conditioned the right of a cable operator to import distant broadcast signals into a local market upon a showing that such an act would not undermine the economic base of local broadcast stations.[64] These early rules showed the power of broadcasters to capture the federal agency that was supposed to regulate them and to use the power of the FCC to insulate broadcasting from serious cable competition for years to come.

In a second major regulatory wave in 1969, the FCC announced that it would apply the Fairness Doctrine, the equal opportunities rule, and the sponsorship identification rule (requiring the sponsor of a program to be announced and identified) to all programs subject to the "exclusive control" of the cable operator. Henceforth these core broadcast regulations applied on all locally originated cable channels but not on leased or public-access channels.[65] The 1969 FCC rules also required cable systems with 3,500 or more subscribers to provide locally originated programming.[66]

In 1972 cable regulation reached its high-water mark with the FCC's announcement of a set of comprehensive rules.[67] Must-carry rules required cable systems to carry the signals of all commercial television stations within a thirty-five mile radius of the community served by the system, as well as other stations in the same television market and all stations "significantly viewed in the community."[68] Nonduplicative distant signals could be imported, according to rules that differed for big cities, small cities, and rural areas. Perhaps most important, the 1972 FCC rules imposed on cable a novel obligation that had never been imposed on broadcasters themselves. Cable systems with greater than 3,500 subscribers had to set aside between one and four "access" channels —one for lease, one channel each for free educational and local government purposes, and a fourth for free public access on a first-come, first-served, free basis.[69] With respect to these access channels, the cable operator was to function as a common carrier.

Another of the 1972 rules imposed wide restrictions on pay cable channels. Fearing that such pay channels would siphon off the audience for free broadcasting, the FCC prohibited pay cable services from televising feature films more than three years but less than ten years old or specific sports events shown on broadcast television within the previous five years. The FCC also prohibited pay cable from accepting commercial advertisers and limited the total overall number of hours that pay operators could devote to sports and feature films to 90 percent of the total pay operation.[70] Bias against cable as a threat to "free TV" was apparent.

Since 1972 both the courts and the FCC itself have whittled down cable regulations. For the courts the problems have been constitutional; for the FCC there has been the additional political problem of how an administrative agency responds to pressure from the broadcast industry it is supposed to regulate. A review of the major post-1972 developments in cable regulation follows.

In *United States* v. *Midwest Video Corp.* (*Midwest Video I*), the Supreme Court upheld the 1972 rule requiring cable operators to engage in locally originated programming, but Chief Justice Burger warned in concurrence that this requirement strained the limits of FCC jurisdiction over cable.[71] In *F.C.C.* v. *Midwest Video Corp.* (*Midwest Video II*), the Supreme Court struck down the access channel rules as falling on the other side of the limit.[72] Avoiding the constitutional issue of whether access requirements violate the cablecaster's First Amendment rights, the Court disposed of the case on narrower, statutory grounds. The Communications Act prohibits the FCC from imposing common carrier obligations on broadcasters.[73] Given that the FCC is entitled to regulate cable only as a means to regulate broadcasters, the Court concluded that the FCC could not impose common carrier restrictions on cable either. Access rules are a kind of common carrier duty and hence lay beyond the commission's statutory authority.

In a 1977 decision that did reach First Amendment issues, the United States Court of Appeals for the District of Columbia struck down the FCC's restrictions on pay cable programming.[74] The court reasoned that while the inherent scarcity of broadcast frequencies justified legal regulation of the content of radio and television programming, cable's abundance of channel capacity left similar "content regulation" unwarranted. In a provocative line, the court found "nothing in the record before [it] to suggest a constitutional distinction between cable television and newspapers."[75]

Meanwhile, the FCC was having its own second thoughts about cable regulation. Beginning as early as 1974, when the FCC dropped the requirement of locally originated programming, there has been a steady movement at the commission to deregulate cable. Indeed, at the time of this writing, virtually all of the 1972 rules are dead. In 1980 the commission deleted the nonduplication rules and lifted virtually all restrictions on importing distant signals; the commission itself now requires no access channels although local franchises may. In 1985 the FCC declined to seek Supreme Court review of a lower court opinion striking down the must-carry rules as unconstitutional.[76] To a substantial degree, broadcast-style regulation of cable by the FCC is a faint shadow of its former self.

But as the broadcast model loses its hold on cable regulation, the common carrier model has come to the fore. In 1984 Congress passed the Cable Communications Policy Act, declaring its purpose in regulating cable to be to "assure that cable communications provide and are encouraged to provide the widest possible diversity of information sources and services to the public."[77] In pursuit of this purpose, Congress imposed two common carrier requirements on cable operators. First, Congress preserved in local governing bodies the discretion to require cable operators to designate a certain amount of channel capacity for public, educational, or governmental use (so-called PEG channels). These channels were to be held out to the public on a first-come, first-served basis,[78] with the operator retaining no editorial control over programming content.[79] Second, Congress required cable operators with thirty-six or more activated channels to set aside a specified amount of channel capacity for paid, commercial leasing by customers on a first-come, first-served basis. The cable operator was to retain no content control over leased channels either.[80] These requirements were not made absolute in the act, because the operator was permitted to program access channels not in fact being used for the purposes designated.[81] But, with this exception, the cable system was expected to be only the conduit, not the programmer of access channels—the cardinal distinction of common carriage regulation.

Cablecasters argue that the mandatory access provisions imposed on them are invalid under the First Amendment. "If a government required a newspaper to publish 10 pages of letters to the editor, you could be sure the publisher would have objections," a lawyer for the National Cable Television Association recently quipped.[82] Basically, the argument remains the familiar complaint that the cardinal premise for broadcast-style regulation—scarcity of channels—is absent in the case of cable television. This issue has never been resolved by the Supreme Court because, as we saw earlier, the major case striking down cable access requirements —*Midwest Video II*—did not reach First Amendment questions.[83] In the absence of a definite Supreme Court opinion, the lower federal courts continue to split over the constitutionality of access requirements. Some courts have remarked that mandatory access requirements for cable "pose particularly troubling constitutional questions"[84] and that *Tornillo* "casts considerable doubt on the government's ability" to impose access requirements on a communications medium that is not technologically scarce.[85] Other courts have upheld the constitutionality of access requirements, on the grounds that they serve the substantial interest muncipalities have in assuring "community participation in cable television production and programming."[86] The exact First Amendment status of the cable industry thus remains murky as of this writing.

Further clouding the picture is a 1986 Supreme Court opinion casting a constitutional shadow on the widespread municipal practice of awarding one cable company an exclusive franchise over a specific geographical area.[87] Cities typically defend the exclusivity of cable franchise awards by pointing out the scarcity of space on public utility poles for cable attachments, as well as the disruptive effect that installing and maintaining a cable system has on the public domain. But, in the case of *Preferred Communications* v. *City of Los Angeles*, a United States Court of Appeals in 1985 found that the public utility structures and other public property in Los Angeles necessary for the installation and operation of a cable system could physically accommodate more than one system. In such a circumstance, the court concluded that the First Amendment forbade Los Angeles from limiting access to a given region of the city to a single cable television company.[88] In 1986 the Supreme Court affirmed the judgment of the Court of Appeals, but in a manner that leaves open the crucial First Amendment issues. The Court agreed that the activities of cable companies "plainly implicate First Amendment interests,"[89] but the Court shied away from endorsing the legal standards set out by the Court of Appeals governing the awarding of franchises. Instead, the Court found that the case's factual record was too incomplete to resolve purely legal questions about the First Amendment rights of cable companies.[90] The case was therefore remanded to the trial court for resolution of all material factual disputes.

As of this writing, therefore, the legal status of cable television remains in flux. For all the legislative victories that the common carrier approach to regulating cable has won in recent years, recent judicial decisions make clear that the cable industry's First Amendment arguments against common carrier obligations retain a great deal of force.

Direct Broadcast Satellite

Direct broadcast satellite (DBS) is a video service in which television signals from earth are transmitted to high-powered satellites. The satellites then retransmit the signals directly to individual homes equipped with satellite receiving dishes. Because DBS satellites are capable of transmitting a signal up to forty times more powerful than conventional satellites, their retransmissions can be picked up by dishes as small as two feet across.

The FCC first approved DBS service in June 1982, setting aside a limited number of frequencies for it.[91] To date, no pure DBS service is operational, although RCA, Western Union, CBS, and COMSAT have received FCC licenses to offer DBS.[92] In 1983 United Satellite Communications did initiate a quasi-DBS service, using less high-powered satellites. But the operation folded in 1985, with a debt of $53 million.[93]

Technically, DBS is a broadcast service to which the full range of broadcast regulations in the Communications Act might seem to apply. However, the FCC has experimented since 1982 with a more flexible approach. Some DBS operators may choose to function as common carriers, providing satellite transmission capacity to customers who do the actual programming. The FCC's 1982 proposal freed DBS services of this sort (so-called common carrier DBS) from all broadcast regulations.[94] On the other hand, the FCC indicated that it would apply broadcast regulations to those DBS operators who elect to program directly through their satellite service.[95]

A 1984 federal appeals court decision throws into question the FCC's proposal to classify common carrier DBS as nonbroadcast in nature. In *National Association of Broadcasters* v. *FCC*,[96] the court held that the plain language of the Communications Act compelled the FCC to regulate DBS as a broadcast medium:

[The] test for whether a particular activity constitutes broadcasting is whether there is "an intent for *public* distribution," and whether the programming is "of interest to the *general* . . . audience." . . . When DBS systems *transmit* signals directly to homes with the intent that those signals be received by the public, such transmission rather clearly fits the definition of broadcasting. . . . That remains true even if a common carrier satellite leases its channels to a customer who does not own any transmission facilities; in such an arrangement, someone—either the lessee or the satellite owner—is broadcasting.[97]

The court left the FCC with discretion to decide whom to regulate as a broadcaster—the DBS satellite owner or the customer-programmer. But

when both the customer-programmer *and* the common carrier through which the former's signal are carried are immunized from broadcast regulation, as they are in the [FCC's] *DBS Order*, the statutory scheme is completely repealed.[98]

The court therefore vacated that part of the FCC's policy which exempted customer-programmers of common carrier DBS from the broadcasting provisions of the Communications Act.[99]

In response to this judicial ruling, the FCC issued a notice of proposed rule making on January 8, 1986.[100] The notice conceded that the court's decision "has a considerable impact on our regulatory policies," potentially affecting "not only common carrier DBS and domestic fixed satellite services but other subscription [video] services that previously had not been classified as broadcasting." Unless the commission "establishes the nonbroadcast status of these subscription offerings, it may be required to apply to these previously unregulated services the broadcast statutory provisions."[101] The FCC then proposed that, the *National Association of Broadcasters* decision nothwithstanding, *all* subscription television services should be reclassified as nonbroadcast technologies. By its very nature, subscription television is not distributed generally to the public but is addressed only to specific paying customers. Moreover,

the contractual relationship between the subscription service and its audience obviates the need for the viewer protections afforded by broadcast regulations because subscription programming is transmitted to discrete audiences that exercise direct economic choice over which services and programs to receive.[102]

These proposed rules for DBS underscore the FCC's intent to free the new pay video services from broadcast regulation, whether or not these media use the electromagnetic spectrum to deliver their signals.

Multipoint Distribution Service

Multipoint distribution service (MDS) is another emerging pay video service. It employs microwave signals in the super-high-frequency broadcast band to deliver text as well as television signals to the home monitor. Subscribers must purchase a special converter to change the MDS signal to the standard television frequency.

Since 1974, the FCC's policy has been to regulate MDS as a common carrier.[103] The MDS operator is to "offer a transmission service for hire and cannot control program material. . . . The carrier's responsibility is to provide a 'pipeline.' "[104] One large exception to this common carrier status is that the MDS operator may program its own channel up to 50 percent of the time, provided that it sets up an independent programming affiliate.[105]

In 1983, a variant of MDS known as multichannel MDS (or MMDS) emerged. The FCC accepted the argument that MDS operators needed multiple channels if they were to compete successfully with cable in the subscription television market. To this end, the commission reallocated eight little-used channels that previously had been reserved for educational use. The reallocation also permitted educators to lease out their own MDS channels for commercial use. In 1985 the FCC held the first lottery to distribute MMDS permits.[106]

Most recently, in March 1986, the FCC proposed new rules that call into question the common carrier classification of MDS. The problem the FCC faced was that many MDS operators in practice retain editorial control over a substantial portion of their programming services. Such control is inconsistent with a common carriage classification and makes these MDS operators seem more like broadcasters than carriers. Nonetheless, the commission refused to reclassify MDS as a broadcast technology, noting that such a reclassification would be inconsistent with its proposal of January 8, 1986, to classify all subscription video services as nonbroadcast technologies. The solution proposed was to "permit MDS carriers to elect to render any kind of point to multipoint communications as either a common carrier or a non–common carrier."[107] As part of this permission for MDS operators to function as non–common carriers, the FCC also proposed to delete the 50-percent rule limiting the amount of programming within the editorial control of the operator.[108]

Subscription Television Service

Subscription television (STV) is one of the oldest and technologically simplest pay video services. Like conventional television, STV uses the electromagnetic spectrum to transmit over-the-air signals. The only difference is that the STV signal is scrambled and can be viewed only by subscribers who have purchased special decoding equipment.

Because STV is so clearly a broadcast technology, the FCC to date has applied the broadcast provisions of the Communications Act to it.[109] However, the FCC's 1986 proposal to classify all subscription video services as nonbroadcast technologies would apply to STV as well.

VHF Drop-ins and Low Power Television

VHF drop-ins "are full-power VHF stations that use more advanced directional signals to avoid interference with nearby stations."[110] The FCC proposes to regulate these drop-ins the same as conventional broadcasting.[111]

Where full-power stations cannot be dropped in, the FCC is experimenting with low-power stations (LPTV) that avoid interfering with existing stations by transmitting very weak, local signals. By contrast to the 5 million watts that may power a conventional VHF signal, LPTV stations are limited to 1,000 watts of power. The result is that LPTV signals reach a radius of ten or fifteen miles, compared to the radius of seventy-five or eighty miles often reached by a full-powered station. Despite this power restriction, the FCC has received thousands of applications for LPTV licenses. The first licenses, about three hundred of them, went to rural stations. Since 1983 the FCC has awarded licenses by lottery, with preference to minority applicants.[112]

The FCC has proposed to regulate LPTV stations on the broadcast model. Noting the potential political uses of localized television, the FCC specifically declared its intent, in 1982, to apply the equal opportunities doctrine to LPTV.[113] Presumably, the FCC's recent move to abolish the political broadcasting rules for conventional television would apply to LPTV and VHF drop-ins as well.

Videocassettes, Videodiscs and VCRs

Although they provide a way of programming the television set, videocassettes played by VCRs do not use the electromagnetic spectrum and so are not regulated by the FCC. To date, feature films make up the bulk of videocassette titles. And, like other ways of distributing feature films, videocassettes would seem entitled to the protection of the print model.

The major controversy has been whether the sale of VCRs capable of recording copyrighted films (when those films are broadcast over television) violates the copyright. In *Sony Corp.* v. *Universal City Studios*, the Supreme Court found no copyright infringement in the sale of VCRs because they are widely used simply to switch the time at which TV viewers watch a film presentation—a "fair use" within the meaning of the copyright law.[114]

Videotex

Like cable, videotex resists classification according to the inherited scheme. It resembles print in that it is the publishing of words and graphics. It resembles broadcasting in that it is displayed on a video monitor. It resembles a common carrier in that it is transmitted through telephone lines or coaxial cable.

The FCC has never applied the political broadcasting rules—the Fairness Doctrine, the reasonable access rule, and the equal time rule[115]—to videotex. This is unimportant, provided that videotex remains a service concentrating on home banking and shopping. But three hints as to how the FCC might respond to a politicized videotex operation follow.

First, in 1983 the FCC authorized television stations to offer teletext services.[116] A close cousin to videotex, teletext permits only a one-way exchange of information. From the technical standpoint, teletext is a broadcast technology in which stations make use of a blank interval on the television screen to transmit words and graphs. But despite these broadcast properties, the FCC has ruled that the reasonable access, equal opportunity, and fairness doctrines do not apply to teletext.[117]

Second, in 1969 the American Newspaper Association questioned whether a newspaper delivered by facsimile on a cable channel would have to abide by the Fairness Doctrine. The FCC responded that, although the doctrine applied (at that time) to cable generally, it did not apply in the case of an electronically published newspaper.[118]

And third, the future of electronic publishing figured prominently in the consent decree divesting AT&T of its twenty-two operating Bell companies. As we saw earlier, in traditional common carrier fashion, the Bell companies were prohibited from entering the electronic information service business. The consent decree similarly prohibited AT&T from engaging in electronic publishing over its own lines for a period of seven years.[119] As mentioned, the Justice Department has now proposed lifting these restrictions and allowing the local Bells to compete in the electronic publishing field. This proposal has not been accepted by the court overseeing the divestment process. Instead, in recent hearings the court's decision was to permit the telephone operating companies to *transmit* electronic information services over their lines, but not to provide the actual services themselves. In essence, the ruling permits the telephone companies to act as intermediaries between customers and videotex providers. Telephone companies will be able to advertise a single number to be dialed for access to any videotex service, and they will handle the billing as part of the telephone bill.[120] As we saw in chapter 6, a similar relation between telephone utilities and videotex providers exists in France.

Four Regulatory Scenarios for the Future

Whither communication policy in the age of new technology? In this section we discuss four possible futures for communications law.

The Pigeonhole Scenario

Conceivably, the FCC could act to maintain the tripartite division among printers, broadcasters, and common carriers, fitting each new technology into the appropriate class. There are a number of reasons why such a pigeonhole approach is inadequate.

First, it ignores what we have emphasized throughout this book as the signpost of modern communications—the blurring of the distinction between print and electronic media. When Knight-Ridder used the technology of videotex to publish a newspaper on the television monitor, was the product print or electronic? More important, why should the legal status of the same words depend on the nature of the delivery system? When the *Wall Street Journal* uses satellite technology to broadcast in facsimile its text to various printing plants throughout the country, which then reproduce the text as a conventional newspaper, does the classification of the text for legal purposes switch from print to broadcast? And what about a data service that is transmitted over interactive cable? Should the information be subject to regulations to which it would not be subject were it delivered by mail?

Cable in particular resists classification according to the traditional legal scheme. If broadcast regulations are a response to channel scarcity and frequency interference, then there is no cause to apply these regulations to cable. But cable is not akin to newspaper publishing either, given the exclusive franchises cable operators enjoy in particular locales.[121] And while cable lays or strings wires like a telephone company, it cannot be classified as a common carrier, because it publishes on its own lines. The pigeonhole approach requires us to ignore the hybrid characteristics of a medium like cable and simply cram it into one slot or another.

The FCC has had similar problems pigeonholing the other new media. Some DBS operators resemble common carriers; others program their own channels. MDS services use the electromagnetic spectrum but function essentially as common carriers; teletext is technically a broadcast service but is a close cousin to print as well. No pigeonhole is adequate for these new hybrid forms of communication.

Another difficulty with the pigeonhole approach is that it disposes of regulatory questions on a technology-by-technology basis, paying scant attention to the new media's cumulative impact.[122] For instance, it may be that DBS service will remain scarce for the foreseeable future, given limited satellite transponder capacity and few frequency allocations by the FCC. But why should anything of import turn on the scarcity of DBS channels? The important question is whether, taken as a whole, television is a scarce or abundant medium today. And this question can be answered only by considering the sum total of broadcasting, cable, DBS, MDS, LPTV, STV, VHF drop-ins, videocassettes, and more. The pigeonhole approach potentially misses the forest for the trees.

The Deregulation Scenario

The FCC's current policy is to deregulate both the old and the new media. For conventional broadcasters, the FCC has recently removed whole blocks of the public trustee structure, including limits on advertising time, the requirement that radio and television stations keep programming logs and make them accessible for public inspection, and the requirement that broadcasters ascertain the needs of the communities they serve. The Fairness Doctrine is but the latest casualty of deregulation. For the new technologies, we have seen that the FCC's newest proposal is to free all subscription video services from the broadcast restrictions of the Communications Act.[123] And in the case of cable, the deregulatory cycle appears to have come full circle, with almost all of the 1972 comprehensive rules scrapped.

The case for deregulation rests on the argument that free competition among multiple media outlets will supply viewers with a diverse set of programming choices. If ever there was a problem of television and scarcity, the deregulationist places the problem in the past and suggests it is high time to permit the electronics explosion to work itself out competitively in the market:

> The first step should be to reject frequency scarcity as a rationale for broadband regulation.[124]

> As systems of broadband distribution make telecommunications resemble print in moving towards market determinations of the number and diversity of programming options, what justification remains for a fundamentally different legal approach to the two types of media?[125]

> The explosion of new media and technology ... means greater diversity through the operation of the marketplace, and thus even less justification for governmental intervention to make up for failures "of the market place of ideas to operate according to the original plan."[126]

Does our study of the new technologies support the deregulationist's free market argument? The deregulationist sees television moving from the oligopoly enjoyed by the three commercial networks to a new age of competition: broadcasting, cable, videocassettes, DBS, MDS, STV, LPTV, videotex, and other services all competing for a fragment of the shattered mass audience. But this portrait of video competition is overdrawn. With the exception of cable and videocassettes, none of the new technologies is a serious contender to network-dominated broadcasting. And even the advent of cable and VCRs, though it has meant some decline in the networks' share of the television audience, has not fractured the mass audience in a way confidently predicted only a decade ago. To be sure, the days when the three networks controlled 90 percent of the prime-time audience are gone. But the networks still garner 73 percent of that audience.[127]

Contrary to the free market argument, cable systems typically enjoy an exclusive government franchise to operate in a given area. Glib comparisons of the cable and newspaper businesses ignore the fact that the cable operator is a publishing monopolist, claiming the right to control a municipality's entire cable medium, even when that medium includes up to 108 channels!

Because cable achieves its monopoly through state action, there are arguably First Amendment grounds for believing that cable should not be left unregulated in the "market." As the political scientist Ithiel de Sola Pool noted:

A cable system is a government franchise that allows one company to dig up the streets in order to put its fifty or one hundred channels in front of every home. Those who seek and are denied access to the channels are so denied not just because economics makes it too expensive for them to publish in competition with the cablecaster, but also because a government franchising body has chosen one licensee. A private person may refuse others access to his facilities under most circumstances, but government under the First Amendment may not give the means of speaking to its favorites and deny them to others. A strong First Amendment case against such restraint by state action can be made on behalf of those seeking to lease cable channels.[128]

The deregulationist is certainly right to emphasize the increased volume of information flowing in our society today. But more information may ironically mean a less informed citizenry. One of the features of conventional broadcasting is that news and public-affairs programs are broadcast over the mass-audience channels themselves, capturing viewers who would not seek out political programming on their own. By contrast, it is entirely possible that there will be more political programs on cable television and yet fewer viewers for that programming. This can happen when a 54- or 108-channel system effectively reserves some channels for mass-entertainment programming and televises the news and public affairs on a separate channel or channels. One result of such separation is that pay movie services on cable (HBO, for example) attract mass audiences, but government meetings are broadcast over public-access channels to an audience too small to measure by Nielsen rating methods.

How do deregulationists respond to such objections? Some argue the facts of the matter—that cable is not relegating the news and information to unwatched channels, that more people are being exposed to more information than ever. But other deregulationists make a stronger response. If viewers prefer not to watch political programming, if they "vote" to watch something else when offered it, and if the market consequently responds to their "elections" by providing less political programming or by scheduling it in nonprime time, then this is simply democracy working to reflect the people's genuine interests. For law to define and enforce good programming strikes these deregulationists as paternalistic and elitist. By contrast, the elections of the market express and respond to popular tastes and preferences. It may be, for instance, that what the people want by diversity is not so much a choice between mass-entertainment programs and public-affairs programs as a choice among a greater number of mass-entertainment offerings. The market ought to be free to respond to this preference.

In this way, arguments over deregulation bring us back to the competing theories of democracy we have traced throughout this book. Market relations, after all, are primarily the relations of individuals seeking to maximize their own private interests. The marketplace may valuably teach us that fulfilling personal interests requires cooperative arrangements and a division of labor. But it does not house a community in the strong sense of that term; it works to realize a common good that is simply the aggregate or sum of individual preferences. Given this underlying view, deregulationists are not concerned that the market in advertiser-supported media selects programs that appeal to the consumer in us, not the citizen. Nor do deregulationists wish the press to aspire to a leadership role in a democracy—to take on the task, for example, of civic education. It is enough that the press fairly reflects and serves the state of popular tastes.

When deregulationists trumpet the new diversity of television, they point to the large menu of programs from which consumers may choose. But this choice is meaningful only if there is diversity at the supplier's end of the pipeline as well. If more of the same sort of programming is coming from the same few sources, the aura of choice and diversity is an illusion. At least one new technology—videorecording—does achieve a victory for heterogeneity at the supplier end. By purchasing a relatively inexpensive VCR, individuals become the programmers of their own television—taping over-the-air offerings and viewing them at their own convenience or watching movies or other prerecorded programs on rented videocassettes. And with a videocamera, any group—from the senior citizens in Reading to congressmen to candidates—are in a position for the first time, as media analyst Les Brown puts it, to make their own television. With the new technology, video equipment is suddenly accessible to the individual in a way printing presses no longer are.

But to date, the political use of videocameras and videocassettes has been quite limited—perhaps the best-known example is the distribution of videocassettes of the antiabortion movie *The Silent Scream* to congressional offices (see chapter 4). On the other hand, videorecorders and videocassettes have already emerged as a prime means of home movie entertainment, impinging on both theater owners and pay cable services. Thus, although VCRs open up the television monitor to an endless library of programs, they are currently solidifying rather than challenging mass-entertainment programming.

What about cable on the supply side? As long as municipalities continue to award exclusive franchises to cable operators, cable will remain a semimonopolistic enterprise. And unless the franchise agreement requires an operator to relinquish programming control over certain channels, cities and towns end up with a private operator deciding what to program on each and every cable channel. Thus what appears to be diversity from the consumer's perspective may in fact be a "mask" for a virtual monopoly on the supply side.[129]

The deregulation argument also fails to acknowledge the trend toward conglomerate control in the cable industry. The original mom-and-pop community antenna operators have given way to huge multisystem operators, owning hundreds of separate cable franchises serving millions of subscribers. Thus, "even as the audience is broken into a hundred splinters, those who control it become fewer and more monopolistic."[130]

The Common Carrier Scenario

Earlier we saw that the FCC favors common carrier status for MDS and for certain DBS operators. But for some time now those who favor the common carrier approach to communications law have fixed their attention on cable. In one way or another, they seek to worry us about one corporation controlling access to the only cable plant in town.

In 1971 the Sloan Commission on Cable Communications endorsed what has become known as a partial common carrier approach to cable regulation.[131] In a pure common carrier model, the cable operator would be totally prohibited from programming its own channels. The Sloan Commission found that pure common carrier status "may, indeed, be the way cable should and will go as it achieves maximum penetration and overtakes or supplants over-the-air broadcasting."[132] But the commission feared that, as of 1971, investors would not "be willing to undertake the substantial capital expenditure of laying cable if they had no control over the use of the channels in the formative years and so were powerless to control the financial destiny of the system."[133] This set up what one commission member called the central dilemma facing cable regulators: the public's interest would undoubtedly be best served by common carrier status but "the economics of the business is such that cable systems will probably not get built" if regulated as common carriers.[134]

Faced with this dilemma, the Sloan Commission recommended a compromise. At some point in the future, it may become appropriate to convert the cable system to a common carrier status. But for the present, cable systems would have to be a legal hybrid. On some channels, the owner of the medium would be allowed to supply the programming; on other channels, the operator would be required to lease time to others commercially, retaining no editorial control over the programming. The franchising authority might also require the operator to designate a third set of channels, which would be programmed independently by local government bodies, schools, or the public on a first-come, first-served basis.[135]

This proposed mixture of owner-operated channels and commercially leased and public-access channels has come to have a powerful place in the regulatory debate. Essentially the same recommendation was given in 1973 by the Cabinet Committee on Cable Communications in the "Whitehead Report." That report again looked forward to a system in which cable would function much like the Postal Service or more appropriately like the United Parcel Service or a trucking company that for a fee will take anyone's package—or, in the case of cable, anyone's television programming —and distribute it . . . to the people who wish to have it. The key point is that the distributors would not be in the business of providing the programming themselves, but would distribute everyone else's programs to viewers that wanted to see them.[136]

But, like the Sloan Commission, the Whitehead Report found the industry not yet ready economically for the legal status most appropriate to a democracy. It put the transition from owner-operated channels to a pure common carrier model at the point when cable would have penetrated 50 percent of the nation's television homes, a target cable is just now reaching.

Is it reasonable to believe that the basic economic and legal structure of the cable industry can be refashioned somewhere down the line? Suppose, asks Pool, we tell potential investors in cable now that the system in which they are investing will change at some indefinite point in the future; would that not chill the decision to invest? There is, by way of historical precedent, evidence that telephone development in Britain lagged behind that in the United States partly because Britain warned private investors that the Post Office might nationalize telephone service at some point (as it did in 1912).[137] There is also reason to believe that over time vested interests in cable as an owner-operated medium will become so strong that postponing the common carrier approach is effectively to make certain the day of reckoning never comes.

While acknowledging these difficulties of conversion, Pool himself argued that

at the maturity of cable, it cannot in a free society be other than a carrier. The transition will not be smooth. A major issue for the 1980's and 1990's will be how to prevent cablecasters from seeking the advantages of becoming publishing monopolists in their own communities, controlling both the conduit and its contents.[138]

Where do things stand today with cable and the common carrier model? In the Cable Communications Policy Act of 1984, Congress legislated the partial carrier model for systems with thirty-five channels or more. The 1984 act, as we have seen, includes two major common carrier restrictions: (1) leased channel requirements with the number of channels to be commercially leased increasing as the channel capacity rises; and (2) public-access channel requirements, with local governments authorized to require such channels as a condition of the franchise award.[139] But despite that legislation, the constitutionality of imposing mandatory access and other common carriage requirements on cable remains as unsettled as ever. An explicit Supreme Court decision on the subject one way or the other would do much to clarify expectations.

The Civic Education Scenario

Last, we turn to those scenarios for the future that rest on expanding the publicly financed telecommunications sector. In chapter 6, we studied two democracies with strong traditions of state-owned or financed media. The opposite is true of the American experience, where private ownership and commercial financing are very much the norm. The American tradition of separating government and the press is so strong that even in the case of public radio and television, government appropriations go to a quasi-independent Corporation for Public Broadcasting.

Neither for the new media nor for the old will the predominance of commercially supported media be reversed in the United States. But, in an effort to make the public sector more robust, three ideas have been put forward.

Charging a Spectrum Fee to Finance Public Radio and Television. For all the talk of market principles, one of the anomalous things about American broadcasting is that the government never attempted to create a market in spectrum. The FCC awards licenses free of charge to the groups it deems most worthy, instead of auctioning off frequency assignments for a market price. In part, this unwillingness to sell licenses at market value may stem from hesitancy to condition entrance into broadcasting on the possession of money. But this hesitancy is idle, because broadcast stations are free to create a secondary market for the resale or purchase of licenses, with mega-profits falling entirely into private hands. Atlanta's CBS outlet was recently sold for $500 million.[140] Overall, in television station sales from 1949 to 1970, the average station had an original cost of $994,000 and a resale price of $3.2

million.[141] None of the profit made when a broadcaster sells its license goes into the public treasury, except for taxes.

Communications analysts as noted as Ithiel de Sola Pool and Henry Geller have separately urged rectifying this situation by charging a spectrum fee—a price for the license.[142] The fees would then go to fund a more robust and viable Corporation for Public Broadcasting. They might also go to fund minority broadcasters or others with clear incentives to contribute to the goal of diverse programming.

Geller defends the spectrum fee as a better way to accomplish the purposes of the Fairness Doctrine. He reluctantly concludes that the doctrine did not succeed in bringing diversity to broadcasting, and that in many cases (especially for small stations shy of lawsuits) it deterred, rather than encouraged, coverage of controversial public issues. He would therefore "let go" or deregulate the commercial sector and pin hopes for public-affairs programs on public broadcasting—public broadcasting at last given adequate funding through the spectrum-fee mechanism:

Why not eliminate the public trustee concept (i.e., renewal and the fairness doctrine) and in its place, exact a modest spectrum fee—say, 1% of the gross revenues, fixed for a 35-year term in a contract. The broadcaster volunteered to be a public trustee, and is now being relieved of that responsibility. But the question then arises—why is the broadcaster on that frequency, with all others enjoined by the government? Why not selection by lot or auction? Clearly this would be too disruptive in light of the long established system, but it is not too disruptive to demand a small fee for the government-granted and protected privilege of "grazing" on the spectrum range.

The monies obtained would go to the general treasury, and could be appropriated by Congress periodically to accomplish more directly and effectively goals not fulfilled in the marketplace—for example, educational, cultural, dramatic, minority, and in-depth informational programming.

This could be done through CPB [the Corporation for Public Broadcasting] for public radio or through funding minority ownership, and would be reviewed periodically in the appropriation process.[143]

Critics are likely to respond that public broadcasting, even better-financed public broadcasting, will never be more than "icing on the cake"—a reserve for high-brow culture watched by a small, highly educated audience and with virtually no impact on the general population. That is to say, even a well-financed public broadcasting sector will not accomplish what continuing the regulation of commercial broadcasting arguably does: requiring the channels that capture the mass audience to capture that audience at times for news, special events, presidential press conferences, public-affairs documentaries, and so forth.

Public broadcasting may never emerge as a mass-audience phenomenon in the United States. But a (relatively) small number of viewers need not itself condemn public radio and television to democratic irrelevance. The current distance between public broadcasting and the concerns of American politics seems to us to have less to do with audience size and more to do with the continued reliance of PBS on imported British programming that does little to engage Americans in contemporary social and political debate. Public broadcasting will become a distinctive voice in American politics only when it turns to programs about indigenous American subjects—programs reflective of life in ethnic neighborhoods as well as in Oxford, of the conditions of poverty as well as of wealth, of black and Hispanic culture as well as of white culture. This kind of indigenous programming is not going to solve the problem of small audience appeal; in the short run, it is likely to aggravate it. But we cannot have things both ways. We cannot fault commercial television for sacrificing political commentary to the imperatives of the ratings game and then expect it to be easy to put public-affairs content and numbers together. The audience for public-affairs television about indigenous subjects will have to be built; it does not yet exist in size. Innovative, quality programming can only begin the process of finding its appropriate audience. Ultimately we are talking about changes in the culture at large, changes beyond the power of the old or new technologies themselves to bring about.

Civic Videotex Services. As computerized information services proliferate, so do worries about the potential of electronic publishing to widen the information gap between rich and poor. To avoid any such antidemocratic result, a variety of proposals have been advanced for publicly subsidizing videotex and other electronic information services. The political philosopher Benjamin Barber has made a case for an independent, civic videotex service, on the model of the Corporation for Public Broadcasting. The new, publicly funded service would be charged by law with developing innovative civic uses for videotex and computerized data services in general.[144] Barber argues persuasively that the democratic potential of electronic publishing hinges precariously on putting the new technologies to civic and not just commercial use. But public uses for the new media are unlikely to be explored unless government subsidizes electronic information services in a way similar to the way it now subsidizes public television.

Barber's proposals are modest; he envisions public information services supplementing rather than replacing commercially owned services. So understood, the idea of a civic videotex service is continuous with our free press traditions, and Barber is certainly right that it is high time to bring the new computer technologies within the reach of the ordinary citizen through some scheme of public financing. Absent some way of dedicating electronic information services to civic use, the bounteous flow of information, which is to provide the new information age with its revolutionary impact, will in fact only prop up the established distributions of knowledge and power.

Public-Access Television. The public scenario is perhaps furthest advanced in the case of cable television. In chapter 5 we saw that public-access stations have come to be used throughout the country to televise live, gavel-to-gavel city council and other local government body meetings. We saw, in the Reading case, that these access channels can be used to mobilize and empower groups of citizens, like shut-in senior citizens, who previously had no way of communicating with one another. Franchise agreements typically speak to these public uses of cable television, by requiring the cable operator to set aside a number of stations for public, educational, and local government use. If one surveys the raw amount of government programming on cable television, it is clear that this new technology, with the surplus channel capacity to support the concept of public-access television, represents a net victory for in-depth political coverage by television.

On the other hand, the public cable scenario is under challenge in three different ways. First, as we stressed earlier, cable operators have mounted an aggressive campaign of litigation against the constitutionality of mandatory access requirements. Second, apart from litigation, cable operators have been pressing city after city to renegotiate franchise terms and the access channel requirements, arguing that they can no longer afford the giveaways originally extracted from them. If either these renegotiations or court litigation proves successful, the future may well hold a dramatic retrenchment in the availability of public-access television. Last, even where public-access television survives, it has yet to find its audience. As we mentioned, the audience for all public-access stations together is still so small as to be unmeasurable on current rating scales, such as the Nielsen service. This fear that public-access television serves an absent audience accounts for Congress's decision to hedge its bet with access television in the Cable Communications Act of 1984. Congress upheld the right of local governments to require access channels but, at the same time, gave the cable operator the authority to program over those access channels when they are not being used for the designated public purposes.

Conclusion

Discussions of communications law can quickly become mired in the intricacies of legal doctrine. In this chapter we have attempted to be fair to the doctrine while discussing the democratic and free speech values that underlie our choices of one doctrinal formulation rather than another. What we have seen is that, like democracy itself, it is possible to understand the concept of free speech in more individualist or more communitarian terms. In the individualist formulation, speech is valued primarily as a form of self-expression, as integral to self-realization. In the communitarian formulation, speech is not primarily about self-expression: it takes its value from its service to self-government, from the dependence of democratic deliberation on a rich and robust debate on the issues. These different understandings of free speech are in turn reflected in two different understandings of free press. One tradition emphasizes the individual rights of publishers to control their own publications, to be independent and autonomous of government; the other tradition stresses that what is important is not so much that the press be autonomous as that it be accessible to the public at large, open to a wide range of diverse points of view. How to strike a balance between press autonomy and public access to the press lies at the heart of the current regulatory debate.

Both the autonomy of the press and access of the public at large to the media are firmly rooted in the best of our free press tradition. Sometimes the two parts of the tradition go together—as when protecting the radical press from political censorship also protects the public's right to know alternative ideas. At other times the two aspects of the tradition threaten to fly apart—as when the Fairness Doctrine assigned oversight responsibility to a federal agency for whether broadcasters were reporting stories in a balanced way. But, unless one retreats into a world of *laissez faire*, governmental regulation of the mass media is likely to remain characteristic of our contemporary free press tradition. Such regulation, when it is bad, is very bad for democracy. But at its best, government regulation can enhance the opportunities to speak and to be heard over the crucial channels of mass communications.

Praise of press autonomy can degenerate into a rather flippant identification of the First Amendment with the politics of deregulation. Nowhere is this flippancy more apparent than in the self-serving invocations of the First Amendment and the autonomy tradition made by cable operators in defense of their right to control the content of each and every one of their system's channels. Rarely do cablecasters show that the public's interest in a free and unfettered exchange of ideas is better served by leaving 108 channels in the exclusive control of the cablecaster than by a system where some number of those channels must be dedicated to public access. We have tried to show in this chapter that the tension between the public's First Amendment rights and those of publishers and broadcasters is greater than any naive, panacea-oriented politics of deregulation allows. So long as the end value remains using the new media to foster a rich and robust public debate on the issues of the day, the First Amendment must make its peace with government regulation of programming content, including the ever-controversial and now mothballed Fairness Doctrine. Nothing in the new technology itself convinces us that the need for government oversight of the prerogatives of private corporate power is now magically at an end.

CHAPTER 8

TOWARD AN ELECTRONIC
COMMONWEALTH

THE NEW MEDIA are here to stay. Video, satellite, and computer technologies have become so basic to modern communications that the new media can no longer be dismissed as a passing fad. For better or worse, we live and will continue to live in a society where information exchange has become torrential. The traditional obstacles to communications of volume, distance, and time have been eliminated for all practical purposes. Ours is now a world accustomed to global telephone and television service via satellite, accustomed to the computer's ability to process data instantly, accustomed to the storage of 100,000 pages of print on a single five-inch disk. Whole sectors of the economy are by now so dependent on communications volume and speed that there is no turning back.

This is not to say that each new medium will find a niche in the marketplace. Currently there is such a proliferation of new video services—from well-known technologies such as cable and videorecording to fledgling satellite delivery services such as direct broadcast satellite—that it is improbable all will prove economically viable. Add to the list the FCC's current experiments with new VHF television technologies such as low-power stations or VHF drop-ins and the potential for a shakeout is obvious. During the years we have been researching and writing this book, that shakeout has already started. CBS aborted its attempt to launch a highbrow cable service; Warner Amex's heralded two-way cable service (QUBE) is in limbo; Knight-Ridder has recently abandoned its videotex experiment with an electronic newspaper (Viewtron). But even a thinning of the video ranks will not carry us back to the scarcity that characterized television prior to 1970. It does not take a crystal ball to see that video has irretrievably moved into a new age of abundance. In combination with computers, modems, and telephones, the television becomes a monitor capable of receiving and electronically publishing not only pictures but text and graphs from the most remote data banks. This convergence of video, computer, and telecommunications technologies into integrated communications networks is not precariously tied to the survival of any one new media. It is solidly embedded in our economic and social ways of life. The entrance of AT&T into the computer market and of IBM into the long-distance telephone business (through the purchase of part ownership of MCI) is testimony to the convergence of formerly separate media fields.[1]

How will politics fare in this new video age? How do we make the best democratic response to the new media environment? With the 1988 presidential campaign, new media politics have come into their own. Pat Robertson, the former president of the Christian Broadcasting Network, has shown that the electronic church can be sufficiently mobilized to mount a plausible presidential campaign. All candidates have learned to make imaginative use of computerized, direct-mail campaigns to target particular audiences for particular messages. Media wizards have also shown how the new satellite technologies permit politicians to bypass reporters and feed their own video productions to local stations. Local cable stations have proved a boon to candidates who do not have the resources to buy conventional television time or who wish to reach the particular audience in their district. Perhaps most visibly, the new technologies have enhanced the already considerable hold that polls have over the electoral process by quickening the results of polling, fine-tuning their accuracy, and providing detailed information about the demographics of those polled. The information candidates now have about the views of their constituents—with all the possibilities for better representation or more deft manipulation that such information creates—has never been greater.

Although in their infancy, these political uses of the new media suggest that we face a basic value choice between two competing visions of democracy's future. The burden of this book has been to bring this dispute over political values into sharper focus.

The Value Choices Ahead

One vision of democracy's future centers on using electronics to keep more constant and instant track of public opinion. In this book we have called this vision plebiscitary democracy. According to the plebiscitarian, technology happily renders obsolete the cumbersome procedures of representative democracy; at long last the people can be empowered to vote on issues directly, using the wizardry of electronic voting from the home. Advocates of such electronic plebiscites speak optimistically about the coming revival of citizen participation and direct democracy.

The vision of citizens voting directly on issues and not just for representatives is certainly alluring. Is it not obvious that we become a more democratic nation if, thanks to electronics, individuals can speak for themselves rather than deputizing representatives to speak for them? This book has argued against the allure of the obvious. Participation in a poll or plebiscite gives only the thinnest experience in self-government. That experience becomes even thinner if electronic communications frees people even from the "inconvenience" of leaving their homes to vote. In the classical conception, participatory democracy required assembly, deliberation, and debate. The value of participation was the education people received in the democratic art of persuading or being persuaded in turn. To persuade others required a person to justify individual opinions in terms of the common good and not merely to vote private interests. At its best, therefore, participation required people to risk their opinions; meetings were hardly idle forums for registering preconceptions on cue. In England and the United States, the jury has long represented this more robust vision of participatory democracy—participation in a process where power goes to the persuasive and not just to the side with the most votes.

In the immediate political present, the electronic voting model has the upper hand in democratic thought. A widespread feeling of powerlessness attracts lay attention to the quick fix of polls and plebiscites. But in our judgment, there is a better and more democratic remedy for lost citizen power—a remedy the new media can help deliver. We have called this alternative vision of democracy's future the electronic commonwealth. The electronic commonwealth takes its political cue from the town meeting. It seeks to use the new age of two-way television to restore practicality and substance to participation in local government. At the same time, the ideal of an electronic commonwealth seeks to expand and enrich the traditional town-meeting format in two ways. First, it looks forward to making civic use of computer power, ending the isolation of communities so far as obtaining information is concerned. Second, the electronic commonwealth guards against the parochialism of local politics by using the scale-conquering properties of video, telephones, and computers to bring communities together for regional discussion of regional issues and national discussion of national issues.

Consider an easy if trivial example of an old electronic technology that overcomes physical obstacles to speaking and being spoken to in turn: the microphone. Only a Luddite would refuse in principle to tamper with traditional ways of conducting a meeting by providing speakers with microphones. Of course, in a democracy providing microphones is not risk-free; words of tyrants can be amplified also. But this merely indicates the obvious point that microphones have no politics. Where the politics of the meeting are already democratic, the microphone will not be monopolized but will be equally distributed to speakers. Used in this way, the microphone enriches democracy by expanding the size of the audience that can hear and be heard in turn. Where the politics of the meeting are authoritarian, the microphone reinforces the tyranny by amplifying the speeches of the leader and leaving others more voiceless than ever.

In essence, the democratic promise in the new media is the democratic promise in the microphone writ large. We now have ways to expand the visual as well as the audio part of the meeting; we now have ways to allow persons attending a meeting via television to speak as well as listen. The approximation of electronic communications to face-to-face meetings is thus qualitatively greater than it has ever been before. Greater also is the size of the audience that can now gather electronically at a school board meeting or even at a party nominating convention. The microphone enlarged participation in meetings but did not explode the constraints of numbers and distance. The new electronic age does just that, with all the threats and promises for democracy implicit in mass participation.

Without electronics, the town-meeting model is suitable only for local government. With electronics, there comes to be the new politics of regional electronic meetings. Consider, for example, local government bodies in New England towns separately wrestling with energy or environmental problems. After a certain point, dealing with those problems requires regional solutions. But it is difficult to find time and place for face-to-face regional meetings. Currently such meetings tend to be held infrequently at best. The new media could do much to put regional politics back on the American political landscape.

A mix of local, regional, and national discussion is the aim of the ideal electronic commonwealth. If all the new media promised was a shift from more national to more local television, then we might be trading one set of democratic vices for another. The democratic vice of broadcasting is the blandness and homogeneity of mass-audience programming. The need for ratings success robs television of the programming diversity appropriate to a pluralist society. But in liberating television from the mass audience, the new narrowcast media could conceivably sponsor the ills of fragmentation and faction: members of closed and insular communities talking among themselves but not to outsiders.

Throughout this book we have stressed that the dangers of faction in our culture are real. Among other special-interest networks, cable television now supports the Christian Broadcasting Network, Music Television, the Nashville Network, the Black Entertainment Network, the Spanish International Network, and the National Jewish Network. However much we welcome the arrival of diversity to television, we must guard against the antidemocratic spectacle of separate but equal television. Democratic conversation is conversation among citizens who see themselves as responsible in common for governing a community. Because they share this responsibility and power, citizens have a stake in communicating across ethnic, religious, racial, income, and cultural lines. For all its blandness, mass-entertainment broadcasting has provided Americans with common channels and common entertainments. It is imperative that these common channels not be lost.

The ideal of an electronic commonwealth guards against the ills of faction and closed communities. Consider the case of school committee meetings televised on the local cable access channels. Suppose at one meeting the discussion centers on the adoption of a new math curriculum for the elementary schools. Those present at such a meeting might want more information about the proposed curriculum—information not locally available. Perhaps the curriculum has been tried in a neighboring district or a district across the country. Perhaps a graduate student is completing a dissertation on the effects of the new curriculum at a distant university. Empowering local citizens to make decisions on local education means getting them in touch with these distant sources of information. And the new media can facilitate the exchange of information across the nation every bit as much as it can facilitate televising local politics to local audiences in the first place. Doing both together—empowering citizens to participate in local government and bringing them the sometimes distant information to participate intelligently—is the goal of the electronic commonwealth.

The marketplace itself is not likely to support electronic information services devoted to exchanges of civic information. Currently, the most successful videotex services are those such as Dow Jones News/Retrieval that concentrate narrowly on commercial information. The technology is the same, whether remote advice is sought on the stock market or the math curriculum; the politics is radically different. If the new media are to be harnessed to civic uses, then intervention in the selections of the market in favor of subsidized civic uses of computers, data bases, videotex, and two-way television must become a political priority.[2]

We have stressed that subsidies for civic communications are in the American tradition and not a violation of it. The free library system is testimony to the importance we attach to subsidizing civic education. We do not yet think of computers and information services as the equivalent of printing presses and libraries. But it is crucial that we make this imaginative leap and provide substantial public financing for civic uses of computerized information. Otherwise, we may soon be talking about a communications counterrevolution. Instead of spreading information, the computer's impact could well be to hoard it on data bases purchased only by well-heeled professional audiences. Dow Jones Information Services advertises itself as accomplishing "the democratization of information." This is true, insofar as it uses computer technology to sell more information to more people at less cost than ever before. But the electronic commonwealth demands democratization of information of another sort. The information a democracy needs is about public as well as private matters. And it is information that is publicly held, not privately held for profit. Only politics, and not technology alone, can deliver this sort of democratized information.

Five Problems for the Future

By way of conclusion, we explore five issues that politics in the United States must particularly address before the electronic commonwealth can arrive. These issues are: (1) ownership of the new media; (2) advertiser financing of the new media; (3) the privatization of American popular culture wrought by the new media; (4) the passivity of television as a medium; and (5) the declining role of the organized press in mediating the news.

Ownership of the New Media

Patterns of ownership of the new media are emerging that conflict with democratic values. Two trends in particular warrant scrutiny and regulation by the FCC and Congress: cross-ownership and conglomeration.

Cross-ownership. Possession of the new and old media is now often in the same hands, with all the conflicts of interest and monopolies that cross-ownership portends. This is especially true in the cable industry. From its inception, broadcasters eyed cable as a dangerous rival that threatened to siphon off the mass audience that made advertisers willing to finance "free" television. As we have seen, until the mid-1960s, the FCC responded to the fears of its broadcast clients by regulating cable in ways that blunted its competitive edge. Although the FCC has largely dropped such antagonistic regulations by now, broadcast corporations have used the intervening years wisely to move into the cable market. Capital Cities/ABC controls three of the largest basic cable services (ESPN, with Nabisco; Arts and Entertainment, with Hearst and RCA; and Lifetime, with Hearst and Viacom). As a result of its takeover by Capital Cities, ABC is also now under the same corporate umbrella as Capital Cities Cable. CBS failed in its attempt to launch a cable network of its own but it retains ownership in the Bravo pay cable channel as well as regional sports cable channels. NBC, through its parent company RCA (now itself owned by General Electric) controls much of the satellite transponder space used to distribute cable signals. RCA also owns RCA Cable and is part owner of the Arts and Entertainment cable network. Turner Broadcasting owns the Cable News Network, the CNN Headline News Network, and Atlanta's superstation WTBS. Persistent attempts by Turner to take over CBS failed in 1986.[3]

Other established media giants have also crossed over into the cable market. Time owns the second largest cable system (American Television and Communications), as well as HBO, Cinemax, and parts of the USA Network and Black Entertainment Television. Warner Communications owns the fifth largest cable system. Viacom owns the tenth largest cable system, in addition to Showtime, The Movie Channel, Nickelodeon, and Lifetime. The Times-Mirror newspaper corporation owns the eleventh largest cable system. Until 1986 Westinghouse owned Group W Cable, the third largest cable operator.[4]

These media giants have crossed over to own other new media as well. The big names in home videocassette distribution are ABC, CBS/Fox, RCA/Columbia, Time-Life, Walt Disney, Paramount, MCA, MGM/UA, and Warner. In the videotex market, IBM and Sears are teaming up in a joint venture videotex service known as Trintex. CBS had been a third partner but withdrew in 1986. Time, AT&T, Bank of America, and Chemical Bank are operating Covidea, a videotex service specializing in home banking. Some of the biggest newspaper corporations, including Knight-Ridder, Times-Mirror, and the *Wall Street Journal,* have also experimented with videotex services. In the fledgling world of MDS, the three commercial broadcast networks have all actively bid for franchises, often in the same cities where the networks already own television or radio stations.[5]

Media cross-ownership on a mammoth scale raises democratic hackles. Unless the FCC and Congress carefully update and enforce cross-ownership rules to prohibit the existing media giants from combining print or broadcast interests with new media outlets in the same market, there is a potential for vast private monopolies of speech. Nothing in our free speech tradition prohibits government from legislating against such monopolies or semimonopolies. Indeed, much of communications law—from common carrier regulations to the public trustee status of broadcasters—is a response to the need to control the private power of media giants such as Western Union or AT&T or RCA.

The recent clash between media mogul Rupert Murdoch and Senator Edward Kennedy illustrates the difficulties of enforcing cross-ownership rules. Shortly before Congress adjourned in 1987, Kennedy secured passage of a law prohibiting the FCC from granting Murdoch any further waiver of the rules against owning a newspaper and a broadcasting station in the same media market. Murdoch had used an earlier FCC waiver to purchase a newspaper and a television station in both New York and Boston.

Public criticism of Kennedy was intense. Some critics charged that Kennedy was using the cross-ownership rules to silence editorial criticism from the Murdoch-owned *Boston Herald.* Others objected to Kennedy's alleged stealth in inserting the antiwaiver provision into another bill as Congress rushed to adjourn. But the most vehement critics questioned the wisdom of enforcing the cross-ownership rules at all. Few seemed concerned about the concentration of media power that Murdoch had been allowed to achieve in New York and Boston. Instead, they were concerned that Murdoch would be forced to put the money-losing *New York Post* up for sale and that a buyer might not be found. As things turned out, a buyer for the *Post* did emerge, but the *Post*'s future remained fragile and dependent on a host of union concessions. The consensus was that an exemption from the cross-ownership rules in this case would have been preferable. In our judgment, this consensus showed far too little concern for the conflict between democratic press traditions and current patterns of press ownership.

Conglomeration. Even apart from the hackles raised by cross-ownership, the sheer size of media corporations is a concern in a democracy. Much of First Amendment law developed to safeguard small press organs and unpopular leafleteers from suppression by a far more powerful government bent on suppressing criticism or unorthodox political views. The importance we attach to leaving the press unregulated by government took root in an era where there was a clear mismatch between big government and a splintered press.[6] Today media power is concentrated in such a few private hands that leaving the press wholly unregulated by government may work against rich and robust public debate. The recent takeovers at ABC and NBC show that the process of conglomeration is far from over and that media corporations themselves are being subsumed into nonmedia giants. In cable television, the clearest evidence of conglomeration is the growth of multisystem operators, or MSOs, controlling numerous franchises and millions of subscribers. The top ten MSOs collectively have 41 percent of all cable subscribers. These top ten, together with numbers of subscribers, are:

1. Tele-Communications, Inc. (4.3 million)
2. American Television and Communications (3.29 million)
3. Storer Communications (1.57 million)
4. Cox Cable Communications (1.33 million)
5. Warner Communications (1.26 million)
6. Continental Cablevision (1.20 million)
7. Comcast Corporation (1.0 million)
8. United Cable Television (1.0 million)
9. Newhouse Broadcasting (970,000)
10. Viacom Cable, Inc. (910,000)[7]

One of the striking features of this list is that so many of the largest cable operators are owned by the established media giants—by familiar names such as Time, Storer, Warner, Newhouse, and Viacom. Clearly, cable financing has come a long way since its mom-and-pop origins.

The power of entrenched media giants over the new technologies exposes the fallacy in the technological determinist's claim that the new media are ushering in a golden age of diversity in video programming. This argument naively avoids any consideration of the political economy of the new media. At the consuming end, the viewer may be able to flip among a greater number of channels. At the supplier end, a few conglomerates still control what programs are produced and purchased. Indeed, a small number of corporations are the dominant owners in all the media fields, new and old. They are empires extending from print to radio and television to movies to cable and satellite transponders. In the face of such concentrated private power, the need for legal regulation remains.

Advertising and the New Media[8]

We do not share the pop criticism of advertising as American society's great bogeyman. Advertising's ability to manipulate minds is greatly exaggerated.[9] Moreover, commercial financing of the media, since the days of the penny press, has coexisted with a fiercely independent press not beholden to government for support. In a country such as France, where broadcasting is state-supported, the adversarial relation between press and government we Americans take for granted seems much less intense.

Nonetheless, we believe the new media can make their greatest contribution to democracy if they eschew advertiser financing and the mass-audience programming advertisers pay for. The importance of liberating television in particular from the advertiser-driven model is illustrated by the recent round of ratings pressure on network news operations. It used to be true that news divisions within the three commercial networks enjoyed a good deal of autonomy within the corporate structure; the expectancy was less that the nightly news would garner a profit or mass audiences and more that it would put the right, public-service face on the broadcast corporation. Just how relaxed ratings pressures once were on television news is indicated by Reuven Frank, the first producer of the *Huntley-Brinkley Report*, who subsequently went on to be a vice president of NBC News:

The Huntley-Brinkley Report started on October 20, 1956. . . . The ratings were terrible for almost a year. The sales were very bad. In those days, when you didn't sell a commercial they aired Smokey the Bear or some other public-service announcement. . . . I believe that for most of the summer of 1957 we did not have one commercial spot on that show. . . . Chet, David and I used to talk about it. And what we decided was that we weren't going to do anything about it. Granted, there was a certain amount of learning to be done, but we were doing the show the way we wanted to do it. It was not a matter of celebrity. We never thought of it in those terms.[10]

The recollections of former CBS News commentator and special correspondent Bill Moyers are to the same effect: "Television news has never been pure. It has always been an alloy of journalism and show business. But at CBS the line between news and show business has traditionally been there and the people in charge have tried to protect news against the intrusion of entertainment values."[11] But Moyers left CBS in November 1986 with a sense that the wall of separation between news and entertainment was fast crumbling. Moyers dates the present erosion to 1984. Having defended the news division against outsiders such as Ted Turner and Senator Jesse Helms, CBS executives then

yielded to the encroachment of entertainment values from within. Not only were these values invited in, they were exalted. The line between entertainment and news was steadily blurred. Our center of gravity shifted from the standards and practices of the news business to show business. In meeting after meeting, "Entertainment Tonight" was touted as the model—breezy, entertaining, and undemanding. In meeting after meeting the discussion was about "moments"—visual images containing a high emotional quotient that are passed on to the viewer unfiltered and unexamined.[12]

These meetings took place at a time when the *CBS Evening News* had slipped from first place in the ratings and when the *CBS Morning News* was an also-ran. One prominent sign of the new ratings pressure was the transfer of *CBS Morning News* out of the news division altogether, its conversion to a much softer sell of the news, then finally threats of cancellation when ratings did not improve. At *CBS Evening News* the whole show packed up and went on periodic tours of the country, the better to break the traditional dominance of hard Washington news and include more people-oriented, human drama stories. Former CBS News President Van Gordon Sauter took the position that "Americans were tired of government, tired of bureaucracy, tired of politics, even." When it was a question of airing a story on the latest vote in Ways and Means or a strike by government workers in Spain, Sauter would ask, "Why should any American care about that?"[13] What he was looking for was "the gripping story," the "story that seems to touch an incredibly responsive chord in people," the "human drama" without which "the facts get lost." One particular story that filled the bill for Sauter was the tragic story of Jeremy Ghiloni from Ohio. On December 18, 1985, both NBC and ABC led their nightly news with the top story out of Washington—the progress of a tax reform bill. But before CBS turned to that story, they showed clips of schoolchildren in Ohio preparing get-well cards for classmate Jeremy who had been rescued and resuscitated the day before after spending forty-five minutes underwater. In all, CBS ran three stories on Jeremy that week, the last about his death.

If there is something to the claim that ratings pressure has increased on network news, what accounts for it? At least two factors seem to be at work. First, competition from the new media—cable television and home videocassettes primarily—has cut into the networks' share of the television audience. Their share of the prime-time audience has declined from near 90 percent during the 1979–80 season to 73 percent in 1986.[14] In this new competitive environment, there is a growing sense in network boardrooms that commercial television simply cannot afford the luxury of yesterday's insulation of the news from the imperatives of television economics. Second, at the very time that networks are worried about overall loss of market share, news itself has emerged as a marketable commodity. This is clearest in the case of local news, where affiliates can sell a thirty-second spot on the local news in a major city for as much as $2,000.[15] This gives local stations a powerful incentive to abandon network news entirely and produce their own news programs using the new technologies provided by satellite and the like. As sober a newsman as former CBS News President Fred Friendly has speculated, in no doubt exaggerated fashion, that "unless the networks make their product appreciably and dramatically superior, I doubt there's much of a future for network news."[16] This is the kind of atmosphere in which the conversion of network news to the tabloid look long popular on the local news is taking place.

It is high time to ask what is so bad, after all, about ratings. Here is a voice raised in their defense: "Ratings are the democratic way; the Nielsen service or Arbitron are but polls of the people to find out what they want from television. In fact, ratings are a way of empowering the people to have the final say on television programming. The networks seek to do nothing other than accurately mirror the state of popular tastes."

But this defense is too cunning about democracy. First, it makes it seem as if the only news democratic citizens need is news that pleases them—news that they watch for the same reasons that they watch a situation comedy. But this is to treat viewers not as democratic citizens but as consumers tuning in to be amused and flattered. But once the news is produced to hook and please the largest possible audience, it is demeaned, as Moyers states, from the "conversation of democracy" to "the small talk of diversion." The news begins "to win viewers the same way Ronald Reagan won voters: by making them feel good."[17] But "feel good" news has to be in principle superficial, episodic, unengaging, and undemanding. It can flatter the culture but not examine it; it can please viewers but not make them think.

The defense of ratings is too cunning about democracy in a second sense as well. The only audience that matters to Nielsen ratings is the mass audience—measured in tens of millions of persons. All power goes to that audience, and even a show that attracts, say, 30 million persons in a time slot while competitors are bringing in 40 million persons is in danger of cancellation. A television documentary such as PBS's history of the civil rights movement (*Eyes on the Prize*) held an audience of 5.9 million persons per segment;[18] but this is mediocre as far as commercial television is concerned. Numbers that would be phenomenal for book sales achieve only a "too small to measure" rating from the Nielsen service in the context of television.

The result is the familiar homogeneity of television programming: each network pushing the same mass-audience fare in each prime-time slot. We are no doubt exaggerating; one long-standing exception is *60 Minutes*, which "has made more money for CBS than any other show at the network ever has."[19] There are also documentaries on topics of public interest, mandatory coverage of presidential speeches from the Oval Office, press conferences, national nominating conventions, and the like. Occasionally there is even entertainment of a different sort, such as the 1986 commercial television presentation of *Death of a Salesman*—a play that hardly fits the usual television notion of what it takes to please an audience. Still, the nation can for the most part conduct its business on broadcast television only on borrowed time; the economics of commercial television are pushed solely by the imperative to capture the largest possible audience for advertisers. This imperative stands against the realization of democratic ideas we commonly associate with diversity in programming or access to the marketplace of ideas for the widest possible array of contending voices.

Advertiser-driven programming on television is in conflict with democratic values in ways that go beyond pressures of the ratings game. In the modern consumer society, possession of personal goods is widely advertised as the key to welfare and happiness. The legitimacy of the state comes to rest on its political ability to maintain a high standard of living for most individuals and to shore up the expectations of the less well off for the future. As historian Daniel Boorstin notes, the only community Americans now share is the "consumption community."[20] Advertising speaks to an ethic of fellowship based on what you eat, drink, smoke, or drive.[21] Such fellowship, Boorstin remarks, is casual and attenuated—"gossamer webs knitting together the trivia of [our] lives."[22]

Commercial television mirrors and magnifies the United States as a consumption community. It is not only the advertisements themselves that lure the consumer and lull the citizen in us. The programming must be bland and apolitical enough to woo the mass audience. Even the dramatic fare must not absorb, disturb, or pain viewers in ways that void attention to the commercials. As a former vice president for programming at ABC put it:

Program makers are supposed to devise and produce shows that will attract mass audiences without offending these audiences or too deeply moving them emotionally. Such ruffling, it is thought, will interfere with their ability to receive, recall and respond to the commercial message. This programming reality is the unwritten, unspoken gemeinschaft of all professional members of the television fraternity.[23]

For these reasons, the communal notions upon which democracy classically depended—the notion that possession of private goods is not the only measure or standard of living; that public welfare can on occasion require a politics of austerity; that participation in the good life requires public service as well as private consumption—all these receive only fuzzy reception on commercial television.

Given the tension between civic and consumer culture, great importance attaches to whether programming on the new television channels comes to be advertiser-driven. The original model for cable television was subscription financing. Whereas dependence on advertising leads to mass-audience programming, dependence on subscriber support allows more specialized and diverse programming formats. Here is a cogent expression of the cultural and political significance in the difference between advertiser-driven media and subscription financing:

Programs paid for by their consumers are generally superior and more diverse than those supported 100 per cent by advertisers. How much advertisers will spend for a program is a function of its ability to sell their product, and that is only slightly dependent on the quality of the program. The number of persons who turn on a television set on a given evening is a function of habit far more than of the programs offered. . . . The willingness of advertisers to spend large amounts to increase the pleasure of the viewer is quite limited. Since only a very small percentage of people who see a commercial will change what they buy the next time they are in a store, a spot commercial is worth only a fraction of a cent per person exposed. In fact, in the 1970s, advertisers spent only about 2 cents per viewer hour to support television. At those levels most television production was "grade B" films. [The] point is that an advertising-based system has limits, set not by what the public wants but by what the advertisers are willing to spend. With that type of income structure, no commercial telecaster can afford to program for a small, specialized audience.[24]

Small audiences who wish to see television address their particular tastes will have to support that television financially. But the dream of subscription cable television is in jeopardy, as dependence on advertising grows. In 1980 cable's total advertising revenue was $58 million. In 1986 advertising revenues were projected at $993 million.[25] Those revenues are still small compared to broadcast revenues ($21 billion in advertising projected in 1986),[26] but they do indicate that cable financing may ultimately go the advertiser route. If so, the much-heralded "cornucopia of channels" on cable will have little political significance; familiar mass-audience programming will fill a dozen or so cable channels and the rest will draw splinter audiences at best.

One sign of the future is cable's current campaign to convince certain advertisers that cable is a better marketing vehicle for their products than broadcast television. The smaller, self-selected audience subscribing to a pay cable channel gives advertisers an opportunity to customize commercials to the tastes of a unified audience. In other words, there would be a shift from mass selling to segmented selling, corresponding to the shift from broadcasting to narrowcasting.[27]

As advertisers experiment with novel ways to extend their empire over the new television channels, the domain of the consumer society is extended as well. Any potential the new media might otherwise have had to support a more civic culture is fast retreating.

The Privatization of Popular Culture

From the marketplace of Athens where youth went to hear Socrates to the Hyde Park soapbox oratory of London to the parades and street demonstrations of American politics, democracy has thrived in open public space. By contrast to the public life of democracy, the popular entertainment culture in the United States is increasingly centered in the home. This privatization of entertainment is largely the work of television, especially as augmented by the VCR and pay cable movie channels. On the surface, television would seem the opposite of a privatizing technology. After all, it vastly increases the number of persons who can simultaneously experience and share the suspense of a live event. But, as Boorstin argues, the sharing is bogus. Before television, to see a performance "was to become part of a visible audience." The desire "to share experience had brought people out of their homes, gathering them together (physically as well as spiritually)." By contrast, the television viewer is isolated, "thrust back on himself." Each person's experience is separate and silent; nobody hears or witnesses any fellow viewer's reaction in another home. Boorstin dubs television's elimination of the visible audience "TV segregation."[28] It is a segregation or privatization that the new media carry forward with a vengeance, as the home videocassette comes to rival the theater, the concert hall, the music house as the "place" for entertainment.

The American preference for private and individualized pastimes has a profound influence on the political and social uses to which any new technology is put. To refer back to an example we considered in chapter 1, the invention of the internal combustion engine could have supported the development of a public-transportation infrastructure; instead politics tilted toward a federally subsidized highway system for private passenger cars. A similar ethos of individualism and privacy is at work in selecting uses for the new media. For all the hoopla about the abundance of channel capacity on the new television, programming on these channels remains devoted to home entertainment of a familiar sort and only infrequently to the public business of the republic. From the democratic point of view, this is unfortunate. Private space for individual tastes and pursuits is a democratic value, but so too is forging a common identity, a sense of shared responsibility for governing according to the common good. Devoting the lion's share of our new video resources to music videos, sports, movies, and broadcast reruns squanders the opportunity to use the new channels to echo and enrich our common life and common purposes.

We do not mean to exaggerate the contradiction between the privatized ways we Americans take our entertainment and the public life of a democracy. The entertainment culture supported by the new media is less something new and ominous and more a continuation of the fare of broadcast television. The point is simply that no communications revolution or democratic revival will occur this way.

The Passivity of Television

When we started research for this book in the early 1980s, it appeared that the technology for two-way or interactive television might make a dramatic contribution to democratizing the electronic media. Traditionally, television has been a passive medium; viewers consume the words and images of governors but do not get to speak back to the tube. As a result, during the first two decades of televised politics, "the citizen felt a frustrating new disproportion between how often and how vividly political leaders could get their message to him and how often and how vividly he could get *his* message to them. Except indirectly, through the opinion polls, Americans were offered no new avenue comparable to television by which they could get their message back."[29]

Two-way cable and videotex promised to change all that. With just a TV set and a keypad, citizens would regain their active voice. No promise of the new media remains more unfulfilled than the arrival of interactive television. Marketwise, two-way cable programming has been a dud. Only QUBE ever offered any substantial amount of interactive programming, and QUBE never made money. As of 1986, only Warner Cable Corporation and Viacom Cable were marketing interactive cable.[30] Only rarely these days does the programming have political or public-affairs content; typically it is home participation in a quiz show.

Videotex is also a two-way video technology, but market penetration here is elusive as well. The pioneer "electronic newspapers"—Knight-Ridder's Viewtron and Times-Mirror's Gateway —folded in 1986.[31] Other specialized videotex services have achieved a market niche by concentrating on commercial information; these services include H&R Block's CompuServe, Reader Digest's The Source, and Dow Jones News/Retrieval.[32] Covidea is a more recent videotex service concentrating on home banking, and Sears and IBM are scheduled to go forward with Trintex in 1988, after years of market research.[33] But to date no videotex service has achieved a market for civic communications. The transformation of television from a passive to an active medium is a key to the democratic promise of the new media. In chapter 5 we reviewed favorably the use of two-way television to support electronic town meetings in Reading, Pennsylvania. Those meetings showed that the electronic commonwealth is an ideal that can inspire real political practice. The vulgarization of two-way cable into a gimmick for quiz shows is an illustration of just how difficult it is to break the mass-entertainment hold on television.

Unmediated News

Any conventional news operation—whether run by a newspaper or television station—requires reporters and editors. The public takes it for granted that it is receiving an edited and narrated version of events. And it judges the quality of journalism in terms of how objective and unbiased the reporting and editing is.

Using the new media technologies for videorecording and videoconferencing, political actors now find themselves in a position to avoid professional journalists entirely and to deliver their own videotape to local broadcast stations. The best example of politicians end-running journalists is the White House News Service, established by Michael Deaver during his years as deputy chief of staff for Ronald Reagan. The president's own news service provided high-quality video clips of the president on a daily basis to non-Washington television stations. The advantage to the president was the capacity to control his own television destiny, without meddling by press middlemen. Another example of the shift from mediated to unmediated news is President Reagan's preference for televised speeches over televised press conferences. In the speech, the president commandeers the resources of television to speak to the American public directly, once more without the press middlemen.

It is far too early to tell whether the role of the organized press in delivering the news to the public is declining. But enough is happening to sound warning bells. In contrast to the three broadcast network news operations, CNN is already a less mediated, more visually oriented production. In general, the dependence of television news on good visuals—and the ability of government to manipulate this need through the staging of media events or the supplying of prerecorded video—opens up the alarming possibility that in the future government and television, once supposed adversaries, will become secret sharers.

Conclusion

It is possible to make a few—but only a few—secure predictions about the future of the new media:
• Television will continue as the principal means of news and entertainment in American society. In fact, the clearest effect of

the new media is to solidify, not to challenge, television's hold on popular culture.

• The three commercial television networks will not collapse as some are still predicting. They have already weathered competition from cable, retaining a 73 percent share of the prime-time audience.

• Television news will not eclipse the traditional newspaper any more than it has in the past. The newspaper will continue its leading role in setting the agenda for news items and in influencing the opinions of the most politically active Americans. Satellite delivery and facsimile transmission technology will support a greater number of national newspapers in the United States than has historically been the case (*USA Today* is an example). But videotex and electronic publishing will not steal the lucrative classified advertising business of the Sunday newspaper.

• The VCR will continue its growth as the most popular new communications technology since color television. Hollywood will respond by tighter control over the marketing of videocassettes of feature films and by releasing films on cassette at an early date.

• Fiber optics and laser lightwave technology will replace copper wire as the principal means for transmitting telephone conversations and data. The advantage of lightwave technology over electromagnetic transmission is its greater capacity, or band width. Once laid, fiber optics networks will support a market in a variety of electronic data services into the home—home banking, shopping, energy monitoring, burglary systems, and the like.

• The word processor or personal computer will replace the typewriter in all but the smallest office situations.[34]

Beyond this short list, all else about the new media is speculation. So much about the politics and economics that control the destiny of technology is in flux. Will the law further regulate the use of backyard dishes to pirate unscrambled satellite signals? How successful will satellite services be in scrambling their signal and selling the necessary decoding equipment? How will cable respond to the unexpected challenge from the VCR in the home movie market? How much spectrum will the FCC reserve for microwave television signals (MDS) or direct broadcast satellite (DBS)? How will Congress and the courts respond to the FCC's abolition of the Fairness Doctrine? Will the process of takeovers and media conglomeration continue? Will any of the new long-distance telephone companies be able to compete successfully with AT&T in the long-distance market? Will legal restrictions prohibiting the local Bell companies from offering electronic information services over their own lines be lifted? Will fiber optics render coaxial cable obsolete? Will the Supreme Court uphold lower court rulings prohibiting cities and towns from awarding exclusive franchises to a single cable company? The list of pending regulatory and economic choices goes on. But the point should be clear that politics and economics, and not technology alone, will shape the media world to come.

Now is the time to raise fundamental value questions about how a democracy may best profit from the marvels of electronic communications. As we see it, the basic choice comes down to this. One choice is to use the new technology to quicken democracy and tighten the hold of public opinion over public policy. This is the politics of polls and plebiscites, electronic voting, and instant feedback schemes. The speed and reach of the new media can put such a politics into practice if we want it. Another choice is to use the new technology to slow down democracy, to involve more citizens than ever in meetings and debates, discussion, and dialogue. This is the politics of the electronic commonwealth and the televised town meeting. The congregating or conferencing capacity of the new media can put such a politics into practice if we want it. The choice between racing democracy and slowing democracy is ours. Only politics, not machines, can make that choice.

NOTES

Chapter 1. The New Media and Democratic Values

1. David Lachenbruch, "VCRs: From Gizmo to Household Word," *The 1986 Essential Field Guide to the Electronic Environment, Channels*, November–December 1985, p. 74 (hereafter cited as *Channels 1986 Field Guide*).

2. Arguments in favor of a communications revolution can be found in Les Brown, "Introduction: When Business and Technology Converge," *Channels 1986 Field Guide*, p. 4; John Naisbitt, *Megatrends: Ten New Directions Transforming Our Lives* (New York: Warner Books, 1982), pp. 23–26. For an argument that no communications revolution is occurring, see Brian Winston, *Misunderstanding Media* (Cambridge, Mass.: Harvard University Press, 1986), pp. 1–14, 363–82.

3. See, for example, Marc U. Porat, "Communications Policy in an Information Society," in *Communications for Tomorrow: Policy Perspectives for the 1980's*, ed. Glen O. Robinson (New York: Praeger, 1978), pp. 3–61; Daniel Bell, "Communications Technology—For Better or for Worse," *Harvard Business Review*, May–June 1979, pp. 20–24.

4. Richard Altick, *The English Common Reader: A Social History of the Mass Reading Public, 1800–1900* (Chicago: University of Chicago Press, 1957), p. 367. The authors are indebted to their research assistant, Stephen Bates, for the examples cited in this note and in notes 5–7. See also Gary Orren and Stephen Bates, "New Communications Technologies" (Washington, D.C.: Roosevelt Center for American Policy Studies, December 1982).

5. Benjamin Compaine, "The Communications 'Revolution': New Rules for New Players," paper presented at the University of Iowa, October 29, 1981, cited in Orren and Bates, "New Communications Technologies," p. 37.

6. Anthony Smith, *Goodbye Gutenberg: The Newspaper Revolution of the 1980s* (New York: Oxford University Press, 1980), p. 241.

7. Miles Orvell, "The Screen Revolution," *Technology Review*, February–March 1982, p. 44.

8. "Dyer Sees Barriers in Television's Way," *New York Times*, November 27, 1938, sec. 9, p. 10.

9. Waldemar Kaempffert, "Big 'Ifs' Cloud the Television Screen," *New York Times Magazine*, June 5, 1938, p. 6.

10. Harry F. Waters, et al., "TV of Tomorrow," *Newsweek*, July 3, 1978, p. 73.

11. E. L. Doctorow, *World's Fair* (New York: Random House, 1985), p. 284.

12. The authors are indebted to Professor Daniel Bell for bringing this example to their attention.

13. "Issues of the Information Age: The Paradox of Power," *New York Times*, September 18, 1987, p. A39. The work cited in this note is an advertisement by the American Telephone and Telegraph Company.

14. Lane Jennings, "Utopia: We Can Get There from Here—By Computer," in *Communications and the Future: Prospects, Promises and Problems*, ed. Howard F. Didsbury, Jr. (Bethesda, Md.: World Future Society, 1982), p. 48.

15. See, for example, Naisbitt, *Megatrends*, pp. 159–61; Alvin Toffler, *The Third Wave* (New York: William Morrow, 1980), pp. 416–32.

16. Ted Becker, "Teledemocracy," *The Futurist*, December 1981, p. 8.

17. John Wicklein, *Electronic Nightmare: The Home Communications Set and Your Freedom* (Boston: Beacon Press, 1982), pp. 1–14; Howard F. Didsbury, Jr., "The Serpent in the Garden," in *Communications and the Future*, ed. Didsbury, p. 311; David Burnham, *The Rise of the Computer State* (New York: Random House, 1983), pp. 49–88, 220–58; Warren Freedman, *The Right of Privacy in the Computer Age* (New York: Quorum Books, 1987), pp. 93–112.

18. Linda Helgerson, "Optical Discs: Advent of the Five-Inch Library," *Channels 1986 Field Guide*, p. 72.

19. Michael Schudson, *Discovering the News: A Social History of American Newspapers* (New York: Basic Books, 1978), p. 15.

20. Ibid., p. 27.

21. For a discussion of the Founders' aversion to direct popular appeals in elections, see James W. Ceaser, *Presidential Selection: Theory and Development* (Princeton: Princeton University Press, 1979), pp. 41–87.

22. Benjamin Barber, "The Second American Revolution," *Channels*, February–March 1982, p. 21.

23. Schudson, *Discovering the News*, pp. 3–11, 121–60.

24. Langdon Winner, "Do Artifacts Have Politics?" *Daedalus* 109 (Winter 1980): 122. The quotation is not indicative of Professor Winner's own views.

25. Ibid. The quotation is not indicative of Professor Winner's own views. For an example of political determinism, see Winston, *Misunderstanding Media*, pp. 23–25.

26. Joseph Schumpeter, "Democracy as Elite Competition," in *Frontiers of Democratic Theory*, ed. Henry Kariel (New York: Random House, 1970), p. 40.

27. See Naisbitt, *Megatrends*, pp. 159–61; Toffler, *Third Wave*, pp. 416–32.

28. The quotation is from Becker, "Teledemocracy," p. 9.

29. See, for example, Ted Becker and Christa Slaton, "Hawaii Televote: Measuring Public Opinion on Complex Policy Issues," *Political Science* 33, no. 1 (July 1981): 52–65. See also Christopher Arterton, Edward H. Lazarus, John Griffen, and Monica C. Andres, "Telecommunications Technologies and Political Participation" (Washington, D.C.: Roosevelt Center for American Policy Studies, 1984), pp. 375–90. The Hawaii televote is discussed at length in chapter 5.

30. Jean-Jacques Rousseau, *A Discourse on Political Economy*, in *The Social Contract and Discourses*, trans. G. D. H. Cole (New York: E. P. Dutton, 1950), p. 307.

31. Jean-Jacques Rousseau, *The Social Contract*, in *The Social Contract and Discourses*, trans. Cole, p. 18.

32. Ibid.

33. Jean Bethke Elshtain, "Democracy and the QUBE Tube," *The Nation*, August 7–14, 1982, p. 108.

34. Alexis de Tocqueville, *Democracy in America* (Henry Reeve Text), ed. Phillips Bradley (New York: Vintage, 1945), vol. 1, pp. 99–100.

35. Ibid., p. 63.

36. Robert Dahl, *A Preface to Democratic Theory* (Chicago: University of Chicago Press, 1956), p. 131.

37. Henry Kariel, "The Pluralist Norm," in *Frontiers of Democratic Theory*, ed. Kariel, p. 158.

38. Robert Dahl, *Dilemmas of Pluralist Democracy: Autonomy vs. Control* (New Haven: Yale University Press, 1982), p. 44.

39. Robert Dahl, *Pluralist Democracy in the United States: Conflict and Consent* (Chicago: Rand McNally, 1967), p. 24.

40. Robert Dahl, *Preface to Democratic Theory*, p. 133.

Chapter 2. What's New About the New Media?

1. Frederick Williams, *The Communications Revolution* (Beverly Hills, Calif.: Sage Publications, 1982), pp. 28–33.

Notes

2. Edward Cornish, "The Coming of an Information Society," *The Futurist*, April 1981, p. 21.

3. Telephone interview with James Sasaki, Cabletelevision Advertising Bureau, conducted by JoAnne Watson, March 1988 (hereafter cited as Sasaki interview).

4. Les Brown, "Cable TV: Wiring for Abundance," *The 1984 Field Guide to the Electronic Media*, *Channels*, November–December 1983, p. 25 (hereafter cited as *Channels 1984 Field Guide*).

5. Sasaki interview. For various predictions see Gary R. Orren and Stephen Bates, "New Communications Technologies" (Washington, D.C.: Roosevelt Center for American Policy Studies, December 1982), p. 127. Also see Cecilia Capuzzi, "Wall Street's Affair with the Wire," *'87 Field Guide to the Electronic Environment*, *Channels*, November–December 1986, p. 68 (hereafter cited as *Channels 1987 Field Guide*).

6. As described in Loy A. Singleton, *Telecommunications in the Information Age* (Cambridge, Mass.: Ballinger, 1983), pp. 31–32.

7. Telephone interview with John Neal, President, Southwest Division of Paragon Communications, conducted by Gary Orren, March 1988.

8. Sasaki interview.

9. John Wicklein, *Electronic Nightmare: The Home Communications Set and Your Freedoms* (Boston: Beacon Press, 1982), p. 107.

10. Singleton, *Telecommunications in the Information Age*, p. 121.

11. Richard M. Neustadt, *The Birth of Electronic Publishing* (White Plains, N.Y.: Knowledge Industry Publications, 1982), p. 8.

12. Ithiel de Sola Pool, "The New Technologies: The Promise of Abundent Channels at Lower Cost," in *What's News: The Media in American Society*, ed. Elie Abel (San Francisco: Institute for Contemporary Society, 1981), p. 87.

13. Doris Graber, *Mass Media and American Politics* (Washington, D.C.: Congressional Quarterly Press, 1980), chapter 9.

14. Daniel Czitrom, *Media and the American Mind: From Morse to McLuhan* (Chapel Hill: University of North Carolina Press, 1982), pp. 15–16.

15. Ibid., p. 3.

16. Interview with Pat Hazan, Associated Press, Broadcast Center, conducted by Karen Skelton, Washington, D.C., October 1984.

17. Interview with Greg Grace, Associated Press, Broadcast Center, conducted by Karen Skelton, Washington, D.C., October 1984.

18. Telephone interview with Brian Kahin, Massachusetts Institute of Technology, conducted by Karen Skelton, October 1984. Telephone interview with Betsy Mikita, Bell Laboratories, conducted by Karen Skelton, October 1984. Some uses of broadband networks are now being applied to telephones as well, expanding both their capacity and speed. Brian Kahin points out that as a telephone service is supplemented with answering machines, call forwarding, and call waiting (made possible through bandwidth), it will conduct point-to-point communication at significantly increased speeds.

19. Michael J. Robinson, "Three Faces of Congressional Media," in *The New Congress*, ed. Thomas Mann and Norman Ornstein (Washington, D.C.: American Enterprise Institute, 1981), pp. 59–61.

20. Interview with Tom Donahue of Senator Edward Kennedy's staff, conducted by Karen Skelton, Washington, D.C., October 1984.

21. Gerald Benjamin, *The Communications Revolution in Politics* (New York: Academy of Political Science, 1982), p. 93.

22. Czitrom, *Media and the American Mind*, p. 3.

23. Anthony Smith, *Goodbye, Gutenberg: The Newspaper Revolution of the 1980s* (New York: Oxford University Press, 1981), p. 21.

24. Czitrom, *Media and the American Mind*, p. 194.

25. "LPTV Gets the Go-Ahead," *Broadcasting*, March 1982, p. 35.

26. Mark Edmundson, "LPTV: The Sleeping Dwarf," *Channels 1984 Field Guide*, p. 55. Also see Singleton, *Telecommunications in the Information Age*, p. 51; Michael Couzens, "They Jes' Keep a-Growin'," *Channels 1987 Field Guide*, p. 54.

27. Charles Tate, "Community Control of Cable Television Systems," in *Talking*

Back: Citizen Feedback and Cable Technology, ed. Ithiel de Sola Pool (Cambridge, Mass: MIT Press, 1973), p. 57.

28. Singleton, *Telecommunications in the Information Age*, p. 29.

29. David Lachenbruch, "From Gizmo to Household Word," *The Essential 1986 Field Guide to the Electronic Environment, Channels*, November–December 1985, p. 74.

30. Lawrence M. Fisher, "Slow Motion for VCRs," *New York Times*, May 24, 1987, sec. 3, p. 1.

31. Smith, *Goodbye, Gutenberg*, p. 21.

32. Ibid., p. 313.

33. We are grateful to sociologist Michael Schudson for stimulating our thinking on the distinction between the content and volume of choice as it applies to user control.

34. James C. Emery, "Electronic Marketplace of Ideas," *Journal of Communication*, Spring 1978, p. 77.

35. F. Christopher Arterton, "Communications Technology and Political Campaigns in 1982: Assessing the Implications" (Washington, D.C.: Roosevelt Center for American Policy Studies, June 1983), p. 43.

36. Ibid., p. 22.

37. Ibid., p. 29.

38. Benjamin, *Communications Revolution in Politics*, p. 4.

39. The following discussion of the use of new media for targeting by political advertisers, incumbents, and interest groups, pages 51 to 53, is drawn from Orren and Bates, "New Communications Technologies," pp. 44–46, 67–68, 78–79, 81.

40. Richard M. Neustadt, "Watch Out, Politics—Technology Is Coming," *Washington Post*, March 14, 1982, p. D5.

41. Anne Haskell, "Live From Capitol Hill," *Washington Journalism Review*, November 1982, p. 49.

42. Jane Perlez, "New Jersey Senator Drops In, Via TV," *New York Times*, March 21, 1984, p. B1.

43. Haskell, "Live From Capitol Hill," p. 48.

44. Ibid., p. 50.

45. Quoted in Andrew Pollack, "A TV Station for Business," *New York Times*, August 27, 1981, p. 8.

46. The following two paragraphs are drawn from Orren and Bates, "New Communications Technologies," pp. 30–31. The interview with political scientist Ithiel de Sola Pool was conducted by Stephen Bates, Cambridge, Mass., September 21, 1982.

47. Orren and Bates, "New Communications Technologies," p. 31.

48. James Traub, "Satellites: The Birds That Make It All Fly," *Channels 1984 Field Guide*, pp. 8–9.

49. Les Brown, "Broadcast TV: Winner—and Still Champion," *Channels 1984 Field Guide*, p. 52.

50. Benjamin Barber, "The Tides in New Channels," *New York Times*, June 22, 1984, p. A27.

51. The following discussion of interactive media, pages 59 to 63, is drawn from Orren and Bates, "New Communications Technologies," pp. 5, 10–13, 57–61.

52. Carolyn Marvin, "Delivering the News of the Future," *Journal of Communication*, Winter 1980, p. 13.

53. Wicklein, *Electronic Nightmare*, p. 101.

54. Interview with Ben Compaine, conducted by Stephen Bates, Cambridge, Mass., August 20, 1982 (hereafter cited as Compaine interview).

55. John Carey, "Videotex: The Past as Prologue," *Journal of Communication*, Spring 1982, p. 83.

56. Compaine interview.

57. Bruce Owen, "Role of Print in an Electronic Society," in *Communications for Tomorrow: Policy Perspectives for the 1980's*, ed. Glen O. Robinson (New York: Praeger, 1978), p. 230.

58. Harry F. Waters and William D. Marbach, "Two-Way Tube," *Newsweek*, July 3, 1978, p. 65.

Notes

59. Ted Becker, "Teledemocracy: Bringing Power Back to the People," *The Futurist*, December 1981, p. 9.

60. Ithiel de Sola Pool and Herbert E. Alexander, "Politics in a Wired Nation," in *Talking Back*, ed. Pool, p. 80.

61. Quoted in Waters and Marbach, "Two-Way Tube," p. 65.

62. Interview with Daniel Bell, conducted by Stephen Bates, Cambridge, Mass., September 30, 1982.

63. F. Christopher Arterton, *Teledemocracy: Can Technology Protect Democracy?* (Newbury Park, Calif.: Sage, 1987).

64. Ithiel de Sola Pool, "Citizen Feedback in Political Philosophy," in *Talking Back*, ed. Pool, p. 244.

65. Ibid., p. 237.

66. Quoted in Alvin Toffler, "And on the Tricentennial . . . ," in *Television Today: A Closeup View*, ed. Barry Cole (New York: Oxford University Press, 1981), p. 464.

67. V. O. Key, *The Responsible Electorate* (Cambridge, Mass.: Harvard University Press, 1966).

68. Russell Neuman, "Putting the Communications Revolution in Perspective," MIT Research Program on Communications Policy, Project on the Future of the Mass Audience, September 1981, p. 17.

Chapter 3. Elections and the Media: Past, Present, and Future

1. Compare Louis Hartz, *The Liberal Tradition in America* (New York: Harcourt Brace, 1955), with: J. G. A. Pocock, *The Machiavellian Moment: Florentine Political Thought and the Atlantic Republican Tradition* (Princeton: Princeton University Press, 1975); Bernard Bailyn, *The Ideological Origins of the American Revolution* (Cambridge, Mass.: Harvard University Press, 1967); and Gordon Wood, *The Creation of the American Republic, 1776–1787* (New York: W. W. Norton, 1969).

2. Kathleen Jamieson, *Packaging the Presidency* (New York: Oxford University Press, 1984), p. 1.

3. Here we have relied on the excellent summary and analysis in James W. Ceaser, *Presidential Selection: Theory and Development* (Princeton: Princeton University Press, 1979), pp. 41–87.

4. Because the Founding Fathers believed that the principal threat to constitutional government would come from the popular side—currents of public opinion and demagogues who might win public confidence—the great challenge facing republican government was to attract wise, virtuous leaders and to design formal arrangements for keeping them virtuous. See Ceaser, *Presidential Selection*, pp. 41–87.

5. Ronald P. Formisano, "Deferential-Participant Politics: The Early Republic's Political Culture, 1789–1840," *American Political Science Review* 68 (June 1974): 473.

6. Paul Goodman, "The First American Party System," in *The American Party Systems*, ed. William Nisbet Chambers and Walter Dean Burnham (New York: Oxford University Press, 1975), p. 86.

7. Walter Dean Burnham, "Party Systems and the Political Process," in *American Party Systems*, ed. Chambers and Burnham, p. 292.

8. Wood, *Creation of the American Republic*, p. 163.

9. James S. Young, *The Washington Community, 1800–1828* (New York: Columbia University Press, 1966), p. 98.

10. Quoted in Thomas Bender, *Community and Social Change in America* (New Brunswick, N.J.: Rutgers University Press, 1978), p. 75.

11. Ibid., pp. 61–108.

12. Young, *Washington Community*, pp. 97–109.

13. The leading exponent of this view was Hartz, *Liberal Tradition in America*.

14. John P. Diggins, *The Lost Soul of American Politics: Virtue, Self-Interest, and the Foundations of Liberalism* (New York: Basic Books, 1984), p. 12.

15. Pocock, *Machiavellian Moment*; Bailyn, *Ideological Origins*; and Wood, *Creation of the American Republic*.

16. Daniel J. Boorstin, *The Americans: The Colonial Experience* (New York: Vintage Books, 1958), p. 326.

17. Frank Luther Mott, *American Journalism* (New York: Macmillan, 1941), pp. 59, 159. Circulation in eighteenth-century America was low compared to the nineteenth century, but high compared to Europe.

18. Richard L. Rubin, *Press, Party and Presidency* (New York: W. W. Norton, 1981), p. 8.

19. Ibid.

20. Ibid., p. 47.

21. Quoted in ibid., p. 47.

22. Boorstin, *The Americans*, pp. 324–25.

23. See Culver H. Smith, *The Press, Politics, and Patronage: The American Government's Use of Newspapers, 1789–1875* (Athens, Ga.: University of Georgia Press, 1977).

24. Thomas Jefferson, letter to Colonel Edward Carrington, January 16, 1787, quoted in Adrienne Koch and William Peden, *The Life and Selected Writings of Thomas Jefferson* (New York: Random House, 1944), pp. 411–12.

25. James Madison, Letter to Thomas Jefferson, June 6, 1787, in *The Records of the Federal Convention of 1787*, vol. 3, ed. Max Farrand (New Haven: Yale University Press, 1911), p. 35; Carl Van Doren, *The Great Rehearsal: The Story of the Making and Ratifying of the Constitution of the United States* (New York: Penguin, 1986), p. 28.

26. Robert Michel, "Politics in the Age of Television," *Washington Post National Weekly Edition*, June 4, 1984, p. 27.

27. Paul Kleppner, *The Third Electoral System, 1853–1892* (Chapel Hill: University of North Carolina Press, 1979), p. 169.

28. Quoted in Stephen A. Salamore and Barbara G. Salamore, *Candidates, Parties, and Campaigns* (Washington, D.C.: Congressional Quarterly Press, 1985), p. 20.

29. Rubin, *Press, Party and Presidency*, pp. 27–28.

30. Ibid., pp. 43–44.

31. Boorstin, *The Americans*, p. 430.

32. Richard J. Jensen, *The Winning of the Midwest: Social and Poitical Conflict, 1888–96* (Chicago: University of Chicago Press, 1971), p. 165.

33. Mott, *American Journalism*, p. 167. There were three times as many papers in the United States as in England or France in 1833 (p. 216). The number, circulation, and influence of newspapers astonished visitors to the United States. As one observer noted in 1833, "The influence and circulation of newspapers is great beyond anything ever known in Europe. In truth, nine tenths of the population read nothing else. . . . Every village, nay, almost every hamlet, has its press. . . . Newspapers penetrate to every crevice of the nation." Thomas Hamilton, *Men and Manners in America*, quoted in Mott, *American Journalism*, p. 168.

34. Rubin, *Press, Party and Presidency*, p. 51; Mott, *American Journalism*, p. 216.

35. Mott, *American Journalism*, pp. 168, 200.

36. Ibid., p. 216.

37. Rubin, *Press, Party and Presidency*, p. 32.

38. On the development of the professional norm of objectivity in journalism, see Michael Schudson, *Discovering the News: A Social History of American Newspapers* (New York: Basic Books, 1978).

39. Mott, *American Journalism*, p. 412.

40. Ibid., pp. 412, 720.

41. Salamore and Salamore, *Candidates, Parties, and Campaigns*, p. 41.

42. Rubin, *Press, Party and Presidency*, p. 147.

43. Quoted in Jamieson, *Packaging the Presidency*, p. 21.

44. Recent studies have questioned whether journalists' personal opinions actually

Notes

color their reporting in a significant way. See, for example, Michael J. Robinson and Margaret A. Sheehan, *Over the Wire and on TV: CBS and UPI in Campaign '80* (New York: Russell Sage, 1983), chap. 3; Michael J. Robinson, "Just How Liberal Is the News? 1980 Revisited," *Public Opinion*, February–March 1983, pp. 55–60; and Maura Clancey and Michael J. Robinson, "General Election Coverage: Part I," *Public Opinion*, December–January 1985, pp. 49–54. To the limited extent that the media are evaluative, they are overwhelmingly negative toward politicians. See Robinson and Sheehan, *Over the Wire and on TV*.

45. Jensen, *Winning of the Midwest*, p. 166.

46. Ibid., p. 154.

47. Rubin, *Press, Party and Presidency*, pp. 191–96.

48. Quoted in Salamore and Salamore, *Candidates, Parties, and Campaigns*, p. 37.

49. "The Electronic Plebiscite," editorial, *New Republic*, October 29, 1984, p. 8.

50. Michael J. Bayer and Joseph Rodota, "Computerized Opposition Research: The Instant Parry," *Campaigns and Elections* 6 (Spring 1985): 26.

51. Ibid.

52. Ibid.

53. Ibid., p. 27.

54. "Secret Reagan Weapon in Race: Computer," *New York Times*, November 13, 1984, p. A25.

55. Dom Bonafede, "Strides in Technology Are Changing the Face of Political Campaigning," *National Journal*, April 7, 1984, p. 657.

56. See Frank L. Tobe, "New Techniques in Computerized Voter Contact," in *New Communications Technologies in Politics*, ed. Robert Meadow (Washington, D.C.: Annenberg School of Communications, Washington Program, 1985), p. 63.

57. Bonafede, "Strides in Technology," pp. 660–61. Both President Reagan and Vice President Bush have used teleconferencing. When Bush was unable to spare the time to attend a Republican fund-raising event in California, he used Washington broadcasting facilities and a satellite connection to appear before the group and field their questions. See Richard M. Neustadt, "Watch Out, Politics—Technology is Coming," *Washington Post*, March 14, 1982, p. D5. Reagan has used the Chamber of Commerce's Washington broadcast facilities to appear before fund-raising and other political functions. See F. Christopher Arterton, "Communications Technology and Political Campaigns in 1982: Assessing the Implications" (Washington, D.C.: Roosevelt Center for American Policy Studies, June 1983), p. 31.

58. Telephone interview with Fred Asbell, Director of Committee Services, Republican National Congressional Committee, conducted by Karen Skelton, July 1985.

59. Andrew Rosenthal, "Campaigning to Instant Response," *New York Times*, July 25, 1987, p. 9.

60. Quoted in Mickey Kaus with Eleanor Clift, "Fresh-Baked Political Wisdom," *Newsweek*, November 2, 1987, p. 83.

61. Eric Freedman, "Plugging in Political Databases," *Empire State Report*, November 1984, pp. 38–39.

62. Bonafede, "Strides in Technology," p. 661.

63. David Doak, quoted in Andrew Rosenthal, "Cable TV Playing Key Role in 1988," *New York Times*, January 16, 1988, p. 8.

64. New Jersey provides a unique opportunity for candidates and officials to reach cable viewers. New Jersey is the only state in the nation with a completely *interconnected* cable system. Therefore, it is not necessary to send programs separately to dozens of local cable franchises. These local systems are connected into a single statewide cable network.

65. Arterton, "Communications Technology," p. 17.

66. Bonafede, "Strides in Technology," pp. 659–60.

67. Tom Wicker, "Showdown Via Satellite," *New York Times*, August 1, 1987, p. 31.

68. Robin Toner, "Of Campaigning in the South: Pool to Pool, Condo to Farm," *New York Times*, March 6, 1988, p. 36; John Aloysius Farrell, "Stumping Out, Media In as March 8 Nears," *Boston Globe*, February 29, 1988, p. 1.

69. See Henry Brady, "Computer-Assisted Survey Methods and Presidential Primaries," *Election Politics*, Summer 1984, pp. 20–23.

70. Stuart Brotman, "New Campaigning of the New Media," *Campaigns and Elections* 2 (Fall 1981): 33.

71. Russell Neuman, "Scenario 4: Politics as Usual," in *Election Communications and the Election of 1992*, ed. Franklin J. Havlicek (Washington, D.C.: American Bar Association Special Committee on Election Law and Voter Participation, 1983), pp. 22–25.

72. David Broder, "Before Letting the Cameras Roll . . . ," *Boston Globe*, February 21, 1982, p. A7.

73. Quoted in Marvin Barrett, "The Cable Revolution," in *Broadcast Journalism*, ed. Marvin Barrett (New York: Everest House, 1982), pp. 90–91.

74. Quoted in Arterton, "Communications Technology," p. 60.

75. Salamore and Salamore, *Candidates, Parties, and Campaigns*, p. 237.

76. For discussion of the history of academic voting theories, see Peter B. Natchez, *Images of Voting/Visions of Democracy* (New York: Basic Books, 1985).

77. Nelson Polsby, *The Consequences of Party Reform* (New York: Oxford University Press, 1983), pp. 132–40.

78. This does not mean totally replacing primaries with party caucuses and conventions. Our preference is for an electoral system that reflects a blend of the three democratic ideals. The current system tilts too far in a plebiscitary direction and requires better balance among the three ideals.

79. For an excellent account of the problems inherent in communitarian politics, see Jane J. Mansbridge, *Beyond Adversary Democracy* (New York: Basic Books, 1980), especially chaps. 7–11.

Chapter 4. Communications Technology and Governance

1. David Easton, *A Systems Analysis of Political Life* (New York: Wiley, 1965), chap. 1.

2. James Madison, "Federalist No. 10," in *The Federalist Papers*, intro. Clinton Rossiter (New York: Mentor, 1961), p. 79.

3. Alexis de Tocqueville, *Democracy in America* (Henry Reeve Text), ed. Phillips Bradley (New York: Vintage, 1945).

4. Arthur Bentley, *The Process of Government* (Chicago: University of Chicago Press, 1908), p. 10.

5. We are indebted to Leslie Tucker for research work on *The Silent Scream* and its reception on Capitol Hill.

6. Quoted in Dudley Clendinen, "President Praises Foes of Abortion," *New York Times*, January 23, 1985, p. A1.

7. Leslie Tucker interviewed the staffs of six congressional offices in gauging their reactions to the videotape.

8. Interview with Larry Kirkman, Director, Labor Institute of Public Affairs, conducted by Christopher Arterton, Washington, D.C., August 1985.

9. Kristin Luker, *Abortion and the Politics of Motherhood* (Berkeley: University of California Press, 1984).

10. Norman Nie and Sidney Verba, *Participation in America: Political Democracy and Social Equality* (New York: Harper & Row, 1972), pp. 95–101.

11. Interview with Arnie Thomas, Vice-President, Legi-Slate, conducted by Christopher Arterton, Washington, D.C., October 4, 1985 (hereafter cited as Thomas interview).

12. Telephone interview with Katherine Rice, National League of Cities, conducted by Christopher Arterton, November 1985; telephone interview with Olivia Pickett, National League of Cities, conducted by Christopher Arterton, February 1986.

Notes

13. Labor Institute of Public Affairs (LIPA), "Satellite Communications" (Washington, D.C.: AFL-CIO, LIPA mimeo, 1986).

14. Telephone interview with Michael Reid, Postal Workers Union, conducted by Christopher Arterton, October 5 and 7, 1985.

15. LIPA, "Satellite Communications," p. 11.

16. Ibid.

17. Ann Cooper, "Lobbying in the '80s: High Tech Takes Hold," *National Journal*, September 14, 1985, p. 2036.

18. Ibid.

19. Ibid.

20. Gary Serota, *The U.S. Congress* (Washington, D.C.: Grassroots Guides on Democracy and Practical Politics, No. 66, 1984).

21. Interview with Milt Mitler, U.S. Chamber of Commerce, conducted by Christopher Arterton, Washington, D.C., April 7, 1983.

22. Thomas W. Lippman, "US Chamber Sets Up Own TV Network," *Washington Post*, February 12, 1982, p. D10.

23. Telephone interview with Frank Allen Philpot, BizNet Syndication, U.S. Chamber of Commerce, conducted by Christopher Arterton, September 30, 1985.

24. Mancur Olson, *The Logic of Collective Action* (Cambridge, Mass.: Harvard University Press, 1965).

25. Interview with Larry Kirkman, conducted by Christopher Arterton, Washington, D.C., September 1985.

26. Jeffrey K. Hadden and Charles E. Swann, *Prime Time Preachers: The Rising Power of Televangelism* (Reading, Mass.: Addison-Wesley, 1981), p. 11. For a more sustained treatment of the political potency of televangelism, see also Peter G. Horsfield, *Religious Television: The American Experience* (New York: Longman, 1984); and Hal Himmelstein, *Television Myth and the American Mind* (New York: Praeger, 1984), pp. 253–77. On direct political involvement by religious groups, see Steven Pressman. "Religious Right: Trying to Link Poll Power and Lobby Muscle," *Congressional Quarterly Weekly Report* 42 (September 22, 1984): 2315–19; and James L. Guth and John C. Green, "Faith and Politics: Religion and Ideology Among Political Contributors," *American Politics Quarterly* 14, no. 3 (July 1986): 186–200.

27. See Richard Hollander, *Video Democracy* (Mt. Airy, Md.: Lomond, 1985); Andrew S. McFarland, *Common Cause: Lobbying in the Public Interest* (Chatham, N.J.: Chatham House, 1984); and Luker, *Abortion and the Politics of Motherhood*.

28. David R. Mayhew, "Congressional Elections: The Case of Vanishing Marginals," *Polity*, Spring 1974, pp. 295–317.

29. Thomas E. Mann, *Unsafe at Any Margin: Interpreting Congressional Elections* (Washington, D.C.: American Enterprise Institute, 1978).

30. Richard F. Fenno, Jr., *Home Styles: House Members in Their Districts* (Boston: Little, Brown, 1978).

31. The network is called CTN (Cable Television Network of New Jersey, Inc.), and the penetration figure is drawn from the network's promotional packet produced in 1985.

32. Interview with Carter Clewes, Executive Director, Senate Republican Conference, conducted by Christopher Arterton, Washington, D.C., October 26, 1982.

33. Paul West, "The Video Connection: Beaming It Straight to Constituents," *Washington Journalism Review*, June 1985, pp. 48–50.

34. Interview with Kevin Childers, Press Secretary to Senator Paula Hawkins, conducted by Christopher Arterton, Washington, D.C., October 7, 1985.

35. David R. Mayhew, *Congress: The Electoral Connection* (New Haven: Yale University Press, 1974).

36. Fred B. Wood, et al., *Videoconferencing Via Satellite: Opening Congress to the People* (Washington, D.C.: Program of Policy Studies in Science and Technology, George Washington University, February 1978).

37. "Worldnet Brings Witnesses for Hill Hearing in from Panama," *Broadcasting,* June 10, 1985, pp. 89–90.

38. David Burnham, "A Channel That Focuses on Government," *New York Times,* February 8, 1984, p. C21; Michael Robinson and Maura Clancy, "Who Watches C-Span?" *C-SPAN Update,* Special Supplement, January 14, 1985.

39. Robinson and Clancy, "Who Watches C-Span?" Note: The authors obtained their figures on the number of homes receiving C-SPAN from the network itself. Its survey sampled 959 respondents.

40. Michael Robinson, "Television and American Politics, 1956–1976," *Public Interest,* Summer 1977, pp. 3–39, cited in Robinson and Clancy, "Who Watches C-Span?" p. S-2.

41. Telephone interview with Brian Lamb, President, C-SPAN, conducted by Wendy O'Donnell, October 7, 1985 (hereafter cited as Lamb interview).

42. Norman J. Ornstein, "Political News," *Video Review,* April 1985, p. 42.

43. Sidney Blumenthal, "Reaganism on Fast Forward," *New Republic,* September 3, 1984, p. 14.

44. Lamb interview.

45. Ibid.

46. Ibid.

47. Blumenthal, "Reaganism on Fast Forward," p. 15.

48. Norman Ornstein, comments at "The New Communication Technologies and the Democratic Process," a conference sponsored by the Aspen Institute for Humanistic Studies, Wye, Md., June 1985.

49. The eleven are: Alaska, Florida, Illinois, Kansas, Montana, Nevada, New Hampshire, New York, North Dakota, Oregon, and Virginia. See Andrea Paterson, "Automating the State Legislatures," *State Legislatures,* May 1985, pp. 9–16; and Eric Freedman, "Plugging in Political Databases," *Empire State Report,* November 1984, pp. 38–39.

50. F. Christopher Arterton, *Teledemocracy: Can Technology Protect Democracy?* (Newbury Park, Calif.: Sage, 1987).

51. In 1985 the State of New York was sued by Legi-Tech, a private firm that wanted to get access to the state's data and resell it to its own subscribers. The U.S. Court of Appeals for the Second Circuit ruled that the state could not completely exclude Legi-Tech, especially if the state's system contained information that could not be obtained otherwise or almost as rapidly. See Legi-Tech, Inc. v. Keiper, 766 F.2d 728 (2d Cir. 1985).

52. Christopher Arterton, Edward H. Lazarus, John Griffen, and Monica C. Andres, "Telecommunication Technologies and Political Participation" (Washington, D.C.: Roosevelt Center for American Policy Studies, 1984) (hereafter cited as Roosevelt Center report).

53. Telephone interviews with Senator William Sederburg, conducted by Christopher Arterton, November 1985 and January 1986.

54. Roosevelt Center report.

55. For information about the available systems, see Committee on House Administration, "HIS Catalogue of Computer and Information Services" (Washington, D.C.: House of Representatives, December 1984).

56. Interview with James Aldensteder, House Information Services, conducted by Christopher Arterton, Washington, D.C., September 1985 (hereafter cited as Aldensteder interview).

57. Richard C. Davis and David Whitman, "The Use of Computers in the House of Representatives" (Cambridge, Mass.: John F. Kennedy School of Government, Case Writing Program, Case Study No. C14-79-242, 1979).

58. Ibid.

59. Michael Malbin, *Unelected Representatives: Congressional Staff and the Future of Representative Government* (New York: Basic Books, 1980).

60. Steve Blakely, "Computers Alter the Way Congress Does Business," *Congressional Quarterly,* July 13, 1985, pp. 1379–82.

61. Aldensteder interview; Committee on House Administration, "HIS Catalogue."

Notes

62. Committee on House Administration, "HIS Catalogue."

63. Quoted in Peggy Watt, "Micros in the White House," *InfoWorld*, August 27, 1984, p. 15.

64. "ADP Outlays—Planning for Rapid Growth," *Government Executive*, October 1984, p. 30.

65. Amitai Etzioni, "A Management Computer for the President," *Technology Review*, January 1983, pp. 39–40.

66. Ibid., p. 40.

67. David Burnham, *The Rise of the Computer State* (New York: Random House, 1980), pp. 114–15.

68. Dudley Clendinen, "New Hampshire Leaders Split Over Computers," *New York Times*, May 6, 1985, p. B1.

69. Ibid.

70. Telephone interview with Frank Haley, Governor's Press Secretary, State of New Hampshire, conducted by Christopher Arterton, October 21, 1985.

71. Chandler Harrison Stevens, "Networking: Legitech Experiments and the Development of Politechs," report to NSF grants DSI 77-27940 and DSI 77-17838 (Winchester, Mass.: Participation Systems, Inc., June 1980).

72. For research on diffusion of innovations, see Everett M. Rogers, *Diffusion of Innovations*, 3d ed. (New York: Free Press, 1983).

73. Mayhew, *Congress*.

74. See Alvin Toffler, *The Third Wave* (New York: William Morrow, 1980); and John Naisbitt, *Megatrends: Ten New Directions Transforming Our Lives* (New York: Warner Books, 1982).

75. See Benjamin Barber, *Strong Democracy: Participatory Politics for a New Age* (Berkeley: University of California Press, 1984).

76. Thomas interview.

77. Christopher Arterton, *Media Politics* (Lexington, Mass: Lexington Books, 1984), chap. 2.

78. Tocqueville, *Democracy in America*.

79. William Kornhauser, *The Politics of Mass Society* (Glencoe, Ill.: Free Press, 1959).

80. R. Kenneth Godwin and Robert L. Mitchell, "The Implications of Direct Mail for Political Organizations," paper presented at the annual meeting of the American Political Science Association, Chicago, September 1983.

81. Nelson Polsby, *The Consequences of Party Reform* (New York: Oxford University Press, 1983), pp. 132–42.

82. Luker, *Abortion and the Politics of Motherhood*.

83. Theodore Lowi, *The End of Liberalism* (New York: W. W. Norton, 1969).

84. For a further discussion of these issues, see Robert Dahl, *Preface to Democratic Theory* (Chicago: University of Chicago Press, 1956); and Gabriel Almond and Sidney Verba, *The Civic Culture* (Boston: Little, Brown, 1963), chap. 13.

85. Philip Converse, "The Nature of Belief Systems in Mass Publics," in *Ideology and Discontent*, ed. David Apter (New York: Free Press, 1964), pp. 206–61.

86. See, for example, the discussion in Lucy Rieselback, *Congressional Reform in the 1970's* (Morrison, N.J.: General Learning Press, 1977), pp. 155–98, 367–416; or in James Sundquist, *The Decline and Resurgence of Congress* (Washington, D.C.: Brookings Institution, 1981).

87. For an intensive discussion of iron triangles, see Harold Seidman, *Politics, Position and Power*, 2d ed. (New York: Oxford University Press, 1976).

88. For example, see Toffler, *Third Wave*; Naisbitt, *Megatrends*; and James Martin, *The Wired Nation* (Englewood Cliffs, N.J.: Prentice-Hall, 1978).

89. James MacGregor Burns, *Leadership* (New York: Harper & Row, 1978); Committee on Political Parties, American Political Science Association, "Toward a More Responsible Two-Party System," *American Political Science Review*, September 1950, supplement.

Notes

Chapter 5. The New Media and Democratic Participation

1. Alvin Toffler, *The Third Wave* (New York: William Morrow, 1980), pp. 429, 417, 382.

2. John Naisbitt, *Megatrends: Ten New Directions Transforming Our Lives* (New York: Warner Books, 1982), p. 160.

3. The account of the Hawaii televote is taken from Ted Becker and Christa Slaton, "Hawaii Televote: Measuring Public Opinion on Complex Policy Issues," *Political Science* 33, no. 1 (July 1981): 52–65. See also Christopher Arterton, Edward H. Lazarus, John Griffen, and Monica C. Andres, "Telecommunications Technologies and Political Participation" (Washington, D.C.: Roosevelt Center for American Policy Studies, 1984), pp. 375–90 (hereafter cited as Roosevelt Center report).

4. Information about the televote procedures appears in Becker and Slaton, "Hawaii Televote," 58–59.

5. Ibid., appendix.

6. Ibid., 58.

7. Ibid.

8. The '84 Vote (New York: ABC News, 1985), pp. 76–77.

9. Roosevelt Center report, p. 285.

10. Ibid., p. 354.

11. Ibid., p. 285.

12. Ibid., p. 450.

13. Ibid., p. 327.

14. Ted Becker, "Teledemocracy," *The Futurist*, December 1981, p. 8.

15. Ibid., p. 9.

16. Les Brown, "Whatever Happened to Cable?" *Channels*, May–June 1984, p. 22. See also Sally Bedell Smith, "Two-Way Cable TV Falters," *New York Times*, March 28, 1984, p. C25.

17. Becker and Slaton, "Hawaii Televote," 60.

18. Ibid.

19. This criticism appears in Kenneth Laudon, *Communications Technology and Democratic Participation* (New York: Praeger, 1977), pp. 31–33, 36.

20. Ibid., p. 39.

21. Becker and Slaton, "Hawaii Televote," 53–54.

22. Ibid., 54.

23. Becker, "Teledemocracy," p. 7.

24. Becker and Slaton, "Hawaii Televote," appendix.

25. Becker, "Teledemocracy," p. 8.

26. Roosevelt Center report, p. 463.

27. Jean Bethke Elshtain, "Democracy and the QUBE Tube," *The Nation*, August 7–14, 1982, p. 110.

28. See Barry Orton, "Phony Polls: The Pollster's Nemesis," *Public Opinion*, June–July 1982, pp. 56–60.

29. Elshtain, "Democracy and the QUBE Tube," p. 109.

30. Ibid.

31. The account of the Reading experiment is taken from Mitchell L. Moss, "Interactive Television: Reading, Pa.: Research on Community Uses," *Journal of Communication* 28, no. 2 (Spring 1978): 160–67.

32. Ibid., 163.

33. Benjamin Barber, *Strong Democracy: Participatory Politics for a New Age* (Berkeley: University of California Press, 1984), p. 276.

34. Ibid.; see also Moss, "Reading, Pa.," 163–67.

35. Barber, *Strong Democracy*, p. 276, n. 22.

36. Roosevelt Center report, pp. 252–53.

37. Richard M. Neustadt, "Watch Out, Politics—Technology Is Coming," *Washington Post*, March 14, 1982, p. D1.

Notes

38. Benjamin Barber, "The Second American Revolution," *Channels*, February–March 1982, p. 62.

39. Peter Kerr, "Public Access TV Ratings Disputed," *New York Times*, March 24, 1984, p. 46.

40. Roosevelt Center report, p. 323.

41. Kerr, "Public Access TV Ratings," p. 46.

42. Laudon, *Communications Technology*, p. 411.

43. "Revising the View of Pay Cable," *Broadcasting*, June 3, 1985, p. 54.

44. W. Russell Neuman, *The Paradox of Mass Politics: Knowledge and Opinion in the American Electorate* (Cambridge, Mass.: Harvard University Press, 1986), p. 155.

45. "A. D. Little Says Cable Will Finish out the Decade with a Bang," *Broadcasting*, June 10, 1985, p. 32.

46. Laudon, *Communications Technology*, p. 49.

47. Richard Sennett, *The Fall of Public Man* (New York: Alfred A. Knopf, 1977), p. 283.

48. Ibid.

49. Ibid.

50. Roosevelt Center report, p. 323.

51. Ibid., p. 321.

52. Ibid., pp. 214–15.

53. Ibid., p. 323.

54. Moss, "Reading, Pa.," 166 (emphasis added).

55. Neustadt, "Watch Out, Politics," p. D5.

56. Ithiel de Sola Pool, *Technologies of Freedom* (Cambridge, Mass.: Harvard University Press, Belknap Press, 1983), p. 172.

57. Benjamin Barber, "The Tides in New Channels," *New York Times*, June 22, 1984, p. A27.

58. Ibid.

59. Barber, "Second American Revolution," p. 22.

60. Gary Arlen, "Videotex: High Rollers with High Hopes," *'87 Field Guide to the Electronic Environment, Channels*, November–December 1986, p. 86.

61. Barber, *Strong Democracy*, p. 278.

62. These figures were provided to Jeffrey Abramson in a telephone conversation with a representative for Mead Data Central, April 14, 1988.

63. Gary Stix, "What Zapped the Electronic Newspaper," *Columbia Journalism Review*, May–June 1987, p. 45.

Chapter 6. Policy in a Comparative Perspective

1. See Erwin G. Krasnow, Lawrence D. Longley, and Herbert A. Terry, *The Politics of Broadcast Regulation*, 3d ed. (New York: St. Martin's Press, 1982).

2. Ithiel de Sola Pool, *Technologies of Freedom* (Cambridge, Mass: Harvard University Press, Belknap Press, 1983).

3. In remarks at "New Communications Technology, Public Policy and Democratic Values," a conference at Harvard University on December 14–15, 1985, Michael Rice of the Aspen Institute cautioned the participants not to accept too quickly the line advanced by PBS officials that public broadcasting exists in a constantly impoverished state on the verge of collapse. In his view, the short history of the complex set of organizations that make up public broadcasting in the United States has been one of considerable and continuing growth.

4. Besides the United States, most of the Latin American nations have privately owned broadcast stations. Italy allows local stations to be privately owned but prevents them from joining together in a network.

5. Pool, *Technologies of Freedom*, p. 17.

6. Daniel Czitrom, *Media and the American Mind: From Morse to McLuhan* (Chapel Hill: University of North Carolina Press, 1982), pp. 6, 27.

7. Quoted in ibid., p. 22.

8. In addition to Czitrom, *Media and the American Mind,* see Robert L. Thompson, *Wiring a Continent: The History of the Telegraph Industry in the United States* (Princeton: Princeton University Press, 1947).

9. Ithiel de Sola Pool, The *Social Impact of the Telephone* (Cambridge, Mass.: MIT Press, 1977).

10. Czitrom, *Media and the American Mind,* p. 27.

11. Pool, *Technologies of Freedom,* p. 26.

12. Quoted in Krasnow, Longley, and Terry, *Politics of Broadcast Regulation,* p. 12.

13. Communications Act of 1934, 47 U.S.C., sec. 303(g).

14. Ayn Rand, "Capitalism," in Krasnow, Longley, and Terry, *Politics of Broadcast Regulation,* p. 29.

15. Pool, *Technologies of Freedom.*

16. This point has been made by numerous observers, including Benno Schmidt, *Freedom of the Press and Public Access* (New York: Praeger, 1976), chap. 1.

17. Communications Act of 1934, 47 U.S.C., sec. 326.

18. Pool, *Technologies of Freedom,* p. 110.

19. Ibid., p. 111.

20. H. G. Knitel, "Advertising in Radio and Television Broadcasts" (Strasbourg, France: Council of Europe, Mass Media File No. 1, 1982).

21. Quoted in Pool, *Technologies of Freedom,* p. 110.

22. Ibid.

23. Of course, informal practice in each country may vary markedly so that a seemingly independent structure may be heavily influenced by the government of the day. See A. Christofides, "Economic and Financial Aspects of the Mass Media" (Strasbourg, France: Council of Europe, Mass Media File No. 3, 1982); J. Dutter, "Comparative Study of Information Structures and Institutions in the Member States of the Council of Europe" (Strasbourg, France: Council of Europe, Committee on the Mass Media, December 13, 1979); and Parliamentary Assembly, Council of Europe, "Report on the Role and Management of Telecommunications in a Democratic Society" (Strasbourg, France: Council of Europe, 1975).

24. Christofides, "Economic and Financial Aspects," p. 10.

25. Howard R. Penniman and Austin Ranney, "The Regulation of Televised Political Advertising in Six Selected Democracies" (Washington, D.C.: Committee for the Study of the American Electorate, 1984), p. 3.

26. Asa Briggs, *Governing the BBC* (London: British Broadcasting Corporation, 1974), pp. 1–4.

27. Ibid., p. 17.

28. See Fred Friendly, *The Good Guys, the Bad Guys and the First Amendment* (New York: Vintage Books, 1975).

29. Alastair Milne, "Future Broadcasting Policy in Britain—Fraught with Ambiguity," *Combroad,* June 1985, pp. 1–4.

30. In Europe, four countries (Belgium, Denmark, Norway, and Sweden) have an absolute ban on television advertising; nine others permit ads as a supplemental source of funding (Austria, Cyprus, the Federal Republic of Germany, France, Ireland, Italy, Spain, Switzerland, and the United Kingdom). Even when permitted, the use of ads is often sharply regulated as to number, time of day, type of product, or broadcasting organization that can accept them. Dutter, "Information Structures and Institutions," pp. 14–15.

31. Harald Wendelbo, "Principles and Criteria Concerning the Content of Television Programmes" (Strasbourg, France: Council of Europe, Mass Media File No. 6, 1983).

32. George Wedell, *Broadcasting and Public Policy* (Manchester, England: European Institute for the Media, 1985).

33. Aaron Lijphart, *The Politics of Accommodation* (Berkeley: University of California Press, 1969), p. 1.

Notes

34. Ibid.

35. Institute of International Communications (IIC), "Broadcasting in the Netherlands," report to the Annen Committee on Broadcasting Policy (London: IIC, July 31, 1975).

36. See principally ibid.

37. Lijphart, *Politics of Accommodation*, pp. 41–48.

38. IIC, "Broadcasting in the Netherlands," p. 17; *Broadcasting News from the Netherlands*, No. 1 (Hilversum, Netherlands: Nederlandse Omroep Stichting, Communications Department, January 1985).

39. Lijphart, *Politics of Accommodation*, pp. 15–22.

40. Herman Wigbold, "The Shaky Pillars of Hilversum," in *Television and Political Life: Studies in Six European Countries*, ed. Anthony Smith (New York: St. Martin's Press, 1976), pp. 192–93.

41. "KRO," in *Broadcasting News from the Netherlands*, p. 9.

42. "EO," in *Broadcasting News from the Netherlands*, p. 10.

43. "TROS," in *Broadcasting News from the Netherlands*, p. 5.

44. IIC, "Broadcasting in the Netherlands," p. 13.

45. As this book went to press, the Dutch were implementing their new broadcasting law. For details as to how the act should work, we have relied upon *HilverSummary* (formerly *Broadcasting News from the Netherlands*), November 1987 (Hilversum, Netherlands: NOS, 1987).

46. Communications Act of 1934, 47 U.S.C., sec. 307.

47. See, for example, David Halberstam, *The Powers That Be* (New York: Alfred A. Knopf, 1979).

48. On the popularity of *60 Minutes*, see Peter J. Boyer, " '60 Minutes': A Hit Confronts the Odds," *New York Times*, September 13, 1987, sec. 2, p. 1.

49. Timothy Green, *The Universal Eye* (New York: Stein and Day, 1972), p. 31.

50. See, for example, Michael J. Robinson and Margaret A. Sheehan, *Over the Wire and on TV: CBS and UPI in Campaign '80* (New York: Russell Sage, 1983); and Thomas Patterson, *Mass Media Politics* (New York: Praeger, 1980).

51. Wigbold, "Shaky Pillars of Hilversum," p. 226.

52. Ibid., p. 218.

53. Penniman and Ranney, "Regulation of Televised Political Advertising," p. 26.

54. Ibid., p. 3; see also Communications Act of 1934, sec. 312.

55. George White, "A Study of Access to Broadcast Media," report to the Campaign Finance Study Group (Cambridge, Mass.: Institute of Politics, Harvard University, 1978).

56. Ibid.; see also Mary Ellen Leary, *Phantom Politics: Campaigning in California* (Washington, D.C.: Public Affairs Press, 1977).

57. Friendly, *Good Guys*.

58. Regarding limitations upon political commercials, see Newton N. Minow and Lee M. Mitchell, "Putting on the Candidates: The Uses of Television in Presidential Elections," *Annals of the American Academy of Political Science* 486 (July 1986): 146–57; and on the use of debates, see Joel Swerdlow, "Beyond Debate: A Paper on Televised Presidential Debates" (New York: The Twentieth Century Fund, 1983). See also the cynical approach of politicians documented in Joseph McGinniss, *The Selling of a President, 1968* (New York: Trident Press, 1969).

59. Christopher Arterton, *Media Politics* (Lexington, Mass.: Lexington Books, 1984). See also Robinson and Sheehan, *Over the Wire*; and Patterson, *Mass Media Politics*.

60. Herbert Gans, *Deciding What's News* (New York: Pantheon, 1979); Leon Sigal, *Reporters and Officials* (Lexington, Mass.: D. C. Heath, 1973).

61. Edie N. Goldenberg, *Making the Papers* (Lexington, Mass.: Lexington Books, 1975); Michael Lipsky, "Protest as a Political Resource," *American Political Science Review* 62 (December 1968): 1144–58.

62. Grace Goldie, *Facing the Nation: Television and Politics, 1936–1976* (London: Bodley Head, 1977).

63. Peter H. Foges, "Two Tribes," *Channels*, May–June 1985, p. 48.

64. Ibid., pp. 48–50.

65. Krasnow, Longley, and Terry, *Politics of Broadcast Regulation*, p. 58.

66. Red Lion Broadcasting Co. v. F.C.C., 395 U.S. 390 (1969).

67. Krasnow, Longley, and Terry, *Politics of Broadcast Regulation*, p. 118.

68. Ibid., pp. 58, 81.

69. CBS v. Democratic National Committee, 412 U.S. 94 (1973).

70. Miami Herald Publishing Co. v. Tornillo, 418 U.S. 241 (1974).

71. In Meredith Corp. v. F.C.C., 809 F.2d 863 (D.C. Cir. 1987), the U.S. Court of Appeals for the District of Columbia Circuit ruled that the FCC could not avoid ruling on the constitutionality of the Fairness Doctrine. As this book went to press, the matter was again before the federal courts.

72. See, for example, the work of the National Federation of Local Cable Programmers (NFLCP), including its report, "Municipal Programming" (Washington, D.C.: NFLCP mimeo, 1984); and its quarterly review, *Community Television Review*, especially the "Government Access" issue (vol. 8, no. 3, 1985).

73. Cable Act of 1984, 47 U.S.C., sec. 531(b) (public, educational, or governmental use), and secs. 541–47 (franchising and regulation).

74. Daniel Czitrom, *Media and the American Mind*, pp. 24–27.

75. George Gerbner, Larry Gross, Michael Morgan, and Nancy Signorielli, "The Mainstreaming of America: Violence Profile No. 11," *Journal of Communication* 30, no. 3 (Summer 1980): 10–29; George Gerbner, Larry Gross, Michael Morgan, and Nancy Signorielli, "Charting the Mainstream: Television's Contribution to Political Orientations," *Journal of Communication* 32, no. 2 (Spring 1982): 100–127.

76. Lord Charles Hill of Luton, Chair of the BBC Board of Governors, quoted in Briggs, *Governing the BBC*, p. 44.

77. Briggs, *Governing the BBC*.

78. Ibid.

79. Krasnow, Longley, and Terry, *Politics of Broadcast Regulation*, p. 59.

80. Ibid.

81. Ibid., p. 55.

82. Ibid., p. 56.

83. Ibid., pp. 60–61.

84. Quoted in ibid., p. 60.

85. *Advertising Age*, March 3, 1981, pp. 1, 80.

86. Arterton, *Media Politics*, chaps. 3, 4.

87. Peter Clarke and Susan H. Evans, *Covering Campaigns: Journalism in Congressional Elections* (Stanford: Stanford University Press, 1983).

88. See Michael Schudson, *Discovering the News: A Social History of American Newspapers* (New York: Basic Books, 1978).

89. Robert A. Dahl, *Preface to Democratic Theory* (Chicago: University of Chicago Press, 1976).

90. Ruth Thomas, *Broadcasting and Democracy in France* (Philadelphia: Temple University Press, 1977).

91. Anthony Smith, *The Shadow in the Cave: The Broadcaster, His Audience and the State* (Champlain: University of Illinois Press, 1973), p. 155.

92. Wigbold, "Shaky Pillars of Hilversum," p. 218.

93. Briggs, *Governing the BBC*, p. 211.

94. Goldie, *Facing the Nation*.

95. Briggs, *Governing the BBC*, p. 211.

96. Wigbold, "Shaky Pillars of Hilversum," p. 204.

97. Ibid.

98. James Perry, *U.S. and Them: How the Press Covered the 1972 Election* (New York: C. N. Potter, 1973); William Rivers, *The Adversaries* (Boston: Beacon Press, 1970).

99. Quoted in Friendly, *Good Guys*, p. 131.

100. Quoted in ibid., pp. 131–32.

101. William E. Porter, *Assault on the Media: The Nixon Years* (Ann Arbor: University of Michigan Press, 1976).

102. Krasnow, Longley, and Terry, *Politics of Broadcast Regulation*, p. 71.

Notes

103. Ibid., p. 85 (based on an interview with Richard M. Neustadt, President Carter's adviser on telecommunications policy).

104. Green, *Universal Eye*, p. 82.

105. For details see Briggs, *Governing the BBC*, pp. 191–92.

106. Quoted in ibid., p. 193.

107. Quoted in ibid., p. 194.

108. Ibid., pp. 120–240.

109. See the coverage in the London *Times*, especially David Hewson, "BBC Cancels Programme with IRA Interview," July 31, 1985, p. 1; and David Hewson, "Divided BBC to Meet Brittan over Film Ban," August 7, 1985, p. 1.

110. Hewson, "Divided BBC," p. 1.

111. Green, *Universal Eye*, p. 146.

112. "TROS," in *Broadcasting News from the Netherlands*, pp. 5–6.

113. David Hewson and Bill Johnstone, "Go-Ahead for Cable TV Likely Despite Opposition," *Times* (London), October 13, 1982, p 1; and "Hunt Report on Cable TV in Summary," *Times* (London), October 13, 1982, p. 5.

114. For a more extensive treatment of how the new media are evolving in European systems, see John Tydeman and Ellen Jakes Kelm, *The New Media in Europe* (Maidenhead, England: McGraw-Hill, 1986).

115. Benjamin Barber, *Strong Democracy: Paritcipatory Politics for a New Age* (Berkeley: University of California Press, 1984).

Chapter 7. Freedom of the Press and the New Media

1. Frohwerk v. United States, 249 U.S. 204 (1919) (prosecution of a Missouri German language newspaper for editorializing against World War I); Schenck v. United States, 249 U.S. 47 (1919) (prosecution for leafleting against the military draft during World War I). See also Masses Publishing Co. v. Patten, 244 F. Supp. 535 (S.D.N.Y. 1917) (prosecution of magazine for publishing cartoons and articles critical of World War I); Gitlow v. New York, 268 U.S. 652 (1925) (prosecution of socialist publication for advocating violent overthrow of government).

2. See, for example, Near v. Minnesota, 283 U.S. 697 (1931) (invalidating a statute that permitted injunctions against newspapers for printing malicious, scandalous or defamatory matter); New York Times v. United States, 403 U.S. 713 (1971) (finding government without power to restrain newspapers from publishing classified Pentagon study of Vietnam War decision making).

3. Red Lion Broadcasting Co. v. F.C.C., 395 U.S. 367, 390 (1969).

4. 47 U.S.C., secs. 301, 307(a), 309(a).

5. See, for example, Alexander Meiklejohn, *Free Speech and its Relation to Self-Government* (New York: Harper and Brothers, 1948), pp. 26–27, 93–94.

6. Compare New York Times Co. v. Sullivan, 376 U.S. 254 (1964) (defamation of public official is actionable only upon proof of actual malice), with Gertz v. Welch, 418 U.S. 323 (1974) (private persons permitted to recover for defamation without proof of actual malice).

7. Garrison v. Louisiana, 379 U.S. 64, 74–75 (1964).

8. New York Times Co. v. Sullivan, 376 U.S. at 270.

9. Meiklejohn, *Free Speech*, p. 25.

10. Red Lion Broadcasting Co. v. F.C.C., 395 U.S. at 390.

11. For instance, John Stuart Mill so relates free speech and truth in *On Liberty* (Indianapolis: Bobbs-Merrill, 1956), chapter 1 generally.

12. Jeffrey Abramson wishes to thank Professor Steven Holmes of the University of Chicago for bringing this point to his attention.

13. Terminiello v. Chicago, 337 U.S. 1 (1949) (overturning arrest of speaker for breaching the peace by stirring the public to anger).

14. Near v. Minnesota, 283 U.S. 697.

15. Cantwell v. Connecticut, 310 U.S. 296 (1940) (overturning arrest of Jehovah's Witnesses for breach of peace).

16. The argument that there has been a change in the paradigmatic free speech case comes from Owen M. Fiss, "Free Speech and Social Structure," 71 Iowa L. Rev. 1405, 1408–13 (1986).

17. See, for example, Near v. Minnesota, 283 U.S. at 716: "No one would question but that a government might prevent actual obstruction to its recruiting service or the publication of the sailing dates of transports or the number and location of troops."

18. See, for example, New York Times Co. v. Sullivan, 376 U.S. at 283 (actual malice standard for defamation suits by public officials against the press); Gertz v. Welch, 418 U.S. at 347 (so long as they do not impose liability without fault, states may define for themselves the appropriate standard of liability for a publisher or broadcaster who defames a private individual).

19. See, for example, Roth v. United States, 354 U.S. 476, 485 (1957) (obscenity is not within the area of constitutionally protected speech or press).

20. See, for example, Brandenburg v. Ohio, 395 U.S. 444, 447 (1969) (state may not forbid advocacy of the use of force or of illegal action "except where such advocacy is directed to inciting or producing imminent lawless action and is likely to incite or produce such action").

21. New York Times v. United States, 403 U.S. 713.

22. Ibid. at 726–27 (Brennan, J., concurring). But compare United States v. Progressive, Inc., 467 F. Supp. 990 (W.D. Wis. 1979) (enjoining a monthly magazine from publishing an article containing technical material on the design of the hydrogen bomb, on the grounds that publication of such matter gravely threatened national security).

23. 418 U.S. 241.

24. Ibid. at 248–50.

25. 47 U.S.C., sec. 301; similar provisions were contained in the Radio Act of 1927, 44 Stat. 1162.

26. 47 U.S.C., secs. 301, 307(a), 309(a).

27. 47 U.S.C., sec. 303 (r).

28. 47 U.S.C., sec. 312(a) (7).

29. 47 U.S.C., sec. 315(b) (1).

30. 47 U.S.C., sec. 315(a).

31. For an account of the partisan press prior to the emergence of the ideal of objective reporting, see James Melvin Lee, *History of American Journalism* (Boston: Houghton Mifflin Company, 1917), pp. 118–64.

32. Robert D. Hershey, Jr., "F.C.C. Votes Down Fairness Doctrine in a 4–0 Decision," *New York Times*, August 5, 1987, p. A1.

33. Great Lakes Broadcasting Co., 3 F.R.C. Ann. Rep. 32, 33 (1929).

34. National Citizens Comm. for Broadcasting v. F.C.C., 567 F.2d 1095, 1099 (D.C. Cir. 1977); see also Red Lion Broadcasting Co. v. F.C.C., 395 U.S. at 375–78.

35. Red Lion Broadcasting Co. v. F.C.C., 395 U.S. at 386–89.

36. 47 U.S.C., sec. 315(a) (1)–(4).

37. 47 U.S.C., sec. 315(a).

38. Red Lion Broadcasting Co. v. F.C.C., 395 U.S. at 380–82.

39. General Fairness Doctrine Obligations of Broadcast Licenses, 102 F.C.C.2d 143 (1985).

40. Ibid., p. 170.

41. Hershey, "F.C.C. Votes Down Fairness Doctrine," p. A1.

42. "Excerpts from F.C.C. Statement," *New York Times*, August 5, 1987, p. C26.

43. 47 C.F.R., secs. 73.123, 73.300, 73.598, 73.679.

44. Ibid.

45. Hershey, "F.C.C. Votes Down Fairness Doctrine," p. C26.

46. "Excerpts from F.C.C. Statement," p. C26.

47. 47 U.S.C., secs. 301, 307(a), (d).

48. Red Lion Broadcasting Co. v. F.C.C., 395 U.S. at 380–82.

Notes

49. Ibid. at 390.

50. Ibid. at 389.

51. The regulations of communications common carriers are set out in 47 U.S.C., sec. 201 et. seq.

52. 47 U.S.C., secs. 201(b), 203(a)–(e), 204, 205

53. 47 U.S.C., sec. 202(a)

54. United States v. American Telephone and Telegraph Co., 552 F. Supp. 131 (D.D.C. 1982), *aff'd*, 460 U.S. 1001 (1983).

55. Ibid at 178.

56. Ibid. at 225.

57. Ibid. at 181.

58. Ibid. at 189.

59. Reginald Stuart, "U.S. Asking Room for 'Baby Bells' to Grow," *New York Times*, February 8, 1987, sec. 4, p. 24.

60. United States v. Southwestern Cable Co., 392 U.S. 157, 178 (1968).

61. First Report and Order, 38 F.C.C. 683 (1965), *modified*, 1 F.C.C.2d 524 (1965); Second Report and Order, 2 F.C.C.2d 725 (1966).

62. First Report and Order, 38 F.C.C. at 716–19.

63. Ibid. at 719–30.

64. Second Report and Order, 2 F.C.C.2d at 782.

65. First Report and Order, 20 F.C.C.2d 201, 223–25 (1969).

66. Ibid. at 223; see also 47 C.F.R., sec. 74.1111(a) (1970).

67. Cable Television Report and Order, 36 F.C.C.2d 143 (1972), codified at 47 C.F.R., secs. 76.57, 76.59, 76.61 (1985), *aff'd sub nom.* American Civil Liberties Union v. F.C.C., 523 F.2d 1344 (9th Cir. 1975).

68. Ibid. at 174.

69. Ibid. at 189–98 (1972). The 1972 access rules were revised in 1976. See Report and Order, 59 F.C.C.2d 294 (1976); 47 C.F.R., secs. 76.254–256 (1976).

70. See Home Box Office, Inc. v. F.C.C., 567 F.2d 9, 18 n. 8 (D.C. Cir. 1977).

71. 406 U.S. 649, 676 (1972) (Burger, C. J., concurring).

72. 440 U.S. 689 (1979).

73. 47 U.S.C., sec. 153(h); Midwest Video II, 440 U.S. at 706.

74. Home Box Office, Inc. v. F.C.C., 567 F.2d 9.

75. Ibid. at 46.

76. Quincy Cable TV, Inc. v. F.C.C., 768 F.2d 1434 (D.C. Cir. 1985). On August 7, 1986, the FCC announced a plan for a transition period during which less stringent must-carry rules would remain in effect; after five years those rules would dissolve. 51 Fed. Reg. 44,608; 44,609; codified at 47 C.F.R., sec. 76.64 (1986).

77. Cable Communications Policy Act of 1984, 47 U.S.C., sec. 521 (4).

78. Ibid., sec. 531(b).

79. Ibid., sec. 531(e).

80. Ibid., sec. 532(c) (2).

81. Ibid., sec. 531(d) (PEG channels); 532(b)(4) (leased channels).

82. Peter Kerr, "Cable TV Pressing Free-Speech Issue," *New York Times*, April 5, 1984, p. C22.

83. See text accompanying notes 72 and 73.

84. Preferred Communications, Inc. v. City of Los Angeles, 754 F.2d 1396, 1401 n. 4 (9th Circ. 1985), *aff'd and remanded*, City of Los Angeles v. Preferred Communications, Inc., 106A S. Ct. 2034, 90 L. Ed. 2d 480 (1986). See also David Saylor, "Commentary: Municipal Ripoff: The Unconstitutionality of Cable Television Franchise Fees and Access Support Payments," 35 Cath. U. L. Rev. 671, 680 (1986).

85. Preferred Communications, Inc. v. City of Los Angeles, 754 F.2d at 1402.

86. Berkshire Cablevision v. Burke, 571 F. Supp. 976, 980 (D.R.I. 1983), *vacated and remanded*, 773 F.2d 382, 386 (1st Cir. 1985).

87. City of Los Angeles v. Preferred Communications, Inc., 90 L. Ed. 2d 480.

88. Preferred Communications, Inc. v. City of Los Angeles, 754 F.2d at 1411.

89. City of Los Angeles v. Preferred Communications, Inc., 90 L. Ed. 2d at 487.

90. Ibid. at 488.

91. 90 F.C.C.2d 676 (1982).

92. Jill Abehouse Stern, Erwin G. Krasnow, and R. Michael Senkowski, "The New Video Marketplace and the Search for a Coherent Regulatory Philosophy," 32 Cath. U. L. Rev. 529, 542 (1983).

93. Ibid. at 543; Richard Barbieri, "DBS By Any Other Name," *The Essential 1986 Field Guide to the Electronic Environment, Channels,* November–December 1985, p. 54.

94. 90 F.C.C.2d at 708.

95. Ibid.

96. 740 F.2d 1190 (D.C. Cir. 1984).

97. Ibid. at 1201 (emphasis in original).

98. Ibid. at 1205 (emphasis in original).

99. Ibid.

100. Notice of Proposed Rulemaking Concerning the Regulatory Classification of STV and DBS, Gen. Doc. 85-305, F.C.C. 85-538 (January 8, 1986). This ruling is now final.

101. Ibid., paragraph 7.

102. Allen Hammond IV, "To Be or Not to Be: FCC Regulation of Video Subscription Technologies," 35 Cath. U. L. Rev. 737, 751 (1986).

103. Multipoint Distribution Service, 45 F.C.C.2d 616 (1974).

104. Ibid. at 618.

105. 47 C.F.R., sec. 21.903(b) (2) (1985).

106. Richard Barbieri, "Wireless Cable: The Quick Fix That Came Late," *'87 Field Guide to the Electronic Environment, Channels,* November–December 1986, p. 57 (hereafter cited as *Channels 1987 Field Guide*).

107. Notice of Proposed Rulemaking, Multipoint Distribution Service, 104 F.C.C.2d 283 (1986).

108. Ibid. at 296–99.

109. 47 C.F.R., sec. 73.643(b) (1981).

110. Robert Koppel, "The Applicability of the Equal Time Doctrine and the Reasonable Access Rule to Elections in the New Media Era," 20 Harv. J. Legis. 499, 527 (1983).

111. Ibid.

112. "Lottery Is Planned for Low-Power TV," *New York Times,* April 1, 1983, p. C25.

113. Daniel Swillinger, "Candidates and the New Technologies: Should Political Broadcasting Rules Apply?" 49 Mo. L. Rev. 85, 93 (1984).

114. 464 U.S. 417 (1984).

115. 47 U.S.C., secs. 315(a), 312(a) (7).

116. Swillinger, "Candidates and the New Technologies," 49 Mo. L. Rev. at 94.

117. Ibid. at 94–95; see also Henry Geller, "Current Government Policy re Mass Communications," paper prepared for the Center for Philosophy and Public Policy, University of Maryland, 1986, pp. 32–33.

118. Memorandum and Order (Cablecasting), 23 F.C.C.2d 825, 829 (1970).

119. United States v. American Telephone and Telegraph Co., 552 F. Supp. at 189, 225.

120. Andrew Pollack, "Ruling May Not Aid Videotex," *New York Times,* September 15, 1987, p. D1.

121. But see text accompanying notes 87–90 for a description of current challenges to the constitutionality of exclusive cable franchises.

122. For a similar criticism, see Koppel, "Applicability of Equal Time Doctrine," 20 Harv. J. Legis. at 536–37.

123. See text accompanying notes 100–102.

124. Benno C. Schmidt, Jr., "Pluralist Programming and Regulation of Mass Communications Media," in *Communications for Tomorrow: Policy Perspectives for the 1980s,* ed. Glenn Robinson (New York: Praeger, 1978), p. 214.

125. Ibid., p. 213.

126. Henry Geller and Donna Lampert, "Cable Content Regulation and the First Amendment," 32 Cath. U. L. Rev. 603, 620 (1983).

Notes

127. Jeri Baker, "The Big Three Networks: Can the Cost-Cutters Beat the System?" *Channels 1987 Field Guide*, p. 41.

128. Ithiel de Sola Pool, *Technologies of Freedom* (Cambridge, Mass.: Harvard University Press, Belknap Press, 1983), p. 174.

129. Benjamin Barber, "The Second American Revolution," *Channels*, February–March 1982, p. 24.

130. Benjamin Barber, "The Tides in New Channels," *New York Times*, June 22, 1984, p. A27.

131. Sloan Commission on Cable Communications, *On the Cable: The Television of Abundance* (New York: McGraw-Hill, 1971), pp. 147–48.

132. Ibid.

133. Ibid., p. 148.

134. Pool, *Technologies of Freedom*, p. 169.

135. Sloan Commission, *On the Cable*, pp. 141–44.

136. *Cabinet Report on Cable Communications, Report to the President* (1974), cited in Pool, *Technologies of Freedom*, p. 169.

137. Pool, *Technologies of Freedom*, p. 170.

138. Ibid., p. 172.

139. See text accompanying notes 76–80 for a more detailed discussion of the Cable Communications Policy Act of 1984.

140. Rinker Buck, "Affiliates: The Year of Living Nervously," *Channels 1987 Field Guide*, p. 44.

141. Pool, *Technologies of Freedom*, p. 140.

142. Ibid., pp. 138–49; Geller, "Current Government Policy," p. 26.

143. Geller, "Current Government Policy," p. 20.

144. Benjamin Barber, *Strong Democracy: Participatory Politics for a New Age* (Berkeley: University of California Press, 1984), pp. 279–80.

Chapter 8. Toward an Electronic Commonwealth

1. See, for example, Steve Behrens, "Toward a United State of Media," *The Essential 1986 Field Guide to the Electronic Environment, Channels*, November–December 1985, pp. 8–10 (hereafter cited as *Channels 1986 Field Guide*). See also Andrew Pollack, "The Battle of the Titans: Part II," *New York Times*, June 30, 1985, sec. 3, p. 1.

2. For concrete suggestions for subsidizing a civic communications system in the electronic age, see Benjamin Barber, *Strong Democracy: Participatory Politics for a New Age* (Berkeley: University of California Press, 1984), pp. 278–79.

3. The information in this paragraph is taken from tables in *'87 Field Guide to the Electronic Environment, Channels*, November–December 1986, pp. 31–33, 73–74 (hereafter cited as *Channels 1987 Field Guide*).

4. Ibid.

5. Mark Kriss, "MDS: The Newest Channels in Town," *The 1984 Field Guide to the Electronic Media, Channels*, November–December 1983, p. 33 (hereafter cited as *Channels 1984 Field Guide*).

6. For amplification of this point, see chapter 7. See also Owen M. Fiss, "Free Speech and Social Structure," 71 Iowa L. Rev. 1405, 1408–13 (1986).

7. "Wired for Growth," *Channels 1987 Field Guide*, p. 69.

8. This section is adapted from Jeffrey Abramson, "Five Criticisms of Press Ethics," paper prepared for the Center for Philosophy and Public Policy, University of Maryland, 1986.

9. See Michael Schudson, *Advertising: The Uneasy Persuasion* (New York: Basic Books, 1984), pp. 14–44.

10. "Seven Voices: Journalists Talk About Their Lives—And How the World in

Which They Work Has Been Transformed," *Columbia Journalism Review*, May–June 1986, p. 48.

11. Jonathan Alter, "Taking CBS to Task," *Newsweek*, September 15, 1986, p. 53.

12. Ibid.

13. Michael Massing, "CBS: Sauterizing the News," *Columbia Journalism Review*, March–April 1986, pp. 27, 30.

14. Ben Brown, "Network Television: Bracing for the Aftershock," *Channels 1986 Field Guide*, p. 22.

15. William J. Drummond, "Is Time Running Out for Network News?" *Columbia Journalism Review*, May–June 1986, p. 52.

16. Ibid.

17. Alter, "Taking CBS to Task," p. 53.

18. *Report on the National Broadcast: Eyes on the Prize, America's Civil Rights Years, 1954–1965* (Boston: WGBH National Productions Department, 1987).

19. Peter J. Boyer, " '60 Minutes': A Hit Confronts the Odds," *New York Times*, September 13, 1987, sec. 2, p. 1.

20. Daniel Boorstin, *The Americans: The Democratic Experience* (New York: Random House, 1973), pp. 89–90.

21. Ibid., p. 147.

22. Ibid., p. 148.

23. Bob Shanks, Vice-President for Programming, ABC Television, quoted in Erik Barnouw, *The Sponsor: Notes on a Modern Potentate* (New York: Oxford University Press, 1978), p. 114.

24. Ithiel de Sola Pool, *Technologies of Freedom* (Cambridge, Mass.: Harvard University Press, Belknap Press, 1983), p. 184.

25. Steve Behrens, "Advertising: Going Soft: The Emergence of a Buyer's Market," *Channels 1987 Field Guide*, p. 16.

26. Ibid.

27. Philip H. Dougherty, "Cable TV's Growth in Ad Spots," *New York Times*, March 29, 1984, p. D21.

28. Boorstin, *The Americans*, p. 393.

29. Ibid., p. 394.

30. "The Powers That Be," *Channels 1986 Field Guide*, pp. 78–79.

31. Gary Arlen, "Videotex: High Rollers with High Hopes," *Channels 1987 Field Guide*, p. 86.

32. Gary Arlen, "Videotex: Information à la Modem," *Channels 1986 Field Guide*, p. 71.

33. Arlen, "Videotex: High Rollers," p. 86.

34. This prediction is taken from Brian Winston, *Misunderstanding Media* (Cambridge, Mass.: Harvard University Press, 1986), p. 4. The authors acknowledge having read Professor Winston's own list of predictions with profit. Our own list differs markedly from his, in accepting the profound influence that television has had on our culture and that many of the new media are likely to have.

INDEX

ABC, 96, 175; cross-ownership and, 281, 283; erosion of hegemony of, 55–56; ratings pressures and, 286; see also Network television

Abortion controversy, 124–27, 160, 265

Absentee ballots, 94

Access issues, 217–22, 233; common carrier law and, 248, 249, 251; First Amendment rights and, 253; free press tradition and, 239–40, 247; pluralist democracy and, 28–29; user control and, 46–47

Action for Children's Television (ACT), 223

Advertising, 29, 42; on cable television, 181–82; and future of new media, 284–90; and history of mass media in U.S., 84; licensing and, 197; mass-circulation newspapers and, 10, 12, 15–16; partisan press and, 82–83; political determinist view and, 17; targeted, 51–52; teletext and, 59; see also Political ads on television

Advertising Age, 224

AFL-CIO, 101, 126, 128, 133, 161

Agnew, Spiro, 228

Albano, Sal, 105

Albany Evening Journal, 81

Alliance for Energy Security, 130

American Cancer Society, 220

American Federation of State, County, and Municipal Employees, 95

American Newspaper Association, 259

American Postal Workers Union, 128

American Revolution, 193

American Telephone & Telegraph (AT&T), 96, 188, 195; common carrier law and, 248, 259–60; in computer market, 275; Covidea and, 38; cross-ownership and, 282; future of, 295; and history of television, 7, 8; "900" poll run by, 167–68n, 175; satellite technology and, 56

American Television and Communications, 56

AP Newspaper 1200, 43

"Apple pie" issues, 116

Arts and Entertainment cable network, 281

Associated Press, 11, 43, 194, 222

Audience targeting, see Targeting

Babbitt, Bruce, 96, 101, 103

Bailey, Douglas, 97

Bank of America, 38, 188, 282

Bank of the United States, 10

Barber, Benjamin, 14, 56, 158, 237, 270, 271

Bayer, Michael J., 92

Becker, Ted, 168, 170, 172

Bell, Alexander Graham, 7, 194

Bell, Daniel, 61

Bell Telephone, 188, 248–49, 259, 295

Benjamin, Gerald, 51

Bentley, Arthur, 123

Berks Community Television (BCTV), 178–80

BizNet News TODAY, 130–33, 157

Black Entertainment Network, 278–79, 281

Blumenthal, Sidney, 144, 145, 146

Boorstein, Daniel, 288, 290

Boston Globe, 38, 97

Boston Herald, 282

"Boutique" radio, 54

Index

Index

Index